OTTO KRETSCHMER

OTTO KRETSCHMER

The Life of Germany's Highest-Scoring U-Boat Commander

Lawrence Paterson

Greenhill Books

Otto Kretschmer
First published in 2018 by
Greenhill Books,
c/o Pen & Sword Books Ltd,
47 Church Street, Barnsley,
S. Yorkshire, S70 2AS

www.greenhillbooks.com
contact@greenhillbooks.com

Published and distributed in the United States of America and Canada
by the Naval Institute Press, 291 Wood Road, Annapolis,
Maryland 21402-5043

www.usni.org

Greenhill Books ISBN: 978–1–78438–192–9
Naval Institute Press ISBN: 978–1–59114–697–1

CIP data records for this title are available from the British Library
Library of Congress Cataloging Number: 2017964283

Designed and typeset by Donald Sommerville

Printed and bound in the UK by TJ International Ltd, Padstow

Typeset in 10.4/14.4 pt Kuenstler 480

Contents

Plates and Charts

The Kriegsmarine ensign is raised aboard *U99*.
Provisioning the boat in Kiel.
One of the golden horseshoes welded to the conning tower of *U99*.
The crew of *U570* attach a horseshoe to their conning tower.
Joachim Schepke and his crouching panther *Wappen*.
A combat U-boat putting to sea.
Kretschmer issuing instructions as *U99* leaves port.
Kretschmer is welcomed to Lorient.
Heinrich Liebe (*U38*) makes his after-action report to Dönitz.
Kretschmer and a welcoming committee for Günther Prien.
Konteradmiral Eberhardt Godt.
Kretschmer on his return to Lorient from a patrol aboard *U99*. *U-Boot Archiv, Altenbruch*

*

Raeder presents Kretschmer with his Knight's Cross, August 1940.
Klaus Bargsten secures the medal around Kretschmer's neck.
Raeder shaking hands with the crew of *U99*.
Kretschmer and his IIIWO, Stabsobersteuermann Heinrich Petersen. *Bundesarchiv, Koblenz*
Kretschmer and his crew enjoy a beer. *Bundesarchiv, Koblenz*
The Hotel Beauséjour on Lorient's Alsace-Lorraine square.
Kretschmer captured on film for the *Deutsche Wochenschau*.
Obermaschinist Edmund Prochnow's family medical card.
U99 in a Lorient dry dock.
Dönitz and members of the BdU staff at their Kernevel headquarters.
Before the interview . . . and during. Kretschmer answers questions from an Army reporter in the summer of 1940. *Bundesarchiv, Koblenz*
Heavy seas in the Atlantic.
Commander Primo Langobardo with Hans-Rudolf Rösing.
Joachim Schepke speaking in Berlin.
An illustration from Schepke's book *U-Boot Fahrer von Heute*.
A British newspaper report of the sinking of SS *Loch Maddy*.
Victory pennants fly from the periscope of *U99*, 22 October 1940.
Kretschmer and the dockside greeting party for a returning U-boat.
Kretschmer at his navigation periscope, November 1940.
Kretschmer meets Hitler, 12 November 1940.

Kretschmer after the Oak Leaves award. *Bundesarchiv, Koblenz*
A member of the technical crew takes an opportunity for fresh air.
Particularly bad Atlantic weather dominated the winter of 1940/41.
U99 returns from patrol, 8 November 1940. *Bundesarchiv, Koblenz*
Klaus Bargsten with his American captor. *US National Archives*
Kretschmer receiving his copy of 'The Kretschmer March'.
The sheet music for 'The Kretschmer March'.
The 'Kretschmer March' ceremony.
Kretschmer speaking to Army officers.
Otto Kretschmer comes ashore in Liverpool and into captivity.
Commander Donald Macintyre aboard HMS *Bickerton*. *Royal Navy Submarine Museum, Gosport*
Hans-Joachim Rahmlow, who surrendered the intact *U570*.
The IWO of *U570*, Bernhard Berndt.
George Creasy, Director of Anti-Submarine Warfare.
The surviving officers of *U99*, Bowmanville, October 1944.
Donald Macintyre and Otto Kretschmer, 1955. *Popperfoto*
A 1940 portrait of Otto Kretschmer.

Charts

Sketch maps of patrols
(copied from the surviving *U23* and *U99* war diaries)

Glossary

General

ASDIC – Term applied to the British equipment used for locating submerged submarines. A powerful and effective weapon, it emitted a distinct "ping" when searching for a target. Equipment of this class is now usually called sonar.

AZ – Aufschlagzündung: impact trigger for the Pi1 pistol fitted to both G7a and G7e torpedoes.

BdU – Befehlshaber der Unterseeboote: Commander U-boats.

DEMS – Defensively Equipped Merchant Ship

Eel – *Aal* – Slang expression for torpedo.

Enigma – Coding machine used by the German armed forces throughout World War Two.

FdU – Führer der Unterseeboote: Flag Officer for submarines, responsible for a particular geographical region.

G7a – German torpedo propelled by steam.

G7e – German torpedo propelled by electric motor.

grt – Gross registered tonnage (a measurement of volume, not weight; one ton equals 100 cubic feet cargo capacity), the standard way of judging commercial shipping size during WWII.

HMS – His Majesty's Ship (Royal Navy).

HMT – His Majesty's Trawler (Royal Navy).

(Ing.) – Ingenieur, engineering trade.

Kriegsmarine – Navy of the Third Reich.

KTB – Kriegstagebuch: war diary. Kept by the commander during a U-boat's patrol, and later entered into official records.

LI – Leitendre Ingenieur, Engineer Officer.

Luftwaffe – Air Force.

MT – Motor Transport

MZ – Magnetzündung: magnetic trigger for the Pi1 pistol fitted to both G7a and G7e torpedoes.

OKM – Oberkommando der Marine; Supreme Navy Command.

OKW – Oberkommando der Wehrmacht; Supreme Armed Forces Command.

PoW – Prisoner of War

Ritterkreuz – Knight's Cross of the Iron Cross.

SKL – Seekriegsleitung; Navy High Command.

Sperrbrecher – Mine destruction ship: generally a converted freighter filled with buoyant material. Designed to escort U-boats and other vessels through potential minefields.

U-Bootwaffe – U-boat service.

UAK – Unterseeboots Abnahme Kommando: new U-boat acceptance commission.

Vorpostenboot – Coastal patrol vessel and escort, usually a converted trawler.

Wachoffizier – Watch Officer. There were three separate U-boat watch crews, each consisting of an officer or senior NCO, petty officer and two ratings. The ship's First Watch Officer (IWO) would be the second in command, the Second Watch Officer (IIWO) the ship's designated second officer, and the Third Watch Officer (IIIWO) often the Obersteuermann (Navigation Officer). The duties of the IWO included torpedo and firing system care and maintenance as well as control of surface attacks; the IIWO handled administration including of food and supplies, as well as the operation of deck and flak weapons.

Wehrmacht – The collective term for Germany's armed forces – Heer, Kriegsmarine and Luftwaffe..

Wintergarten – Winter garden: nickname given to the open-railed extension astern of the conning tower, built to accommodate increased flak weaponry. Known to the Allies as a 'bandstand'.

Kriegsmarine Ranks

Seamen

Matrose	Ordinary Seaman
Matrosengefreiter	Able Seaman
Matrosenobergefreiter	Leading Seaman
Matrosenhauptgefreiter	Leading Seaman (4.5 years service)
Matrosenstabsgefreiter	Senior Leading Seaman
Matrosenstabsobergefreiter	Senior Leading Seaman

(For equivalents to the above for members of the engine room branch, replace '*Matrosen*' with '*Maschinen*')

Junior NCOs

—maat	Petty Officer (e.g. Matrosenmaat)
Ober-maat	Chief Petty Officer (e.g. Obermaschinenmaat)

Senior NCOs/Warrant Officers

Bootsmann	Boatswain
Stabsbootsmann	Senior Boatswain
Oberbootsmann	Chief Boatswain
Stabsoberbootsmann	Senior Chief Boatswain
Obersteurmann	Quartermaster
Stabsobersteuermann	Senior Quartermaster

Officers

Fähnrich zur See		Midshipman
Oberfähnrich zur See		Sub-Lieutenant
Leutnant zur See	(L.z.S.)	Lieutenant (Junior)
Oberleutnant zur See	(Oblt.z.S.)	Lieutenant (Senior)
Kapitänleutnant	(Kaptlt.)	Lieutenant-Commander
Korvettenkapitän	(Korvkpt.)	Commander
Fregattenkapitän	(F.K.)	Captain (Junior)
Kapitän zur See	(Kapt.z.S.)	Captain
Kommodore		Commodore
Konteradmiral		Rear-Admiral
Vizeadmiral		Vice-Admiral
Admiral		Admiral
Generaladmiral		no equivalent
Grossadmiral		Admiral of the Fleet

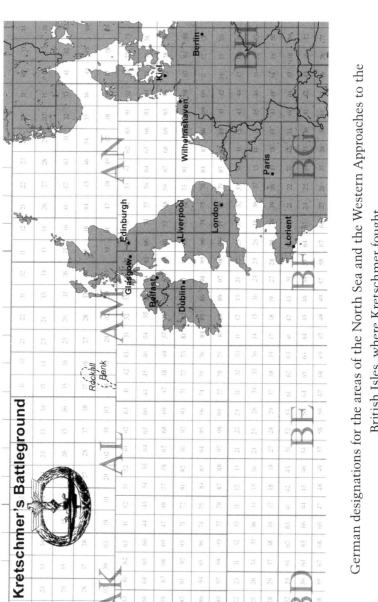

German designations for the areas of the North Sea and the Western Approaches to the British Isles, where Kretschmer fought.

Foreword

Otto Kretschmer remains almost legendary within the annals of submarine warfare. During the Second World War he was the highest scoring 'ace' of the German U-boat service, about which so much has been written. Kretschmer was not history's most successful U-boat commander; that honour belongs to Lothar von Arnauld de la Perière who between 1915 and 1918 was credited with destroying 453,716 tons of enemy commercial shipping. Kretschmer's credited tally of commercial shipping lies at 273,043 tons sunk and five other ships damaged, plus four warships destroyed. That ranks Kretschmer as the fourth most successful U-boat commander ever. However, the Second World War presented considerably greater difficulties for Kretschmer and his fellow second generation of German U-boat commanders. During the previous conflict, submarine warfare was fresh territory, whereas by 1939 weaponry and tactics for combating U-boats had already been developed and successfully used. That is not to say that further development was not required – it most certainly was – but the obstacles faced by a man like Kretschmer would not have been present for Arnauld de la Perière during his years of combat. Additionally, the U-boats of the First World War that claimed such a terrifying tally of destruction were frequently operating within the Mediterranean Sea against independently sailing ships, a far easier target than Atlantic or even North Sea convoys. In a letter dated 12 July 1989 Kretschmer himself expressed an opinion on this:

> The top scorer of WWI, Arnauld de la Perière, has told a friend
> of mine, Herbert Schultze – captain of *U48* – that in his time

everything was much easier because there was no ASDIC and he almost never experienced a depth charge, which in WWII was almost our daily bread, dropped from both aircraft and escorts.[1]

Kretschmer was a serving U-boat captain at the outbreak of war in 1939, his apprenticeship spent in peace-time exercises and as part of the overt international forces sent to monitor the Spanish Civil War. Following the beginning of hostilities against Great Britain in 1939, his early achievements appear somewhat modest. However, this reflects the nature of the tasks assigned to him and the limited capabilities of a Type IIB U-boat. Additionally, his early success was only modest if purely measured in terms of tonnage sunk as the feats of seamanship and daring that took his boat into relatively easily defended British anchorages within the Shetland and Orkney Islands were remarkable for their courage, skill, and precision. From his earliest days as a U-boat captain he truly did possess a resolve and analytical determination that was almost unmatched.

This book is a biography of Otto Kretschmer. However, by its nature, it is also an operational history of *U23* and *U99* during the years 1939–41. The U-boat was arguably an extension of its commander's will, and therefore a reflection of the personal stamp that he made on its crew. Kretschmer's boat was always highly rated by observers and highly efficient in action. He has been described as running his boat like a martinet, and there is a degree of accuracy to this. He was a stickler for discipline and procedure and saw the opportunity to wear the German military uniform both at sea and ashore as an honour not to be sullied by inappropriate or lax behaviour. He demanded – and achieved – a high degree of proficiency in every aspect of a U-boat's operation, both from his men and from himself. However, these hard-line demands only paint a part of the picture of this complex man. He was widely considered quiet, reserved, even shy by comparison to most of his peers. But he also possessed a biting, dry wit that he could deploy at any time and was capable of wry observation of events, even if he was to become the butt of whatever joke was to be made. His crews held him in high esteem and displayed a loyal affection for Kretschmer even once captured and separated individually for interrogation. That kind of devotion can rarely be achieved by a tyrannical approach to command. Kretschmer, in turn, was immensely loyal to his crew and remained genuinely concerned for their welfare before and after capture. By contrast, Günther Prien, perhaps the most famous U-boat officer in history and a friend and flotilla-mate of Kretschmer, was highly successful in action, but apparently generated little genuine affection from his crew. He was reputedly a strict disciplinarian who rarely allowed humanity to interfere with the running of his ship, and his crew apparently despised him for it. Prien was a man who harboured much bitterness, carried with him from a difficult early life, and though amongst fellow officers he could be raucously genial, his reputation with subordinates was considerably less flattering.

This book is based on a combination of official records, personal anecdotes, snippets of interviews and secondary material, though only those that can be verified as fact. There are a surprising number of legends that have built up around many of the Wehrmacht's major figures, often repeated as true but frequently no more than apocryphal tales. I make no attempt to write a book of 're-created conversations', a popular method of attempting to 'novelise' history and perhaps make it as approachable as reading a work of fiction. Unless what was said between people is known via the people themselves, or eyewitnesses, then it would be disingenuous to attempt to re-create personal interactions for the sake of getting across the truths of any particular event. For example, there is no verbatim record at any of Dönitz's meetings with Kretschmer; therefore I make no attempt to re-create their exchanges. There has been a scattering of books about Otto Kretschmer, including Terence Robertson's excellent and ground-breaking biography of 1955. Of course, the majority of the subjects of that book were still alive and in good health at that time, which allows the recounting of 'conversational history' with a high degree of accuracy. The same is not true in 2017, unfortunately. Nonetheless, it is surprising how many inaccuracies can creep into a story and become repeated as reliable fact, losing a fragment of truth with each subsequent retelling. This can sometimes be caused by relying on the supposedly infallible memories of protagonists, though it is to be hoped almost never for the sake of enhancing an already fascinating tale. On occasion, however, it can also be the result of a man's desire to have some fun with the topic, telling yarns of the sea to impressionable listeners, all with a twinkle of merriment in the eye. The genuinely hospitable and accommodating Erich Topp would sometimes do this, as did Heinrich Timm when he told of putting men ashore in New Zealand to milk cows. These men exercised their sense of humour, and it subsequently became written elsewhere as fact.

Therefore, rather than run the risk of mutating an interesting story, the text that follows sticks to what is verifiable or rightly judged to be accurate. A mainstay of such a story is the U-boat's war diary – *Kriegstagebuch* or KTB. The KTB was a written record of a U-boat's operational life, broken down into patrols and dockyard time. They were often kept in handwriting aboard the U-boat at sea during the early stages of the war and typed once ashore. The KTB recorded significant events, weather conditions, distance travelled and so forth. Some are written like personal diaries, full of tension and excitement, others are more matter of fact and detached. They also included torpedo shooting reports (*Schussmeldung*) filled out by the Torpedo Officer (a duty of the First Watch Officer), track charts and radio logs (*Funkkladddenauszüge*). Other officers of the boat *could* contribute material to be included in the KTB – particularly the Navigator (*Obersteuermann*, Third Watch Officer) and radio operators – though they were not obligated to do so. The boat's KTB therefore provided an all-encompassing single record. Once typed it was read and signed by the captain who would then present it to Dönitz (if possible) or a ranking member of the FdU or BdU Staff. Once the events of the patrol had been weighed, discussed and explained, it remained on file at BdU; copies were sent to the flotilla commander, BdU Operations, BdU Organisation, and two copies to OKM, one to be passed on to SKL. This is the heartbeat of a U-boat patrol, and though it can contain unverified guesswork regarding targets, or inaccurate estimation of ship and escort numbers, it is the 'go to' reference for any U-boat operation. As a result, this book is heavy on detail – something lacking elsewhere – which has resulted in major inaccuracies in the retelling of Kretschmer's personal story. In the early drafts of this book even the types of torpedoes fired in every attack were listed, but this is not necessary to the story itself and therefore some of the minutiae that could slow the text down have been removed. Nonetheless, no attempt has been made to guess what may or may not have been Kretschmer's point of view on various topics.

Perhaps the most significant question that therefore arises is exactly what he thought of the National Socialist government and his *Führer*, Adolf Hitler. It would have been very interesting to discover his exact feelings – as it has been when interviewing other German veterans – but the opportunity to do so no longer exists. Certainly, he and his family would no doubt have been affected by the turbulent relationship with Poland during the interwar period, and one can infer certain things by 'reading between the lines' of what we know Kretschmer has said to people such as Donald Macintyre. However, to speculate beyond that would be a disservice to this biography.

The majority of this book concerns Kretschmer's time in action, though of course his biography does not end with his capture in March 1941. Otto Kretschmer was a celebrity of the Wehrmacht, despite his aversion to that fact. However, for his Allied captors he remained something of an enigma: on the one hand refined and 'correct', on the other a stubborn and unrelenting opponent to whom barbed wire mattered little and who carried on fighting the war from his prison camps. He was certainly a unique individual and the author would like to dedicate this book to this remarkable man and all of those who sailed with him.

Acknowledgements

As well as the many people who have helped over the years with my U-boat research, I would especially like to acknowledge the assistance of the U-Boot Archiv in Altenbruch, Germany, in the preparation of this book. Copies of the full war diaries of both *U23* and *U99* – complete with the attached track charts – have proved invaluable in tracing the combat missions of both U-boats. Though the clarity of the charts themselves has not have always stood the test of time, they provide a fascinating glimpse at the administrative detail required and recorded by a U-boat at war so I have reproducd a selection in the pages of this book. I am also indebted to the Royal Navy Submarine Museum, where I once worked as a member of the Archive Working Party, which holds many personal papers collected by the late Gus Britton. Amongst these are the letters to Mr Priddey written by Otto Kretschmer. They too have provided new sources of information, in Kretschmer's own words. The online presence of the BBC People's War series has helped with first-hand accounts, and, as always, the remarkable website www.uboat.net is an ever-useful place to cross-check references and access information.

Chapter One

Between the Wars

On 1 May 1912, Otto August Wilhelm Kretschmer was born to Friedrich Wilhelm Otto Kretschmer and his wife Alice (née Herbig) in Ober-Heidau within the Prussian *Landkreis* (county) of Liegnitz, Silesia. Now named Golanka Dolna and a part of Poland, the small Silesian town was barely a speck on the map in 1921 and numbered only 283 inhabitants in a 1925 census. Friedrich was a school teacher of the Heidau *Volksschule* (elementary school) which Otto attended between 1918 and 1921 before later enrolling in the Wahlstatt *Realgymnasium*, the equivalent of a British grammar school. This institute of learning had various famous military alumni who had become luminaries of the First World War such as Paul von Hindenburg, Manfred von Richthofen and Lothar von Arnauld de la Perière, the last the most successful U-boat commander of the First World War.

Otto Kretschmer's early years were spent during a tumultuous period for Germany. As the guns fell silent on 11 November 1918, Germany ended the First World War a broken nation. Bolshevik revolution sparked amongst the listless crews of the Imperial German Navy's High Seas Fleet that had lain ineffectively at anchor for two years after the inconclusive Battle of Jutland eliminated the Navy's offensive doctrine. Restless, bored and unhappy, the smouldering crews of stagnating sailors were soon fanned into the flames of full-scale revolt that soon spread throughout Germany as the war ended. Revolution polarised political and nationalist groups as never before in what was still a relatively young nation.

Meanwhile, the harsh dictated terms of the Treaty of Versailles severely curtailed German military power, with U-boats, tanks and military aircraft strictly forbidden. Territorial losses, a forced acceptance of total responsibility for the outbreak of war and crippling reparation payments sowed seeds of resentment that took root in extreme politics. Unable to face the humiliation of defeat, many Germans took refuge within the myth that disloyal elements of the home front had 'stabbed the German soldier in the back'. Those perceived to be of questionable loyalty – notably socialists, communists, and Jews – were viewed with suspicion and hostility and the atmosphere became ripe for Adolf Hitler's incendiary brand of politics.

While Germany endured years of turbulence, the Kretschmers remained a largely apolitical family. Otto's father's passion for languages and scientific subjects infected the young teenager and he developed into a studious young man. His character developed to that of calm reserve, capable of intense concentration that could occasionally flash to irritation if disturbed by unwelcome intrusion. Though quiet and unassuming, he was not introverted and accumulated a wide circle of friends, though never became the centre of any social group. Perhaps incongruously in such a scholarly outlook, Kretschmer also excelled at sports, particularly skiing. He harboured a healthy sense of competitiveness, though his primary motivation was perhaps more internal than external. He simply believed that any man who applied himself to any task should attempt to achieve mastery for his own satisfaction.

Kretschmer achieved good grades in mathematics, chemistry and physical education. His final *Abitur* qualification, issued when he had reached the age of seventeen, ended with the following statement: 'Kretschmer demonstrated his extraordinary courage in many instances. He wants to be a naval officer.' Since Otto was still too young to enlist in the Reichsmarine, Kretschmer's father arranged for his son to spend time in Britain in order to broaden his knowledge of languages and science. He stayed in Exeter for eight months and was privately tutored there by Professor Jacob Wilhelm Schopp. Schopp, born in Germany in 1871, was a naturalised Briton who had made Exeter his home and lectured in modern languages at what was then the University College of South West England. Otto's time in Britain left an indelible mark on him. Not only did he achieve mastery of the English language but he observed what he considered to be a distinctly practical approach in British education rather than the theoretical, scientific experience of his

German schooling. This would later cause him intuitively to believe rumours of ingenious advances in anti-submarine warfare weapons and code-breaking as he felt that the British possessed both the intellect and the mechanical ability to excel at such projects. His cautious acceptance of these possibilities later stood him in good stead as a combat U-boat commander.

Family tragedy during his first term forced his temporary return home for a brief period when his mother unexpectedly died of tetanus as a result of medical malpractice. Following this unwelcome hiatus, as part of his continuing schooling Kretschmer took part in an organised study trip that passed through Paris, Geneva, Milan, Pisa, Rome, Naples, Capri, Pompeii, Florence, Venice and back into Switzerland. Kretschmer's absorption of English language and customs was augmented by basic Italian that he learned while abroad. Not long afterward, during his second term back in Germany, Kretschmer officially applied to join the Reichsmarine in Bremerhaven, travelling to the port city during a trip to Kiel to study the Schleswig-Holstein education system. The application process complete, Kretschmer was declared fit for service following the standard introductory medical examination. Despite his father's wishes that he would follow in his academic trail and become a teacher, Kretschmer remained determined to pursue a naval career. Though clearly disappointed with their son's choice, neither his father nor late mother had ever placed any obstacles before him so that he finally joined the Reichsmarine on 1 April 1930, one month short of his eighteenth birthday, as a *See Offizier Anwärter* (Naval Officer Candidate).

Germany's navy had been severely limited by the Treaty of Versailles that followed the end of hostilities in 1918, with more applications than there were positions to be filled within the maximum of 1,500 officers allowed under the treaty terms. Thus, the Reichsmarine could carefully select who it accepted into the ranks and by 1930 it truly was a highly specialised and elite force, still several years away from possessing a U-boat arm although covert experiments with new U-boat designs had already begun outside of Germany's borders. Each intake of officer cadets into the Reichsmarine, and later the Kriegsmarine, was known as a Crew and of the seventy-eight cadets who comprised Crew 30, twenty would go on to subsequent careers as U-boat officers.[1] Though Kretschmer's well-known reputation is one of a certain reflective gravity in all situations, this was clearly only one facet of his character as, amongst the fellow cadets of Crew 30, Kretschmer was a popular figure who melded well with all. Within the wide association of friends, he formed a firm and close friendship with at least one other who would later become one of the 'Three U-boat Aces': Joachim Schepke.

> Schepke was a tall, fair-haired, blue-eyed good-looking man. When we, the Crew 30, started in the navy at Stralsund at No. 4 Company I (on the island of Dänholm) of the 2nd Abteilung (Battalion) of the Schiffsstammdivision der Ostsee, the company was subdivided into eight *Korporalschaften* (groups under the command of a Petty Officer). Number 1 *Korporalschaft* was composed of the tallest, No. 8 of the shortest young men (of about 18 to 20 years of age). I came into No. 4 with my 179 cm. I guess Schepke must have been in about No. 1 or 2. Schepke was not at all a heavy drinker – not more than any one of his fellow officers. He was happily married and had, I think, two children: a boy and a girl.[2]

The young men of Crew 30 included many who would later make indelible marks during the Second World War and in their company Kretschmer excelled. The community of the naval 'Crew' of officer cadets was forged over a total period of fifty-four months of training and remained an indelible bond that was a cornerstone of German naval officer development. Traits of each man were frequently highlighted in yearbooks as running 'in-jokes' that would even last through wartime and into the peace that followed Germany's second defeat. For example, the gregarious and handsome Schepke was nicknamed *Ihrer Majestät bestaussehender Offizier* ('Her Majesty's best-looking officer') by his crewmates, exuding an easy-going charm that almost belied his intelligence and exceptional abilities as a naval officer. German cadets spent six months in basic training at Stralsund before moving on to three and a half months of practical instruction aboard the sail training ship *Niobe* as a *Seekadet*. This beautiful ship was used for the instruction of both officer cadets and aspiring non-commissioned officers. On board, the men would learn practical seamanship while also building experience and character worthy of a naval officer.

Following the end of the First World War, the two sail-training ships that had been used by the Imperial Navy – *Grossherzog Friedrich August* and *Prinzess Eitel Friedrich* – were seized by the Allied powers as war reparations. Not until 1922 did the Reichsmarine purchase a new tall ship for training, buying a Danish-built four-masted schooner and rechristening it *Niobe*. The elegant ship had begun life in the Danish Frederikshavn Værft og Flydedok shipyard, originally named *Morten Jensen* and sailing as a freighter before being sold to a Norwegian shipping line in 1916 and renamed *Thyholmen*. On 21 November that same year, it was intercepted in the North Sea by Oblt.z.S. Friedrich Karl Schiart von Sichartshofen's *UB41* and taken as prize as it was carrying mine props from Scandinavia to Britain. Once in German hands it drifted through various companies for diverse purposes before its purchase by the Reichsmarine.

The steel-hulled ship was re-rigged as a three-masted barque and served successfully as a training ship for the entire decade that followed. Though the Reichsmarine had, of course, been severely curtailed by the Versailles Treaty, there were stirrings of covert rearmament and a slow increase in military strength even before the rise of Hitler's National Socialist Party. However, on 26 July 1932 – long after Kretschmer had departed the vessel – tragedy that would have far-reaching consequences for the German Navy overtook *Niobe*.

Sailing with a full complement of trainees aboard in full summer heat, *Niobe* was suddenly engulfed in what is known as a 'white squall'. This phenomenon refers to a sudden violent windstorm that is not presaged by the usual weather warnings such as darkening skies or a freshening breeze and can occur with alarming speed even on clear cloudless days. The *Niobe* was between the German Fehmarn Island and Denmark in the Baltic Sea, caught so abruptly that it heeled dramatically, allowing water to flood through portholes and hatches that had been left open to provide ventilation in the stifling heat below decks. The ship capsized and sank within four minutes. Of the 109 men aboard, sixty-nine were lost and the remaining forty rescued by German freighter SS *Theresia L. M. Russ*. Of those killed, thirty-six young men were from Crew 32: twenty-seven officer cadets, two NCO candidates and seven medical officer candidates.

An immediate enquiry followed and, despite a desire to assign blame for the tragedy, no fault was found during the subsequent court-martial proceedings of the ship's captain, Heinrich Rufus, who had survived the sinking, or indeed with the conduct of any of his complement.

The hulk was raised and the dead recovered from where they had been trapped below decks, and later buried with military honours. The wreck was subsequently sunk once more, this time in a ceremony attended by almost all of the fledgling German Navy in which it was torpedoed and sent to the bottom one final time. With the Navy now bereft of a training vessel, the Prussian state mint struck a memorial coin the equivalent of a five-mark piece that was sold to banks at a profit for the sole purpose of fund raising for 'Project 1115', building a replacement training ship. Though many had begun debating the efficacy and relevance of using sail training, the Reichsmarine had committed to replacing *Niobe*. A total of 200,000 marks was raised by the sale of the coin and the *Gorch Fock* built within a hundred days and launched from the Blohm & Voss shipyard in Hamburg on 3 May 1933. Two more ships – *Horst Wessel* and *Albert Leo Schlageter* – followed in 1936 and 1937 respectively.

The sinking of the *Niobe* and loss of so many officer cadets resulted in a direct appeal by Admiral Erich Raeder, head of the Navy, to Germany's merchant navy for volunteers to join the naval officer corps as an additional draft for Crew 32. The shipping industry was wallowing in the doldrums because of the worldwide Great Depression, the longest-lasting economic decline of the Western industrialised nations that began in 1929 and lasted for ten years. Many qualified sea-going officers were unemployed as a result and took the opportunity to join the military, amongst them Günther Prien, who had been languishing in the Labour Corps in land-locked Oelsnitz in the Vogtlandkreis, Saxony, after achieving his master's ticket but failing to secure a working position.

Prien had been born in the Hanseatic city of Lübeck before moving with his mother and two siblings to a life of near poverty in Leipzig following his parents' separation. Obsessed with Vasco da Gama as a child, he dreamed of a life at sea and had begun his career as a fifteen-year-old cabin boy aboard SS *Hamburg*. After his arduous climb to master only resulted in sustained unemployment in a depressed shipping industry, Prien had enrolled in the National Socialist Party in desperation and fury at the state of joblessness within Germany. He then enlisted in the voluntary Labour Corps that provided free board and lodging in exchange for civic construction jobs, working at the camp situated within Oelsnitz's Schloß Voigtsberg. With at least temporary purpose and structure to his life, he rose to Group Leader, though amidst a contentious atmosphere that culminated in a disciplinary incident and dismissal by Prien of thirty men. Prien had developed a tangible air of authority, but it was backed by bitter cynicism and barely restrained anger at his perception of worldly injustice, hallmarks that appear never to have left him.

> A few days later I heard that the Navy were giving commissions to officers of the Merchant Navy to bring the establishment up to strength. All the time I had longed to go back to the sea and now the longing gripped me irresistibly. Thus, I joined the Navy in Stralsund in January 1933. Once again I began from the bottom as an ordinary sailor.[3]

Prien would also rise meteorically through the ranks of the Kriegsmarine and later go on to become the last member of the famed 'Three Aces' in Lorient during 1940. However, that still lay some years in the future.

Kretschmer was posted to the light cruiser *Emden* on 10 October 1930, which would sail international training cruises showing the German flag. Serving as an ordinary seaman, he remained assigned to *Emden* until 4 January 1932, by which time he had achieved the rank of *Matrosengefreiter*. During this period the *Emden* was commanded by Fregattenkapitän Robert Witthoeft-Emden, the third commander of the cruiser, who replaced the First World War U-boat ace Lothar von Arnauld de la Perière in the same month that Kretschmer joined the ship. Kretschmer's training officer was Kaptlt. Jürgen Wattenberg, who would later serve aboard the *Graf Spee* before transferring to U-boats in 1941. Wattenberg was nicknamed *Der Uhrmacher* ('The Watchmaker') because of his constant striving for precision and accuracy in all that he and his cadets did and was perhaps an influential man in reinforcing a trait that Kretschmer already possessed and would later make him particularly effective in action.

Of course, this particular demeanour also included a strict code of discipline which Kretschmer rarely fell foul of. However, on one particular occasion Kretschmer and Schepke purchased US Navy underwear from a nearby visiting ship anchored in harbour to replace their unpopular and uncomfortable Kriegsmarine issue. Wattenberg apparently was informed and during the next inspection ordered

Kretschmer to drop his trousers, revealing the US Navy boxer shorts; he reprimanded the young *Fähnrich* with an official note in the daily record, 'Otto Kretschmer is wearing sport trunks under his uniform.'

The *Emden* sailed for the Far East on 1 December 1930. Travelling through the Mediterranean and Suez Canal, the ship called at Ceylon, Siam, Philippines, China, Japan, Guam, Batavia, the Cocos Islands, Durban, Angola, Freetown, Canary Islands and Santander before returning to Wilhelmshaven on 2 December 1931.[4] On 1 April 1932 Kretschmer and his crewmates were promoted to *Fähnrich zur See* (midshipman) and sent to continue their studies at the Flensburg academy, absorbing lessons in ordnance and communications alongside sports competitions and instruction in the social etiquette expected of a naval officer. Kretschmer briefly served aboard the survey ship *Meteor* for navigation training as an *Oberfähnrich zur See* and the pocket battleship *Deutschland* as a gunnery officer during a visit to Denmark. He was transferred to the light cruiser *Köln* during December 1934, after having completed his officer candidacy and having finally been commissioned as *Leutnant zur See* at the beginning of October, serving initially as the ship's Second Torpedo Officer. Somewhat ironically, Kretschmer was unhappy at his new assignment: 'Then I was put in the torpedo department, but I didn't want to go, because I liked gunnery better. It was more modernised, and our torpedo weapon department was still like World War One.'[5]

Deutschland had initially been used for trials and training purposes but joined the fleet at the beginning of 1934, sailing to Madeira during that year. Kretschmer served aboard while the ship also exercised close to German territorial waters within the North and Baltic Seas. On 26 and 27 July 1935, *Deutschland* was engaged in gunnery exercises off Eckernförde with the new Chancellor Adolf Hitler aboard to observe the event, driven, no doubt, by his noted interest in naval artillery.

Hitler's rise to power from the tumult of German politics had culminated in his appointment as Chancellor in 1933, followed by a referendum to the German people during the following year that merged the posts of Chancellor and President, the new title of *Führer und Reichskanzler* (Leader and Chancellor) finally giving Hitler total dictatorial power. The race for rearmament subsequently intensified. During 1933 Germany had withdrawn from the League of Nations, established to foster international peace, as well as its disarmament conference in Geneva after the German delegation, headed by Josef Goebbels, had proposed international disarmament to Germany's level and been thoroughly rebuffed by France.

In 1935 Hitler formally repudiated the Treaty of Versailles and announced overt German rearmament following two years of covert development both within Germany and beyond its borders. Fearing that French intransigence would once again provoke a German-led European arms race of the kind that resulted in war in 1914, Britain signed a bilateral deal with Germany on 18 June 1935, that became the 'Anglo-German Naval Agreement'. In tacit acceptance of Germany's flagrant breach of the Versailles Treaty, the agreement limited the Kriegsmarine's size to 35 per cent of that of the Royal Navy, though there was a specific clause that gave Germany 'the right to possess a submarine tonnage equal to the total submarine tonnage possessed by the Members of the British Commonwealth of Nations'.

This agreement, which provoked strong French condemnation, was designed to allay fears of German expansionist aims in Europe, though it would ultimately, and comprehensively, fail to do so. However, combined with a German–Polish non-aggression pact signed in 1934, it appeared at least for the time being as though Nazi Germany was only interested in regaining the international standing denied by the Versailles Treaty, though seemingly unbeknownst to all but the most astute observers, Hitler's rearmament plans were secretly set on supporting wider territorial ambition.

During January 1936, Kretschmer finally transferred to the fledgling U-boat service, which offered greater advancement and an opportunity to be at the cutting edge of a developing 'service within a service'. After completion of his initial U-boat training, Kretschmer was promoted to the rank of *Oberleutnant zur See* on 1 June 1936, and posted to the *Saltzwedel* Flotilla on 3 October, and the position of First Watch Officer (IWO) aboard the Type VII *U35*.

Germany had launched its first new U-boat on 15 June 1935 when the floating crane at Kiel lifted the diminutive Type IIA *U1* into the water. Based on a design perfected through the prototype *Vessiko* in Finland and covert experience gained by international construction beyond the sight of the Versailles Treaty Commission, *U1* was a 250-ton U-boat designed for coastal operations and its commander *Kapitänleutnant* Klaus Ewerth commissioned the boat into the newly established U-boat

School Flotilla, which soon numbered six U-boats. The first of the new Type IIA boats, construction of *U1* had begun during February 1935. By 27 September, improved Type IIB U-boats *U7*, *U8* and *U9* had also been launched and the combat *Weddigen* Flotilla was formed in Kiel with a nucleus of these three. *Fregattenkapitän* Karl Dönitz arrived to take command of the small flotilla, was promoted to *Kapitän zur See* within a month and at the beginning of 1936 relinquished his flotilla command to become the *Führer der Unterseeboote* (FdU). During June 1936, the first medium U-boat – the 750-ton Type VII *U27* – was launched and three months later the *Saltzwedel* Flotilla formed in Kiel, moving to Wilhelmshaven within weeks of creation. Two disappointing prototype heavier boats – the Type Is *U25* and *U26* – were also attached to *Saltzwedel*, though they proved an unsuccessful design. On 2 March 1936, the keel was laid for *U35* at Friedrich Krupp Germaniawerft shipyard, Kiel, building work number 558.

Kretschmer attended what is known as *Baubelehrung*, the pre-commissioning phase in which a prospective U-boat crew familiarised themselves with their new boat as its construction was finalised. It also allowed an opportunity for the men to become acquainted with each other before being thrown into training at sea. For much of the course of the U-boat's construction, the engineer officer supervised work on the boat within the shipyard, and was also able to suggest alterations as it progressed. He generally arrived twelve weeks before the vessel was launched and was followed in stages by other engineering crewmen in descending rank order who all used the time to observe the creation of their new boat and learn the intricacies involved. With four weeks left before launch the commander and watch officers generally arrived to begin their own familiarisation process, followed by the remainder of the crew from the seaman branch.

U35 was commissioned on 3 November 1936, by Kaptlt. Klaus Ewerth who had moved on from his command of *U1*. Ewerth held the post for a little over a month before being replaced by Kaptlt. Hans-Rudolf Rösing. Rösing, a veteran submariner and naval officer since 1925, had been involved in the clandestine construction of U-boats overseas and been placed in command of the boat ahead of the scheduled captain, Kaptlt. Hermann Michahelles.

The flotilla's tenders provided targets for U-boats to attempt interception and simulated attacks, though the Baltic was too small for

Dönitz fully to test his theories regarding the potential efficacy of U-boat group operations. However, despite repeated appeals for permission to stage Atlantic exercises, Hitler and Generaladmiral Raeder refused to allow U-boats to operate in any strength within the Atlantic while the civil war in Spain raged, lest their presence be misinterpreted by British naval units monitoring the fighting. On the other hand, approval was granted to hold small-scale test-cruises to assess the handling of Germany's new submarines within the expansive Atlantic Ocean.[6] In Wilhelmshaven Kaptlt. Wilhelm Ambrosius of *U28* was temporarily replaced by the veteran Kaptlt. Hans-Günther Looff, while Rösing handled *U35*

> This was to be the first time that the boats had been into the Atlantic. I took over from Michahelles, as Dönitz was of the opinion that Michahelles had not enough experience [and] therefore one of the 'old horses' was put in. At that time, there was the Spanish Civil War and our two submarines were initially to be sent to the Spanish Civil War, but when we were equipped and fully ready the Spanish War was practically over and so we were sent to the Azores.[7]

Rösing had been the commander of the Type II *U11* and he brought with him his own IWO, Oblt.z.S. Dietrich von der Ropp. Nonetheless, Kretschmer remained with the boat, though at the temporarily reduced post of IIWO.

> I was a lieutenant on *U35*, in the second submarine flotilla, and together with *U28*, we were the first to go into the Atlantic, to Ponta Delgada in the Azores. As was customary, the boat went out for practice manoeuvres in the Bay of Lübeck before departure.[8]

The training was arduous and maintained a punishing schedule of gunnery, torpedo firing, and emergency dives within the cold wind-swept Baltic of December. During the course of one of the training days Kretschmer and Rösing were atop the conning tower when Kretschmer lit up one of his customary cheroot cigars that he had begun smoking since enlisting in the Navy. 'I thought maybe he would let me smoke it to the end, but I looked at his eyes and thought, "No, he will not."'

To attempt to delay the onset of more diving drill, Kretschmer declared that he was going to inspect the deck gun – the domain of

the IIWO, who was the boat's gunnery officer – and empty any water
that might have entered through the tampion clamped in place over the
barrel mouth.

> I was on the foredeck, adjusting the gun, when PSSSSSSH he was
> diving. Then up came the green sea, and I ran to the conning
> tower and tried to climb the periscope, hoping that I could be
> seen in the optics. But of course it was too oily, and I couldn't
> get up. When the water was dark green I let loose and popped up
> again.

Kretschmer had been dragged underwater and was lucky to reach the
surface of the frigid Baltic. However, he would not survive for long in
the near-freezing temperature.

> It was December, and I had on heavy clothing – my leather suit
> with rubber at wrists and ankles – so it kept in some air to help
> me float. Also, I had sea boots, and they held air but in the end, I
> had to paddle like a dog because the air was disappearing.

Fortunately, his presence had been missed, Rösing looking through
the periscope as the boat dipped under and noticed that something was
'funny' and perhaps there was a man in the water. *U35* rapidly surfaced
once more, and lookouts spotted the struggling officer, throwing a life
ring to him. Kretschmer had just enough energy to grab the ring but was
unable to pull himself aboard as numbness spread rapidly through his
body, which threatened to succumb to the deadly effects of exposure.

> They pulled me out, pushed me up onto the conning tower, and
> then I said to the captain, 'Reporting back on board, sir.' He said,
> 'Thank you, thank you very much. Please go down.' No apology.
> When I got down I took off all my wet things and drank a good
> deal of rum. You see, there was no heating in the boat. I lay down
> on the bunk and vigorously exercised my arms and legs, and then
> I asked for hot water bottles to put on myself so I could get warm
> again. Otherwise I would have died there on the bunk.

After the boat's arrival in port a crew-member appears to have told
the story to a local reporter and an article was soon published that
related a tale of Kretschmer surviving a near-fatal accident in the Baltic
with a cigar still clamped between his teeth, the latter point obviously a

media fabrication, but one that neither Kretschmer nor his crew denied as it enhanced the young officer's image amongst both the public and his peers.

Kretschmer was made responsible for provisioning the boat before their departure for the Azores, Rösing reminding him of the profound effect a well-fed and healthy crew can have on a U-boat's operational efficiency. Correspondingly, Kretschmer was directed to allow the crew unfettered access to the food stores while at sea with the predictable result that consumption far exceeded expectations and went over the budget allocated to the boat.

> I was going to have to pay for all that myself, so I told the authorities that I had only followed the commander's instructions. But the commander denied knowing anything about it, and even though I said I would swear to it and that others had witnessed, I still had to make it good.

Kretschmer was furious, his relationship with Rösing, never particularly close to begin with, thereafter remaining civil at best. Following negotiations with the flotilla staff, Kretschmer reached a deal whereby cuts could be made elsewhere within the scheduled rationing and the credit applied to his debt. Therefore, from that point onward, the free access was removed and the crew could only have tinned fish as a supplement to their normal late meal of bread and butter. The oily fish cost only ten pfennigs per tin and, despite appeals from the crew to rescind his decision, Kretschmer successfully narrowed the margins of his considerable, though unexpected, debt.

The voyage to Ponta Delgada had proved the seaworthiness of the Type VII boats; *U28* and *U35* both encountered violent storms during their passage and were able to submerge when conditions became intolerable for men atop the conning tower. Rösing suffered from his usual period of seasickness before he found his sea legs, his condition normally only lasting for the first two days at sea. *U35* left Wilhelmshaven on 11 January 1937 and returned less than a month later, on 3 February. Upon the boat's homecoming, Von der Ropp returned to *U11* and Rösing handed command of *U35* to Kaptlt. Hermann Michahelles.[9] A graduate of Crew 27, Michahelles had skippered *U2* from 25 July 1935 until 30 September 1936 as *Oberleutnant zur See*, and was then promoted on 1 October 1936 and transferred to the *Saltzwedel* Flotilla, where he was held in readiness until *U35* had returned from the Azores under Rösing's command.

Under his leadership the boat completed a single patrol in Spanish waters as part of the overt international presence during their civil war that had been agreed by the Nyon conference of September 1937, held to address Italian submarine attacks on international shipping in the Mediterranean Sea during the conflict. The war inside Spain between the Republicans, who were largely assisted by the Comintern, and Fascists, who benefited from German and Italian support, was particularly bitter. The strategic location of Spain put it astride the great trading routes of the world and both belligerents completely ignored international maritime law whenever it suited. As an example of this, between November 1936 and April 1937, eighteen Dutch, twenty-six Danish, and thirty Norwegian ships were either intercepted or impounded and had their cargoes confiscated. The international naval community mounted several civilian evacuations and numerous patrols to ensure that the fighting stayed within the Iberian Peninsula.

The U-boats engaged as part of the Nyon presence had their conning towers painted in Germany's national colours and were tasked with guarding Spain's borders against troop reinforcement of volunteers from other countries. *U35* was allocated a patrol zone near the French border in the Bay of Biscay, the German crew sometimes going ashore in the resort town of San Sebastian, and was based for nearly a month near the Illa de Arousa while performing its duties before rotating back to Germany. Unfortunately, five days after the boat's return to Wilhelmshaven on 25 July 1937, Hermann Michahelles was killed in an automobile accident in Haunstetten near Augsburg. Kretschmer therefore found himself the temporary commander (*Kommandant in Vertretung*) of *U35* for a little over two weeks until the arrival of Kaptlt. Werner Lott, of Crew 26.

Lott did not return *U35* to Spanish waters until February 1938, by which time Kretschmer had been transferred. After having gained considerable experience aboard *U35*, Kretschmer attended his own commander's course and was named captain of the Type IIB *U23* of the *Weddigen* Flotilla on 1 October 1937, replacing Kaptlt. Hans-Günther Looff, who moved on to the *Saltzwedel* boat *U28*.

Chapter Two

Command: War in the North Sea with U23

Kretschmer took command of the Type IIB U-boat *U23* on the first day of October 1937. The small boat was one of the second wave of U-boats that had been constructed for the fledgling Kriegsmarine. Following the launch of *U1* and subsequent trials, technical improvements were planned for the second generation of the coastal design and only six Type IIA boats were launched in total. The Type IIB was essentially a lengthened version of its forerunner. Three additional compartments had been placed into the hull amidships plus the addition of diesel fuel tanks beneath the central control room (*Zentrale*) that carried an added nine tons of fuel which nearly doubled the Type II's surfaced range from 1,000 nautical miles to 1,800 at an average speed of 8 knots. The lengthened hull also allowed installation of additional batteries which correspondingly increased the underwater range of the boat by as much as 23 per cent.

The Type II U-boat had a single-skinned hull and no watertight compartments. There were three torpedo tubes mounted in the bow, each of which was loaded before leaving port, with an additional two torpedoes, carried inside the pressure hull, for reloads. A single 20 mm anti-aircraft gun was provided on the forward deck for flak protection or surface firing, though its stopping power in the latter role was minimal. The interior space aboard the boat was extremely limited, the two spare torpedoes extending from just behind the torpedo tube doors to the edge of the small control room that was the nerve centre of every U-boat. The majority of the twenty-four-man crew lived in this forward area around the torpedoes, sharing twelve bunks between them, while a further four were provided in the absolute stern of the boat, past the engine room and the single WC. Both the cooking and sanitary facilities were basic; U-boats catered little for the creature comforts of their crews, particularly in relation to other nations' submarine designs.

U23's keel was laid in Kiel's Germaniawerft shipyard on 11 April 1936 and the boat was launched a little over four months later, commissioning into the Kriegsmarine on 24 September 1936. The small boat's first commander was Eberhard Godt, who held the command until January 1938 whereupon he joined FdU Staff, becoming Dönitz's operations officer and, later, Chief of Operations at BdU. Kaptlt. Hans-Günther Looff then commanded the boat until September 1937 before he passed command to Kretschmer and himself moved to the position of chief of the *Weddigen* Flotilla.

U23 had been in service for a year by the time of Kretschmer's arrival and many of its crew had served with the boat throughout. However, amongst the fresh draft that followed Kretschmer's assumption of captaincy was a new IWO, L.z.S. Adalbert 'Adi' Schnee. Schnee arrived at the end of September and would remain IWO until 2 January 1940, with two short periods as a training officer at the Torpedo School in Flensburg-Mürwik during 1938. Part of Crew 34, Schnee would prove an adept pupil, learning his own future craft as a U-boat commander from his new captain, who had already established a reputation for being the finest torpedo shot in the U-boat service during Baltic combat drills as IWO on *U35*. Orthodox U-boat training instructed that attacks were to be made while submerged at a close enough range to ensure the probability of a hit with at least one of a fan of three torpedoes fired. It was a wasteful exercise, particularly for small Type II boats that carried five torpedoes as standard and Kretschmer knew instinctively that such a wastage of available ammunition was not the way to wage effective U-boat warfare. He was yet to develop his theories of attacking while surfaced wherever possible, but he already viewed the principle of U-boat combat as being to achieve maximum results with minimum expenditure. The phrase 'one torpedo for one ship' still lay in the future, but the thinking behind it had already taken shape. Kretschmer was, even at this young age and early stage of his career, the consummate professional and devoted his scholarly and methodical approach to all issues leading to the development of a truly effective mode of combat.

Aboard a combat U-boat, the entire task of sighting and firing a torpedo while submerged was led by the commander at the periscope. However, while surfaced, the captain's job was to choose targets, hold an overall view of the developing attack, and exercise the final say regarding the mechanics of the attack, while the boat's IWO handled the actual sighting and firing of the torpedo. Both the IWO and IIWO (and IIIWO if present) were generally invited to put forward their own estimates of target speed, size and range, but ultimate control and authority always deferred to the captain.

Although war remained months away, *U23* took part in emergency alerts during Hitler's period of triumphant international gambling. During March 1938 Austria was amalgamated into the Third Reich and during September Hitler demanded the annexation of the Sudetenland, former Austro-Hungarian territory that had been ceded to the newly created Czechoslovak state after the First World War. British Prime Minister Neville Chamberlain met Hitler in Berchtesgaden on 15 September and, following two further meetings, agreed to his demands, French Prime Minister Édouard Daladier following suit three days later. The Czechs were not invited to either meeting, after which Neville Chamberlain declared from the steps of Number 10 Downing Street that the accord signed between the western powers and Nazi Germany signified 'peace for our time'. On 4 March 1939, the Wehrmacht occupied the Czech provinces of Bohemia and Moravia, including Prague, and all illusions that Hitler's ambition could be contained were finally gone. Germany also annexed the Klaipėda (Memel in German) region from Lithuania on 23rd of the same month. The city and district was occupied by Wehrmacht troops – this former East Prussian territory, with 160,000 inhabitants, having been ceded to Lithuania after 1918. Each time that international tensions reached these potential crisis points, Dönitz's U-boats put to sea on 'exercises' as the attitude of the likely foes Britain and France remained unknown and war threatened to erupt. On 'active service' during these events, Kretschmer qualified for the commemorative medals presented to members of the Wehrmacht, though the final conflagration was avoided in each instance.[1]

During the Austrian *Anschluss*, Dönitz had sent his boats to sea while Hitler met with Neville Chamberlain in Munich, and Europe waited to see whether the latest gamble by the German Chancellor would prove one step too far. The U-boats took station with sealed envelopes to be opened in the event of conflict, their deployment in the Baltic and North Seas explained internationally as routine fleet exercises. *U23* was allocated a patrol area to the east of the Humber River, the boat carrying a mixed weapon load of torpedoes and mines.

According to Terence Robertson's excellent biography published in 1955, while they waited Schnee and Kretschmer were discussing reports of a new form of listening device with which the Royal Navy had located the wreck of the large aircraft-carrying submarine HMS *M2*. In January 1932, the British submarine had sunk in an accident during exercises in Lyme Bay, Dorset, its entire crew of sixty men killed in the disaster. Over a week after *M2* had gone down it was finally located by searching ships, the ASDIC-equipped HMS *Torrid* identifying a stationary submarine on 3 February, which was subsequently positively identified by divers. The first prototype ASDIC sets had actually been produced by both France and Britain in 1918, the Royal Navy mounting theirs aboard HMS *Antrim* in 1920, and beginning production of the tested equipment two years later in the utmost secrecy. Within one year, the 6th Destroyer Flotilla contained front-line ASDIC-equipped vessels.

News of the device began to leak out to the wider world; after all, the concept was not unique to the British, Germany having been interested in echo-sounder technology since 1913. Oddly, while those within German naval circles who were aware of the potential dangers of British ASDIC generally harboured a healthy respect for its potential, Dönitz appears at first to have been quite dismissive of the entire technology. However, it boded ill for the U-boats that the Royal Navy had clearly mastered the concept.

> 'Well, we will soon know what the Royal Navy has ready for us if we have to open those sealed orders,' Kretschmer told [Schnee]. 'I don't like carrying mines. It is not too comfortable to think that we might have to close the coast to lay them.'[2]

Somewhat ironically, torpedo mines would actually go on to be more effective for U-boats than torpedoes themselves during the early days of the Second World War. The first of the mines capable of being launched from a torpedo tube was the TMA (*Torpedomine* A), a moored mine that detached from its weighted plate after launching. Two could be carried in each torpedo tube and they were capable of being moored in water up to 270 metres deep, the 215 kg warhead floating on a chain designed to keep it just below the water's surface where it would be detonated by its magnetic influence trigger. The next model – the TMB – was a ground mine and therefore only able to function at a maximum of twenty metres. Initial instructions had briefed commanders to lay the mines at thirty metres, but questions arose regarding their reliability at this depth of water and subsequently orders were given to lay them in no more than twenty-five metres of water, though U-boat captains subsequently began sowing such fields in progressively shallower areas despite the vulnerability of a submerged U-boat at such depths. Measuring only 2.3 metres in length as opposed to the 3.4-metre-long TMA, up to three TMBs could be carried in each torpedo tube. Another unearthed magnetic mine, a timer activated the fuse in order to allow the firing boat to move out of range before the mine went live. The warhead of a TMB comprised 576 kg of TNT, twice that of German torpedoes used during the period. Like the magnetically fused torpedoes, the mine was designed to explode beneath a ship's keel once triggered by the magnetic field generated by the metal-hulled ship above. The resultant shock wave amplified through incompressible water was generally more effective than any contact hit against a hull side or bottom and was designed to snap the ship's spine and send it under. A third torpedo mine variant – TMC – was later developed following Dönitz's concerns that the TMB warhead was insufficient to sink capital ships. Measuring 3.4 metres in length, only one TMC could be carried in each tube, but the warhead was packed with 1,000 kg of explosive which was considered effective from depths up to thirty-six metres.

For three days, *U23* remained on station, avoiding coastal freighters and fishing boats, until recalled by Dönitz as Chamberlain returned to Britain with the signed agreement that sealed the fate of the Sudetenland and, ultimately, Czechoslovakia. However, though nobody could foresee it, this was the final act of failed appeasement in which Hitler successfully outmanoeuvred his opposite numbers and by September 1939, the stage was set for him to undertake one gamble too many.

The likelihood of war with Great Britain increased greatly in March 1939. Neville Chamberlain obtained French agreement to guarantee Poland's independence and come to its aid if threatened. Incensed by the action, Hitler promptly renounced the Anglo-German Naval Agreement along with his non-aggression pact with Poland. With international tension rising, Generaladmiral Raeder was gratified by Hitler's approval of an intensive building plan (named 'Plan Z') to bring about a greater measure of surface fleet parity with the Royal Navy. Privately, Hitler assured his naval chief that there would be no chance of war before 1944 at the earliest and Plan Z was scheduled for completion by 1948. Raeder remained convinced that any naval struggle with Britain or France would be fought with grand fleets, despite Dönitz's intense lobbying for greater consideration of his U-boat service.

The conflicting demands of German rearmament left the Kriegsmarine as the orphan of all resource allocation. Priority was given to Army and Luftwaffe units and by the outbreak of war none of the ships scheduled as part of Plan Z had achieved any significant stages of construction. Within a year, the grand scheme was scrapped and only those major surface vessels that predated Plan Z were eventually completed. There is little doubt that much of the scarce resources available would have been better used in U-boat construction. Mindful of 1917, Dönitz maintained that to strangle Britain's maritime trade and establish an effective blockade he would need 300 U-boats: one third on station, one third in transit and one third undergoing refit and repair. As war was declared he faced the Royal Navy with fifty-seven U-boats, only twenty of them suitable for Atlantic operations. Opposing the Kriegsmarine was a Royal Navy fleet that included 7 aircraft carriers, 15 battleships and battlecruisers, 66 cruisers, 184 destroyers and 60 submarines.

Preparations for another U-boat 'exercise' were well advanced by August 1939 with the plan for the invasion of Poland already decided on in Berlin; Hitler's original intention was to begin on 26 August. However, an 'Agreement of Mutual Assistance' signed between Great Britain and Poland at noon the previous day guaranteeing military support to either party should any other 'European country' attack, prompted a nervous Hitler to postpone his assault, delaying until the morning of 1 September. Nonetheless, Dönitz's U-boats were already at sea. There existed a firm mobilisation plan that had been decided during April and the appropriate orders were issued on 15 August. U-boats sailed to assigned bases and sea areas where they would execute instructions between 19 and 23 August, in line with the expected opening of hostile action against Poland. Dönitz had divided his FdU Command into two subordinate offices: FdU West, dealing with the North Sea and Atlantic, and FdU Ost that was concerned with the Baltic Sea. The *Weddigen*

Flotilla was attached to FdU West. Senior Officer Kaptlt. Looff returned from abroad on 20 August and immediately set about having his boats prepared for sea, seven boats being ready by the evening of 21 August. In total, Dönitz had thirty-five U-boats ready, with eight more available by the end of the month. There were a number that would remain unavailable: *U2*, *U8* and *U10* of the U-boat school, *U42* and *U51* in the middle of extended dockyard periods, *U49*, *U60* and *U61* with the U-boat trials group and *U11* with the Communications Experimental Department.

> In order to occupy the positions, which are not many, without a break with the minimum of boats I would need a further 43 boats and an additional 43 boats which, as experience shows, would be in dock undergoing overhaul. Thus, for a war of some length, 130 U-boats should be necessary.
>
> Even then I would have no reserves, so that I could send out 3 or 4 boats from home against a worthwhile transport reported by the intelligence service. Also, there are not enough boats for the Atlantic and none for remote sea areas. Therefore, the minimum requirement to be aimed at is 300 U-boats.[3]

While ocean-going U-boats headed early for the Western Approaches and the Atlantic gateway to Great Britain, the six boats of the *Weddigen* flotilla were tasked with the North Sea mission Operation *Ulla*, their orders to monitor the north-eastern English Channel and the sea areas off the English east coast up to 0° longitude. On 25 August Hitler ordered *Ulla* extended to northern harbours and the Great Fisher Bank. At 0130 hrs on 25 August, the code-word 'Special Command Ulla' was received at Dönitz's headquarters and re-transmitted with emergency priority by Naval Communications Officers at Wilhelmshaven, List and Borkum. At 0350 hrs Kretschmer's *U23* slipped from Wilhelmshaven harbour.

Once past the Nordeney lightship Kretschmer headed north until noon that day when the bows were turned to point due west towards the entrance to the English Channel, passing flotilla-mate *U15* later that night as Kaptlt. Heinz Buchholz took his boat to patrol the English east coast. Kretschmer quickly reached his operational patrol area north of the Dutch West Frisian island of Terschelling and slowly patrolled the area allocated to him. Aircraft were frequently sighted, initially positively identified as Luftwaffe flying boats though by the beginning of September neither Kretschmer nor his lookouts were any longer certain whether they were sighting Heinkel He 111 bombers or British Avro Ansons. The morning of 1 September dawned overcast and hazy with only a slight breeze sweeping from the east. In Poland, war had begun as Hitler finally threw caution to the wind and launched the German invasion; the Kriegsmarine's obsolete battleship *Schleswig Holstein* fired the opening salvo against the Polish bastion at Westerplatte. The tension amongst the young submariners aboard *U23* was palpable: would Britain and France honour their declaration of solidarity with Poland? Or had the *Führer* managed yet another miracle of iron-fisted diplomacy. Within days they had their answer.

At 1100 hrs on 3 September, the *Weddigen* Flotilla war diary recorded 'War with Britain'. Eight hours later France had followed suit and also declared war and Germany was in conflict with two of the most powerful naval forces in Europe. All Kriegsmarine vessels and shore stations received the following message at 1256 hrs German time: 'Hostilities with Britain effective immediately.' A little over an hour later, a second message was relayed from Berlin: 'U-boats to make war on commercial shipping in accordance with operations order.' This instruction related to the ordered adherence to Prize Laws countermanding a previous directive that U-boats were only to engage in combat as a matter of self-defence. Momentary confusion aboard the combat boats was removed after Dönitz himself clarified matters with his own message transmitted later that afternoon: 'Open hostilities against Britain immediately. Do not wait to be attacked first.'

Restrictions were kept in place regarding action against French ships as the French government appeared more hesitant in its declaration of war and Berlin harboured hopes that they could be dissuaded from military action. Therefore, convoys were to be attacked only if it were absolutely confirmed that no French vessels sailed amongst them. French ships were still strictly only to be engaged in a clear case of self-defence.

These restrictive measures robbed U-boats of their greatest asset of surprise, but were of little concern to Kretschmer. He broke open the sealed orders that he had carried in the event of hostilities and found them to be almost identical to those he had carried during previous sailings. *U23* was to leave its reconnaissance lines and head west to the

Humber estuary to lay mines. However, he did not have long to register his disappointment as even these instructions were short-lived.

As night fell a little after 1800 hrs on 4 September, *U23* received radio instructions from FdU to abort the mission and return to Wilhelms-haven. Kretschmer followed the returning cruiser *Emden* into harbour during the following afternoon, his entry coinciding with the first British air raid of the war to use bombs instead of leaflets. At the outbreak of hostilities, the RAF's initial strategy was to launch raids against German shipping located by verified aerial reconnaissance. Flying Officer Andrew McPherson, flying a Bristol Blenheim of 139 Squadron RAF, sighted a large German naval force in the Schillig Roads off Wilhelmshaven on the 4th, though failure of the aircraft's radio meant that the information was not relayed to other attack squadrons until after his return to base. Hours later, fifteen Handley Page Hampdens and nine Vickers Wellington bombers were despatched, but failed to find the target in poor visibility. The next day, McPherson again spotted warships off Brunsbüttel, Wilhelmshaven and in the Schillig Roads, though yet again his radio malfunctioned and no attack could be launched until after his return.

This time, fourteen Vickers Wellingtons of 9 and 149 Squadrons and fifteen Bristol Blenheims of 107, 110 and 139 Squadrons successfully took off to attack warships at all three locations in a raid that became disastrous for the attackers. As well as demonstrating the RAF's unpreparedness for war by one aircraft nearly departing without any bombs being loaded and another suffering malfunctions of all defensive weapons, five Blenheims and five Wellingtons each failed to locate targets. Two Wellingtons mistakenly bombed Esbjerg in Denmark – 110 miles north of their intended target of Brunsbüttel – and though three bombs hit the pocket battleship *Admiral Scheer* in Wilhelmshaven, none of them exploded. *Emden* was damaged when (ironically) Flying Officer Henry Lovell Emden's 110 Squadron Blenheim was shot down and crashed on its deck, killing eleven sailors and injuring thirty more.[4] Emden's Blenheim and four more from 107 Squadron were lost over Wilhelmshaven; fourteen crewmen were killed and two captured, the first prisoners of war taken from RAF Bomber Command in the Second World War. During the raid, Kretschmer had taken his small U-boat into the centre of the harbour basin away from the expected target, but as quickly as it had begun the attack was over, leaving smoking aircraft wreckage and little bomb damage behind.

It had been a disappointing and brief first war patrol and Kretschmer strained at the leash to have his boat back at sea. While sailors traditionally indulged in alternative pastimes whilst ashore, Kretschmer maintained a slightly priggish demeanour that would set him apart from many of his contemporaries and increase the air of aloof detachment that he had acquired. Kretschmer remained at all times a Prussian officer and professional seaman, actively pursuing fresh instructions for his next war patrol as the boat underwent routine maintenance work.

U23 sailed for its second patrol on 9 September, slipping from Wilhelmshaven at 1130 hrs. Kretschmer swung west-northwest once past Wangerooge, dusk settling on clear skies and the sea relatively calm, when a warning message was received from his nearby old boat *U35* of the presence of enemy submarines. Lieutenant-Commander George Chesterman Phillips, RN, had fired the first British torpedoes of the war when he attacked *U35* from HMS *Ursula*, a salvo of five torpedoes all missing Lott's U-boat. The warning proved valid as at 1950 hrs *U23* also evaded three torpedo tracks, all visible by their tell-tale bubble trails created by steam propulsion. Kretschmer 'combed the tracks' pointing the bow into the oncoming torpedoes and removing a broadside target, before showing a clean pair of heels and escaping at full surface speed from their submerged assailant.

The remainder of the voyage into British waters was relatively uneventful and by 12 September *U23* lay approximately seven nautical miles east of Montrose, Scotland, though they sighted no targets of opportunity – only the steady presence of British patrol boats. Weather conditions had deteriorated a little, a moderate wind whipping up the sea into whitecaps before rain arrived to obscure visibility further. Kretschmer was soon forced to retreat from the area at speed: *U23* was cruising surfaced during the early hours of 14 September when an aged British destroyer emerged from a thick squall at close range. Attacking the Royal Navy ship was not possible at a distance of only 200 metres and in the strongly gusting wind. Neither party opened fire and *U23* crept back to its previous position through the course of the next day as the weather gradually cleared. Finally, Kretschmer was rewarded with the sighting of a laden tanker estimated at 3,000–4,000 tons. The ship was under escort by armed trawlers and zig-zagging dramatically. Kretschmer shadowed the small convoy until, finally,

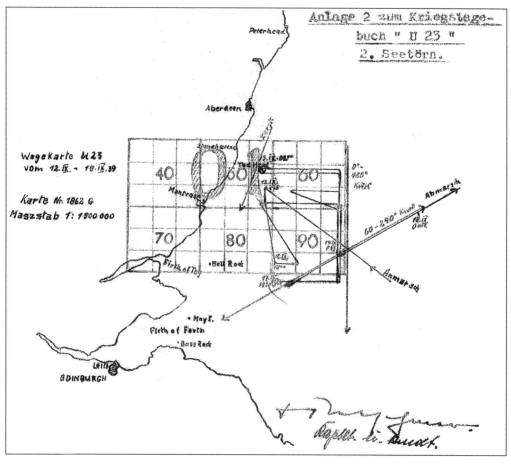

Detail from the track chart of *U23*'s second patrol, showing the operations close to the Scottish coast.

he fired three single shots at the close range of between 500 and 300 metres. The seconds ticked by with no detonation until his hydrophone operator detected a distant explosion: not an impact but the 'end of run' detonation generally caused when a torpedo that has missed is exploded by the increasing water pressure as it sinks once its fuel had been exhausted. The 'end of run' explosion is sometimes incorrectly attributed to a mechanical process intended to destroy any errant weapon, but this is not so. There was no 'device' that caused a German torpedo to explode at the end of its intended run or afterwards, rather it was generally caused by the aforementioned pressure, impact with the seafloor or another obstacle, or by pure malfunction.

Kretschmer was furious and retreated from the scene to study his calculations and confer with Schnee and his torpedo crew on the possible causes of the failed shots. He remained certain of the firing solution that had been plotted and firmly believed that all three torpedoes had passed beneath the hull of the tanker. Equipped as they were with magnetic firing pistols, this was the optimal place for the warheads to explode, using the physical properties of the dense water and compression wave transmitted between the explosion and the ship's hull to snap the ship's spine in two. If successful, this was a far deadlier method of attack than using conventional contact fuses that merely punched a hole in the ship's side. However, the premise only offered success if the magnetic pistols were efficient and already Kretschmer was beginning to form doubts regarding the efficacy of the U-boat's primary offensive weapon.

Three days later, inshore near Todhead, Kretschmer fired his fourth torpedo at a steamer sailing an independent zig-zag course. At a range of 800 metres, Kretschmer made his final shot of the patrol and it too missed. Despondent, Kretschmer ordered course set for Kiel. Two days later *U23* passed through the Skagerrak and, in accordance with Prize Law, intercepted five vessels which were searched for contraband.

Dating to the earliest days of sail, Prize Law governed the acquisition of equipment, vessels and cargo captured from an enemy belligerent. By the time of submarine warfare, the application of these rules demanded that enemy merchant vessels, or neutral ships suspected of carrying contraband through a declared blockade area, be stopped and searched before either being sunk or taken as a 'prize' to the nearest friendly port. Furthermore, before any vessel judged to be a legitimate target could be sunk, all passengers and crews had to be taken to a place of safety. The rules were waived if target ships were clearly armed, displayed a persistent refusal to stop once requested or offered active resistance. U-boats entered the Second World War ordered to abide by Prize Rules, thereby robbing them of the element of surprise. The U-boats were also highly vulnerable to Q-ships, merchant ships heavily armed with concealed weapons designed to lure surfaced U-boats into range before opening fire. However, though feared by U-boat crews, the effectiveness of the Q-ship was somewhat exaggerated. During the First World War from a total of 150 engagements, British Q-ships destroyed only fourteen U-boats and damaged sixty for a loss of twenty-seven of their own.

Coupled with obedience to Prize Law, U-boats had already been forbidden to attack any French ships, though this order was finally cancelled by 24 September, alongside a gradual loosening of restrictions on U-boat operations. By the end of September, strict U-boat adherence to Prize Law was relaxed in the North Sea and two days later permission was given to attack any darkened ship sighted near the British and French coasts. By 4 October, the zone in which Prize Law had been removed was extended to 15° West, well into the Atlantic Ocean. British merchant ships were armed in response and Dönitz subsequently designated several British coastal zones as open to unrestricted submarine warfare, although it was strictly forbidden by Hitler to use the phrase openly as he was aware of the emotive power it still exerted following its use during the First World War, particularly within the United States that still vividly recalled the sinking of the *Lusitania* in 1915. The areas in which restrictions were removed gradually expanded until, by January 1940, U-boats were free to operate at maximum efficiency, torpedoing suspected enemy ships without warning. It had taken only four months for the Kriegsmarine to reach a state of unrestricted submarine warfare, for which Dönitz would later be charged with 'crimes against peace' at the post-war Nuremberg trials. Used in his defence was an affidavit from Admiral Chester Nimitz who, in his role as Commander-in-Chief, United States Pacific Fleet, had ordered an unrestricted submarine campaign initiated on the first day of the United States' entry into war against Japan.

Within the Skagerrak, *U23* stopped the vessels *Saturnus* (sailing from Karlstadt, Sweden), *Nemrac* (from Käsmu, Estonia), *Sedia* (from Copenhagen, Denmark), *Stella* (Esbjerg fishing boat) and *Emily* (from Mariehamn, Finland). No forbidden goods were found and each ship left to go on its way unhindered. After dodging another torpedo attack in the Samsö Belt, Kretschmer brought his boat into Kiel's naval harbour on 21 September and reported the usage of three G7e torpedoes, one G7a and a single shell from his boat's 20 mm C/30 flak weapon, used to halt *Saturnus* with the traditional 'shot across the bow'. At the end of his war diary, Kretschmer also recorded items he deemed significant:

Special Observations:
1. British navigation lights at Todhead and Scurdy Ness.

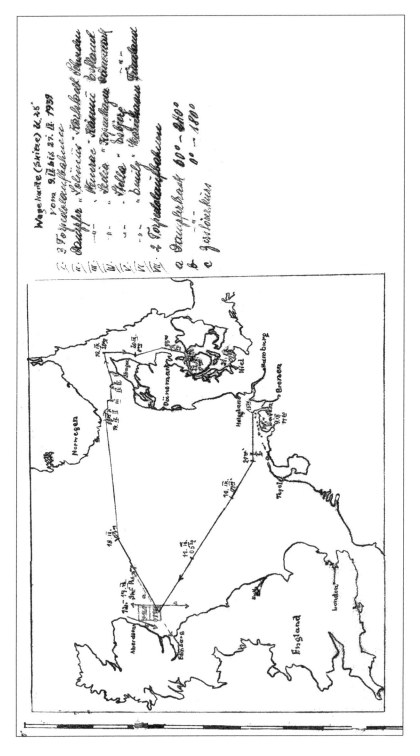

The full track chart of the second patrol, with the locations of *U23*'s encounters in the Skagerrak.

2. The quadrants AN 0160 and 0190 were constantly occupied by guardships (trawlers, apparently new builds) which often had nets.
3. Apart from the above-mentioned destroyer (older build), no warships sighted.
4. Two main steamer tracks were observed:
   a. Bass Rock in 240° (traffic flowing both in- and outbound)
   b. Eastern edge of quadrant AN0160 and 0190.
5. Neutral shipping travelling with navigation lights set, British merchant ships without flags by day, darkened at night.
6. Picket boats travelling at night with lights set (very lightweight) and without the required fishing lights.
7. Pickets boats often join incoming steamers in quadrant AN0196.
8. British torpedoes show bubble head [*Blasenkopf*] and bubble trails like the G7a torpedo, but the oil track is more prominent.

FdU West war diary:

U23 arrived in Kiel. Report of the commander:
1. A picture of the trade traffic before the Firth of Forth.
2. The fact that there were not any British warships sighted except for one destroyer.
3. In the case of a double attack of a British submarine on *U23*, well-defined bubble heads and strong oil track spurs were sighted. Since the attacks in both cases took place at a very advanced dusk, the British submarines must have very good night vision. These experiences have been reported to all parties.

While *U23* had been at sea, Dönitz had been promoted to the rank of *Konteradmiral* and named BdU (*Befehlshaber der U-Boote*: Commander-in-Chief U-Boats) on 19 September. Beneath BdU, two separate offices were created: BdU Operations, headed by Korvettenkäpitan Eberhard Godt, who would oversee all operational matters; and BdU Organisation, headed by Kapitän zur See Hans-Georg von Friedeburg, who would deal with logistics and organisational tasks for the expanding U-boat service.

Following the overhaul required after a thirteen-day patrol, *U23* passed through the Kaiser Wilhelm Canal to Brunsbüttel at the mouth

of the Elbe River, and onward to Wilhelmshaven in preparation for
the boat's third mission, arriving on 30 September in the military
harbour and departing early the following day. *U23* had been ordered
to patrol the western entrance to the Pentland Firth and sailed from
Wilhelmshaven under escort by the converted trawler Vorpostenboot
V404 *Deutschland*, passing Heligoland and proceeding towards the
southern tip of Norway before heading north-west in the direction of
the Orkney and Shetland Islands. Kretschmer was determined to take
advantage of his stationing at the entrance approaches to the Orkney
Islands' famous Scapa Flow anchorage, one of the primary bases used
by the Royal Navy since the beginning of the twentieth century and
developed as a direct answer to the growing German naval capabilities
of Kaiser Wilhelm's Imperial Navy before the First World War. He was
certain that it would be possible to penetrate the sheltered basin and
attack whatever lay beyond. However, such an attack had twice been
attempted unsuccessfully during the previous war: in these attempts
U18 was rammed and sunk by a patrolling trawler in November 1914, and
UB116 detected by hydrophones in October 1918 and disabled by shore-
triggered mines before being finished off with depth charges. Aboard
the latter, Oblt.z.S. Hans-Joachim Emsmann had planned to enter the
anchorage through Hoxa Sound, and Kretschmer had decided to do the
same despite the fierce currents to be found there that made successful
navigation of the passage difficult under the best of circumstances.

Approaching the Orkney Islands, at 0445 hrs on 4 October, lookouts
sighted a single steamer travelling darkened towards Scotland. *U23*
successfully evaded an evident picket line of fishing boats as he
pushed his boat at high speed, trimmed down low on the surface in
pursuit. Closing the ship, which he estimated at 3,000 tons fully laden,
Kretschmer ordered a burst of fire from the boat's 20 mm deck cannon
across its bows. Unlike the Swedish vessel of the previous patrol,
the target ship immediately began to accelerate and transmit a plain
language radio message reporting gunfire attack by U-boat. Seventeen
more shots were fired into the bridge and superstructure before it finally
stopped engines a little before 0600 hrs. Kretschmer and his lookouts
could plainly see the crew getting into their lifeboats and waited until
they were clear of the ship before Schnee fired a single G7a torpedo from
Tube III at a range of 300 metres. After a run of only fifteen seconds,
the torpedo exploded opposite the smoke stack and SS *Glen Farg* began

to sink. After thirty seconds, the ship's spine broke and it went under in two pieces within another minute. The two-year-old steamer owned by the Anglo-Norwegian South Georgia Company and based in Aberdeen, was en route from Trondheim for Methil and Grangemouth carrying general pulp, carbide, paper and ferro chrome, though Kretschmer had greatly overestimated its size as it was registered at 876 grt. The merchant's master, Robert Galloway Hall, had supervised the evacuation of his crew, though *Glen Farg* went down with the body of 46-year-old donkeyman David Thomson Couper, killed by shrapnel caused by the U-boat's cannon fire. Royal Navy destroyer HMS *Firedrake* picked up the sixteen surviving crewmen twenty-five miles east of the Orkneys later that day.

With his proximity to land and the likelihood of *Glen Farg*'s radio distress call being speedily answered by British forces, Kretschmer departed immediately without questioning the shipwrecked survivors and identifying his victim. Only an hour and a half later, *U23* made an emergency dive to escape aircraft and, before he could resume his planned approach on Scapa Flow, fresh instructions were received from FdU ordering *U23* into a new search area of the North Sea away from the Orkneys. Kretschmer was disappointed, but acknowledged the navigational orders and *U23* arrived at its new station in quadrant AN2672 by 1600 hrs. A tedious sequence of orders relocating the boat to north and then south again was punctuated by alarm dives caused by aircraft, but little else. British trawlers were periodically visible in their picket lines; otherwise the North Sea appeared barren.

Unbeknownst to Kretschmer, his movement order had been the result of an operational plan to attack Scapa Flow that had already been formulated with the task allocated to *U47* and Günther Prien. As the FdU West war diary recorded:

> To lessen suspicion, five U-boats operating around the Orkneys were withdrawn from these waters on 4 October in order to avoid potential disturbances in the Orkney sea area and thus potentially alert the British. Everything was being staked on the one card.

Prien had passed around the Orkneys on his previous patrol into the Western Approaches during which he had sunk three ships. The additional underwater capabilities and weapon load of a Type VIIB U-boat were considered essential to capitalise on any successful penetration of the British Scapa Flow defences; the opportunity to launch such an attack was unlikely to be available twice. *U14* had conducted a detailed reconnaissance of the approaches to Scapa Flow during September and armed with all the latest intelligence available, including Luftwaffe aerial reconnaissance, Prien made his successful penetration of the Scapa Flow anchorage on the night of 13/14 October and sank HMS *Royal Oak* by torpedo. Although the tragedy of 836 Royal Navy men killed by the sinking of the aged battleship was a catastrophic loss, Prien's attack could have caused greater devastation if the sound had not been virtually empty, the bulk of the Home Fleet having sailed that night. Furthermore, *U47* fired seven torpedoes of which three were duds.

Meanwhile *U23* had received orders to return once more via the Skagerrak to Kiel, its North Sea station to be taken over by *U18*. This proximity to another U-boat almost spelled disaster for Adalbert Schnee as he controlled the watch on 13 October. While Kretschmer rested in his bunk, *U23* battered through large waves whipped up by a strong south-southeast wind. In the bad visibility, an unexpected submarine appeared at close range and Schnee immediately ordered an alarm dive. The conning tower was cleared in seconds and as Schnee readied himself to race below, his final glimpse showed the approaching boat to be German, whereupon Schnee frantically attempted to stop the dive. Those moments of hesitation almost meant disaster as *U23* tilted downward with both hatches still open. Kretschmer was immediately on his feet and reached the control room as cold water began crashing through the open hatch. Assisted by others, he managed to close the main watertight hatch as *U23* submerged, immediately noticing the absence of his IWO and assuming Schnee likely to have been lost at sea in what could only be called a tragic diving accident. Once *U23* was at trim and the hydrophone operator had established no trace of the other submarine, Kretschmer returned to periscope depth to ensure the sea was clear before ordering the boat surfaced, expecting to begin a search for Schnee's body. Draining the flooded conning tower into the bilges of the control room, they were surprised at the small amount of water that came forth, opening the hatch to find a damp, but very much alive, Schnee huddled inside. He had had the presence of mind to jump into the tower and slam the hatch above as the hatch below was shut in front of him and patiently waited for the boat to resurface.

On 14 October, they encountered a far more dangerous submarine when HMS *Sturgeon*, travelling submerged on patrol twenty nautical miles west-northwest of Skagen, Denmark, found a surfaced U-boat approaching.

1435 hrs: Sighted a vessel bearing 000°. Enemy course 110°. Range 4,500 yards. Identified the target as a German submarine. Started attack.

1452 hrs: Fired three torpedoes. Lost trim on firing and went deep to prevent *Sturgeon* from broaching.

1457 hrs: Heard distinct explosion.

1501 hrs: Heard two more explosions. *Sturgeon* meanwhile had returned to periscope depth. The U-boat was not seen again.

On Kretschmer's part the attack appears to have taken him completely by surprise, as his war diary recorded: 'Two heavy underwater explosions near the boat. Probably torpedoes. No bubbles sighted.' All three torpedoes had missed and *U23* made haste from the area, reaching Kiel two days later at 0745 hrs, a single success pennant flying from the periscope.

Tragically, there was bad news arriving for Kretschmer shortly after his return to Kiel when his brother, Hans-Joachim, was shot down and killed on 17 October over the North Sea. Leutnant Kretschmer belonged to Major Werner Kriepe's reconnaissance unit Aufklärungsgruppe 122, and his aircraft was flying solo hunting for traces of HMS *Hood* which the Germans believed to be in the Firth of Forth at that time. The Heinkel He 111 H-1 (F6+PK) was piloted by Oberfeldwebel Eugen Lange, the crew rounded out by radio operator Unteroffizier Bernhard Hochstuhl and gunner Hugo Sauer. Flying northwards at an altitude of 10,000 feet nine miles from the Whitby coast, Lange was sighted by three Spitfires of Green Flight, 41 Squadron, RAF, that were on a routine defensive patrol from Catterick airbase. Pilot Officer Peter Blatchford led his two wingmen Flight Sergeants E. A. Shipman and Albert Harris and it was Shipman who spotted the German at approximately 1630 hrs.

Shipman led the attack, expending 2,000 rounds in his first pass that raked the fuselage as far as the gunners' positions before creeping on to both engine housings. A brief flurry of returning fire from Sauer passed by the Spitfire's left wing before he was silenced; both of the Heinkel's engines were also soon smoking after being raked with bullets. As the other Spitfires added their own fire to the attack, the dorsal machine gun could be plainly seen pointing harmlessly skyward, Sauer killed in Shipman's initial attack. Inside the cockpit Kretschmer, too, was already dead, shot through the head.

The Heinkel was doomed and came down in a shallow dive into the sea twenty miles east of Whitby, the impact stopping Lange's watch at 1700 hrs. Blatchford radioed a position report and that he had seen two survivors clambering out of the sinking aircraft and into a tiny liferaft. Though lifeboats from Whitby and Runswick Bay had put to sea to find the Germans, they were not recovered as the weather conditions worsened. Not until two days later, after forty-three hours at sea, was the dinghy washed ashore in a rocky cove to the north of Sandsend village. With Lange nearly unconscious from exposure, Hochstuhl clambered inland, despite having been wounded in the leg by flying shrapnel, and surrendered himself and his comrade to Special Constable George Thomas, who had been charged with guarding the entrance to the nearby Sandsend railway tunnel. The two Germans held the dubious distinction of being only the second and third Luftwaffe fliers captured on British soil during the Second World War. Sauer's body later washed ashore near Whitby on 30 October and he now lies in the German Military Cemetery at Cannock Chase. Hans-Joachim Kretschmer's was never found, presumably entombed within the remains of his aircraft at the bottom of the North Sea.

Otto Kretschmer was back at sea on his fourth patrol on 1 November, the newly awarded decoration of the Iron Cross Second Class adorning his shore uniform. This time he was tasked with minelaying, *U23* carrying nine TMB mines (numbered 163 to 171) to the waters directly off Cromarty Firth, an inlet within the Moray Firth, Scotland. Two days from port the U-boat gyrocompass failed, requiring an extended period travelling submerged in which to repair it, though this also gave the opportunity to prepare the tubes with the TMB mines. The gyrocompass was an essential tool for the U-boat: a non-magnetic compass, it was unaffected by the metal construction of the vessel itself or by weather and ship movement.

On 4 November Kretschmer began approaching his target area, passing submerged astern of a patrolling destroyer as he noted occasional

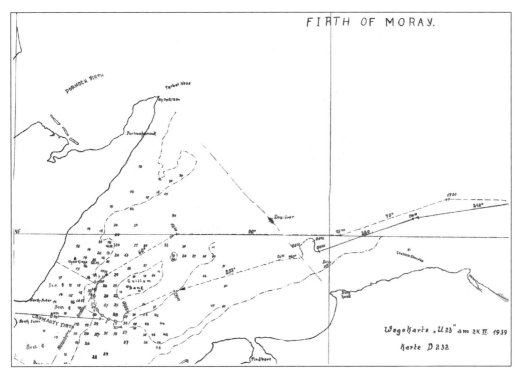

FIRTH OF MORAY.

Wegekarte "U 23" am 24. XI. 1939

Karte D 232

U23's fourth war patrol, showing the careful navigation
essential for successful minelaying.

naval trawlers also positioned nearby as stationary pickets. Undeterred,
he began the minelaying operation at 1008 hrs and by 1054 hrs the last
of the nine TMBs had left the tubes. Kretschmer had laid his small
minefield in a sweeping curve that edged on to the border of the military
harbour limits, mirroring the contour of the shallows of the Guillam
Bank to the east and depositing each mine at 500-metre intervals
between twenty-four and thirty-three metres depth. The minelaying
had been a complete success and *U23* traced a reciprocal path east
towards the open sea, slipping undetected once more past the single
patrolling destroyer. Though the mines were not specifically recorded
as swept, they claimed no victims. Shortly afterwards, a moored mine
was recovered by a fisherman off the Cromarty Firth, prompting extra
minesweeping vigilance on behalf of the Royal Navy defences, which
perhaps also accounted for the field sown by *U23*.

Concerned at the potential unreliability of his boat's compass,
Kretschmer opted not to return through the Kriegsmarine minefields

that defended the German Bight, and instead headed east for Norwegian waters and through the Skagerrak to Kiel. The boat's attack periscope also failed on the morning of 6 November because of what Kretschmer deduced was a simple design flaw. Early U-boats were equipped with a sighting column known as a TUZA (*Torpedo-U-Boot-Zielapparat* – U-boat Torpedo Target Apparatus) for making surfaced attacks. The TUZA mounted a pair of Zeiss binoculars atop a pedestal from which the target bearing could be transmitted below to the control room by means of a Bowden cable. In order to calculate the necessary deflection angle for firing a torpedo, the torpedo officer read the target bearing from the mechanical receiver and, combining this information with the U-boat's course, was then able to calculate the angle on the bow to target by means of tables or the use of a 'torpedo calculating disc'. He then passed this information orally to the bridge and the officer at the TUZA. Once his information was set on the sight column, the U-boat was turned to bring the target into the targeting crosshairs, the launch order passed to the torpedo room, and the weapon was fired manually. A salvo spread of torpedoes was launched by firing torpedoes while the U-boat was still turning.

However, the primary disadvantage of this sight was the necessity to demount the instrument before the U-boat submerged, something rectified when Zeiss developed the TUZA 3 which was pressure-proof up to a depth of 100 metres. The TUZA would eventually be superseded by the UZO (*U-Boot-Ziel-Optik*) introduced from 1939 onwards, though many of the smaller boats did not have the newly developed system, which electrically transmitted target information to the torpedo calculator by means of a synchro link rather than from man to man with the data entered manually. However, on Kretschmer's boat the TUZA was mounted atop a retracted attack periscope which apparently had caused the problem that disabled the periscope. Kretschmer recorded his observations for improving the design of this unwieldy system in his war diary, :

> The attack periscope was repaired; apparently a foreign body fell into the top of the periscope housing. This trouble could happen again at any time, as long as the TUZA in its present version is mounted on the front periscope. Because the periscope must be completely retracted, the result is that the periscope housing

remains open at the top. I therefore consider it essential that
I have a hinged cover plate attached to the TUZA mounting.

Kretschmer took *U23* through the Little Belt and into Kiel Fjord,
unchallenged by German patrol ships along his path, much to the
young commander's chagrin. Indeed, the pilot vessel designated to
escort *U23* into harbour only appeared to notice the U-boat when it lay
stopped with navigation lights showing. Kretschmer was not impressed
with the lack of effective security when he was acutely aware of the
threat posed by British submarines, and included in his war diary his
impression that security vessels within the Western Baltic and Little
Belt were in a 'deep sleep'. *U23* finally tied up in Kiel's military harbour
on 9 November, the war diary of the FdU West recording:

> *U23* in Kiel through Little Belt. The boat has carried out its
> mining task immediately before Invergordon in a determined and
> skilful execution, despite the failure of the gyro and numerous
> guard ships [*Bewachung*].

Navigation officer and IIIWO, Heinrich Petersen received the Iron
Cross Second Class on 19 November in recognition of his sterling
performance at navigating under difficult circumstances. Minelaying
was not to Kretschmer's taste, and remained unpopular throughout the
U-boat service. While there were pragmatic reasons for this – primarily
the fact that to lay effective minefields, U-boats had to operate inshore
under the noses of prowling defensive craft and within easy range
of shore batteries – the fact that any 'kills' made by the mines were
frequently unrecorded and therefore did not reflect on either the
successful commander or crew was also a cause of dissatisfaction with
the entire task. Therefore, it was with some relief that Kretschmer's
next mission was planned as a torpedo patrol, destined for the Scottish
coast of the North Sea and with freedom to explore the inner waters
of the Orkney Islands: *U23* was ordered to hunt for any traces of the
British fleet that was reported to have relocated following Prien's attack
on Scapa Flow.

Kretschmer slipped from the Tirpitzmole in Kiel at 2200 hrs
on 5 December, sailing through the icy Kaiser Wilhelm Canal to
Brunsbüttel. The canal was a little under 100 kilometres in length
(approximately 53 nautical miles) and with a maximum depth of

only eleven metres; all vessels travelled surfaced and at low speed lest excessive wake damage the canal banks. After passing into the North Sea and after two days on patrol, *U23* dived for long enough to let a neutral steamer pass beyond the line of sight before resurfacing when, at 1600 hrs, four smoke columns were spotted almost dead ahead by lookouts atop the conning tower. The ships gradually hove into view with visible lights showing from more than one of them. Leading the small convoy was a trawler making enough speed to send strong plumes of smoke through its single stack, followed by a steamer showing clearly illuminated Danish markings and a second larger steamer that displayed no markings at all. Another trawler trailed in the rear and at 2326 hrs, *U23* made a surfaced attack on the second freighter, which Kretschmer estimated at 5,000 tons.

Surfaced at a range of 600 metres, while Kretschmer maintained his overall view Schnee fired a slightly oblique shot, though Kretschmer had overestimated the target speed and the torpedo passed ahead of the freighter, which continued oblivious to the near miss. A second attack was immediately plotted, this time at the decreased range of 500 metres. An electric G7e was launched a little after midnight and hit neutral Dane SS *Scotia* in the bow. The 2,400-ton steamer was travelling from Denmark to the United Kingdom in ballast, a large Danish flag painted on each side of the hull but obviously not illuminated nor observed by Kretschmer or his crew. It started to sink slowly by the bow and within seventeen minutes was gone, a strong detonation observed as the boilers exploded underwater. Of the twenty-one men aboard, nineteen were killed, including the master, 42-year-old Paul Albert von Achen. The accompanying freighter SS *Hafnia* rescued the only two survivors from the freezing water.

Kretschmer left the scene unobserved and later submerged in order to load the two reserve torpedoes before returning to his surfaced path towards the Orkneys. That evening, in rough seas, *U23* began to reconnoitre the inner sounds of both the Orkney and Shetland islands, alternating between running submerged and surfaced by night with the boat trimmed down to lower its silhouette. Conditions around the Orkneys were particularly difficult with strong currents and treacherous underwater topography, although Petersen's superb navigation allowed Kretschmer to avoid natural obstacles in what could be dangerous waterways even without the presence of enemy patrols.

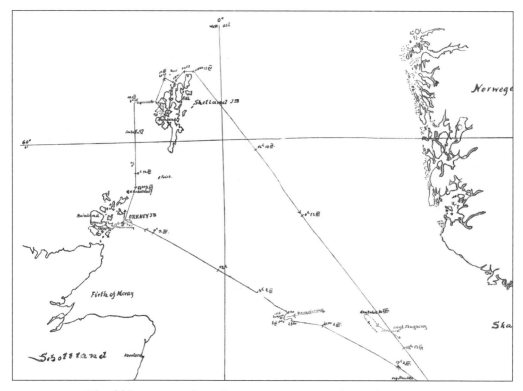

The fifth war patrol, with its incursion into the inshore waters
around Orkney and Shetland.

They sighted nothing but picket ships and decided to move onwards
to the Shetlands, though once more there was little to be seen except
patrolling trawlers until the early hours of 12 December. During the
darkness, in bad weather with variable visibility, the unmistakable
silhouette of an enemy warship at anchor was sighted on the north-west
coast of Yell Island. *U23* crept slowly forward for a surfaced attack and
at 0208 hrs two G7e torpedoes were fired from tubes one and two at
the target only 600 metres distant. The estimated torpedo run would
have been 48 seconds, but from the first torpedo there was only silence
as the shot disappeared completely. However, the second impacted
the darkened ship, throwing a fireball twenty metres into the night
sky, though the shock waves felt through the boat were surprisingly
mild. Within seconds the reason was obvious as the target was vividly
illuminated and revealed to be a large rock formation. *U23* hurriedly
reversed from the scene, Kretschmer initially fearing that he might

actually have fallen into a deliberate trap, but the lack of enemy response soon allowed him to relax.

The U-boat sailed from the scene while the KTB was dutifully filled out for an attack on a 'Rock (mistakenly identified as warship).' Kretschmer reckoned the first torpedo had failed to detonate due to what was probably the sloping bottom leading upwards to the rock formation; the torpedo likely ran aground at an angle too oblique to activate the 'whiskers' of the contact pistol.

A possibly apocryphal story related in Terence Robertson's book tells that Kretschmer then issued a brief radio transmission to FdU West that said: '*Felsen torpediert, aber nicht versenkt.*' ('Rock torpedoed but not sunk.') As the story relates, the message was mistyped by the receiving signals officer who replaced 'Felsen' with 'Nelson'; the battleship HMS *Nelson* was a prestigious and actively sought target for the Kriegsmarine and had already been attacked on 30 October by Kaptlt. Wilhelm Zahn's *U56* near the Orkney Islands with three torpedoes, all of which failed to explode. Following Kretschmer's radio message, Goebbels's Propaganda Ministry was apparently already preparing a broadcast with which to taunt the British Admiralty about the condition of their precious battleship, until Dönitz managed to intervene and get the broadcast amended after debriefing Kretschmer on his successful return to Kiel on 15 December under *Vorpostenboot* escort.

Despite various re-tellings of the story, both in my own book *First U-boat Flotilla* and by others, it does not really stand up to careful scrutiny and – while we might like it to be true – there seems little historical basis for this message being sent. Kretschmer was averse to broadcasting all but the most necessary signals from his U-boat at the best of times as he correctly surmised that British scientific advances would soon turn the numerous U-boat radio transmissions against them through advances in direction finding. It was this reluctance to use his radio – particularly after he joined the Atlantic war aboard *U99* – that led to his famous nickname 'Silent Otto'; the fact that it also suited the taciturn nature of the man once ashore just enhanced the suitability of the name. Therefore, with that in mind, it appears highly unlikely that he would have made such a frivolous transmission for the sake of humour. Furthermore, that would not explain the time lag between the transmission apparently made at sea and the expected broadcast being only stopped days later following *U23*'s return. I suspect that the tale is merely U-boat folklore.

Kretschmer's war diary listed the following conclusions from his detailed study of the target area:

1. All beacon lights of the Orkneys, Fair Isle and the Shetlands completely extinguished. North Ronaldsay light burning on 9 December from 0400 until morning light.
2. The entrance to the harbours can nevertheless be recognised by the illuminated guard ships located there.
3. A specially large number of guard ships (trawlers) was found in St Magnus Bay.
4. In the entrance to the Yell Sound there is an upwardly shielded light ship with a solid white light at about 60° 40.5' N – 01° 14.5' W. There is a guard nearby.
5. The descriptions of currents within the maritime manual [*Seehandbuches*] give good indications of the actual currents and are generally correct. The sheer cliffs of the Shetlands are, after having recognised their form by day, good as navigational indications for night-time activities, especially as they are mostly in deeper waters.
6. I believe that further activities in this maritime area are easily feasible by taking advantage of the appropriate weather conditions.

From the war diary of FdU West:

Commander *U23* arrives from Kiel with the report about the area Orkneys–Shetlands. He probed, with great courage, into the potential hiding places of the British surface fleet, such as Ura Firth, Busta Voe, Olna Firth and Aith Voe, all of which he found empty. I intend to send him there again on the basis of his knowledge of the place, since a penetration, especially of Sullom Voe, appears to be quite possible according to his report.

Kretschmer was awarded the Iron Cross First Class on 17 December 1939 for his sterling record thus far. At the end of the year Dönitz forwarded to the Kriegsmarine Operations Division (SKL) the report written by outgoing chief of the *Weddigen* Flotilla, Kaptlt. Hans-Günther Looff, in which he assessed all of the commanders within his unit, Kretschmer amongst them:

Kapitänleutnant Kretschmer has been commander of *U23* attached to the U-Flotilla *Weddigen* since the autumn change of commands in 1937.

He is, for his age, unusually quiet, but has an extremely strong and defined character. Very pleasant, modest and comfortable in form and appearance. Never tries to pretend there is anything special about himself. Exceptionally well-kept and of good appearance, well versed though socially reserved. With a good mental disposition, he is very versatile and well-read, stimulating in conversation, as soon as he has overcome a certain shyness and reserve. Tends to be a loner and will make up his mind about matters on his own, although he is very popular in the comrades' circle with his basically cheerful and especially comedic manner, as well as his dry sense of humour.

He has already served faultlessly for two years during peacetime as a U-boat commander; his crew is well trained and led, and his boat has operated well in every respect, with particularly good seamanship noted. Navigation is always prudent and safe. In exercises, he shows good tactical skills and understanding. During several war patrols, Kretschmer has proved himself extremely reliable, and, after having already been awarded the Iron Cross Second Class, he was awarded the Iron Cross First Class in December, after a difficult special operation that he performed with daring and care.

His most striking features when in action are the ease, calmness, determination and great ability with which patrols have been carried out. He is a U-boat commander who is particularly suited for carrying out difficult tasks and is physically and mentally fresh with an excellent temperament, so that a successful career is to be expected from him. Kretschmer is an especially suitable commander for a large U-boat. Possible post as a flotilla commander as well as an advisor or Admiralty staff officer appears to be appropriate when the requisite seniority is reached. He will fully fill any position in his own right, and deserves attention for the future.[5]

Chapter Three

1940

From the beginning of hostilities against France and the British Empire to the end of 1939, nine U-boats had been sunk, six by enemy warships and another three by mines. In return, 114 enemy vessels had been sent to the bottom, amounting to some 420,000 tons of commercial shipping. While on the surface this would appear to show a German surge in fortune, given the number of combat U-boats available to Dönitz, the loss of nine was almost crippling, proving the lie of U-boat domination frequently assumed in many post-war histories. Kretschmer's point of view regarding the 'Happy Time' of U-boat 'dominance' will be seen later.

For the Kriegsmarine, the beginning of 1940 was punctuated by an organisational restructuring of the U-boat service. Where previously flotillas had been identified by the name of a First World War hero, they were henceforth given numerical designations. The original flotilla – *Weddigen* – was now given the title '1st U-boat Flotilla' and to the eight existing flotilla U-boats, came the additional Type IIs of the now defunct *Lohs* and *Emsmann* flotillas bringing the 1st U-boat Flotilla's strength to a total of seventeen boats.

On 3 January, three days after his twenty-sixth birthday, Schnee finally departed his post as IWO aboard *U23*. He was transferred to the manpower pool of the U-boat training flotilla (U-Ausbildungsflottille) in Plön in preparation for assuming command of his own boat. At the end of the month he was assigned captaincy of the training boat *U6* as part of the 24th U-Flotilla based in Memel on the Baltic Sea. Finally, on 19 July 1940, he would become skipper of the 1st U-Flotilla's combat boat *U60* and began an illustrious career that would see most spectacular success in the Atlantic as captain of the Type VIIC *U201* from the beginning of 1941. Schnee was one of the brightest of the 'second generation' of U-boat commanders and had learned a great deal of his future capabilities from his time aboard Kretschmer's *U23*.

His replacement as IWO was a fellow member of Crew 34, Latvian-born Oblt.z.S. Hans-Diedrich Freiherr von Tiesenhausen. He arrived to take up his new post on 28 December 1939, briefed in full by his predecessor about the exacting standards expected of him by his new commander. Tiesenhausen had served aboard the light cruiser *Nürnberg* during 1937 and 1938, and subsequently as a platoon leader in the flak company of Pillau's 5. Marine-Artillerie-Abteilung (5th Naval Artillery Battalion), later becoming the battalion adjutant on 27 June 1939. Unhappy in the naval artillery be requested a transfer to U-boats and began training at the U-boat school at the beginning of October 1939. *U23* was his first active U-boat posting.

Otto Kretschmer began his sixth war patrol when northern Europe was in the grip of the most severe winter for decades, parts of Germany experiencing the coldest temperatures recorded for a hundred years. By mid-December 1939, sea ice had formed along the German Bight and it remained there for up to a hundred days. Strong patches of drift ice were flowing from the Elbe, and the temperature in the great port city of Hamburg would be measured at −29.1 °C on 13 February 1940. *U23* cast off from the Tirpitzmole at 2357 hrs on 8 January 1940 to begin transiting the Kaiser Wilhelm Canal, assisted by the tug boat *Monsun* and an icebreaker. Past Brunsbüttel, in the mouth of the Elbe, the escort changed to the tug *Eisfuchs* before handing over once again to a *Sperrbrecher* mine-clearance vessel assisted by another icebreaker.

In addition to the potential for general hull damage from the ice, the bow-caps of U-boat torpedo tubes were relatively delicate and susceptible to impacts that could render them inoperative, so *U23* crept gradually seaward until the marker buoy Elbe 1, where Kretschmer took the boat down for its customary test dive to check hull integrity following shipyard repair, and to sharpen the crew after days spent ashore.

Kretschmer had been ordered once again to patrol the Orkney Islands, opting to take *U23* north and into Inganess Bay to hunt for potential targets that might have eluded reconnaissance flights. With conditions on the surface bright and calm, though bitterly cold, *U23* proceeded largely submerged during the day on 10 January; enemy submarines had been reported ahead, though hydrophone sweeps at a maximum depth of sixty metres failed to show any indication of any prowling enemy.

At 1632 hrs the following day, approximately sixty nautical miles east of Wick, a distant steamer was seen to starboard headed west towards Scotland, sailing a course that would cross the U-boat's path. Kretschmer dived *U23* as the ship drew near and prepared for a submerged torpedo attack. The target was estimated at 3,000 tons and wrongly identified as a tanker, and at 1833 hrs Kretschmer fired his first torpedo, a G7a which ran true until it detonated prematurely near the starboard side of the target ship after a distance travelled of about 260 metres. Aboard the Norwegian SS *Fredville* the master, Ole N. Johansen, immediately ordered all engines stopped and his crew of sixteen to prepare to abandon ship. Although no hostile vessel had been sighted, Johansen feared either a mine or sabotage, as the so-called 'Wollweber League' had been responsible for planting of explosives aboard several freighters in Scandinavia.[1] Johansen probably did not suspect U-boat attack as his

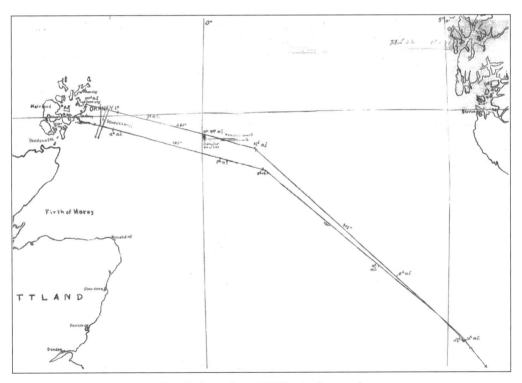

Track chart from *U23*'s sixth patrol.

ship was travelling in ballast from Drammen to Methil to collect coal bound for Oslo and carried a brightly illuminated neutral flag painted on both sides of the hull and plainly visible by night and day.

While the crew took to the lifeboats, Johansen remained aboard and soon recalled his men as no damage could be found following the unexplained explosion. Second Mate Arthur E. S. Knudsen descended into the *Fredville'*s cargo hold and confirmed that there had been no serious weakening of the hull or other obvious effects. Meanwhile, Kretschmer had taken *U23* in a slow loop around the stationary freighter, evidently still ignorant of its neutral markings. At 1911 hrs he fired a second torpedo, but with no visible result as the electric G7e left no track that could be followed: it was either a clear miss or a malfunctioning torpedo. As some of the Norwegian crew continued to check the outside of the hull using torches while sitting in the small lifeboat secured by ropes, they too found no obvious damage and reboarded as Johansen prepared to get under way again. At the moment that the small boat was being lifted onto its davits Kretschmer fired his third torpedo; this one ran straight and true and hit the port side astern near the funnel, rupturing the hull. As cold water cascaded through the torn skin of the ship and into the engine room, the hot triple expansion steam engine and boiler exploded, breaking the ship in two near Number 4 hatch. The stern sank in less than three minutes, but the forward part of the ship stubbornly refused to go down. In no doubt that his victim was doomed, Kretschmer opted to leave immediately while still submerged in order to maintain his planned schedule dictated by tides, currents and the cycle of day and night.

> We cannot wait to observe the sinking of the bow, since the time draws near for the planned operation within Inganess Bay. For this purpose, the boat should be near Auskerry at around 0400 hrs, so that it can still run out of the Stronsay Firth surfaced under cover of darkness.[2]

Kretschmer took *U23* away from the stricken Norwegian, which slowly sank behind him. Of the sixteen crewmen, eleven were killed, including Knudsen, who was still in the cargo hold when the torpedo exploded. The ship sank so slowly that the five survivors took the opportunity to leave their lifeboat periodically, reboard and hunt for any other survivors. They were later picked up by a Swedish vessel and taken to

Kopervik in Norway. Days later, on 16 January, maritime hearings were conducted in Arendal in which the survivors were carefully questioned. With no visible vessels nearby, and the vessel under close guard while in port thereby negating sabotage, the conclusion was reached that the SS *Fredville* had been sunk by a mine.

Though successful, Kretschmer was disappointed at the performance of his torpedoes. He would have been further depressed if he had correctly identified the target as an ordinary freighter rather than a tanker and of only half the tonnage he had estimated. It seems that he carried only four torpedoes rather than the capacity of five and therefore had expended nearly all of his ammunition. German torpedo stocks were relatively low during 1939, production taking place in five locations: Deutsche Werke in Kiel, Julius Pintsch in Berlin, Auto-Union in Zwickau, Borgward in Bremen, and Planeta in Dresden. Before the war a paltry seventy were produced per month, and though by the spring of 1941 this number had risen to 1,000, stocks were low for all Kriegsmarine forces during 1939 and 1940.

> 2015 hrs: Loading the reserve torpedo (G7e) into Tube III. Unfortunately, after shooting three torpedoes, only one is left for the main operation. But I had thought it necessary to destroy the tanker.

Shrouded by early morning darkness on 12 January, Stronsay Island came into sight to port; almost exactly on schedule at 0430 hrs. The weather had moderated considerably and barely any wind ruffled the calm sea surface. Petersen steered *U23* sharply south at that point and by 0510 hrs the boat was passing between British picket ships arrayed east of Auskerry Sound, taking advantage of the period of new moon and almost total darkness as Kretschmer counted as many as eleven trawlers floating silently on the gentle swell.

U23 passed the north-eastern tip of Deerness at 0612 hrs and a little over twenty minutes later was easing surfaced into Inganess Bay, past a single guard ship that showed no signs of having detected the prowling U-boat. There, lying silently at anchor within the bay, Kretschmer's lookouts sighted a large anchored tanker estimated at between 8,000 and 10,000 tons, the consolation prize that Kretschmer had hoped for if unable to find Royal Navy capital ships. With only a single torpedo left aboard, the firing solution was carefully and exactingly worked out and he let it go at 0650 hrs, seeing it explode almost dead centre. The Danish 10,517-ton tanker MV *Danmark* was carrying 8,200 tons of petrol and 5,760 tons of kerosene from Aruba, destined eventually for Nyborg, and the blast broke the ship in two, the stern sinking and forepart drifting slowly ashore to ground in shallow water. A constructive loss, the forepart was later refloated and served as a British fuel oil storage hulk in Inverkeithing. There were no casualties from the forty-man crew of the Danish ship, most of whom were ashore, and the British authorities remained ignorant of what had caused the explosion, believing it most likely to have been an aerial mine. The U-boat's new IIWO, L.z.S. Hans-Joachim von Knebel-Döberitz (often known as Hans-Jochen), who was on his first voyage aboard *U23*, later recalled the event:

> We were very proud and happy. The British didn't believe we could be so close by in the anchorage, and when the torpedo exploded they searched the air with lights because they thought we were the Luftwaffe. They were even firing into the air. Of course, for me on this first voyage, it was quite an experience. Then we turned back and again we sailed very close to the lookouts, but got out of there in one piece.[3]

Although the guard ship nearby showed no signs of having seen them, Kretschmer took *U23* out of the shallow bay at full speed, heading towards open water and the potential safety that depth provided if submerging became necessary. At 0820 hrs another steamer was seen headed towards Kirkwall, but Kretschmer was out of ammunition. Directed to return to Wilhelmshaven, *U23* entered port with a tug and icebreaker in thick fog at 0932 hrs on 15 January.

> Special Observations:
> 1. A steamer track in quadrant 1228 east on both eastern and western courses.
> 2. A steamer track high in the Orkneys between 2° W and 2° 10' W heading on both northerly and southerly courses.

From the war diary of FdU West:

> *U23* entered Wilhelmshaven after mission to the Orkneys. Following a short rest, on about 19 January he will return to the operating area of Orkney–Shetlands.

Kretschmer drove both himself and his crew hard. Though he maintained a clinically professional demeanour at sea and on land, and went as far as to admonish crewmen of his boat who were seen drunk in public between patrols, he still demonstrated humanity and compassion in his dealings with his men. While Günther Prien is reputed to have been unpopular on a personal level with his crew, though revered for his military accomplishments, Kretschmer earned a level of devotion that would have been impossible if he had acted purely as a military disciplinarian. Though success by a commander in combat reflected well on his crew and could be enough to maintain their loyalty, it did not serve to generate the camaraderie that Kretschmer managed to instil in the men aboard *U23* and his next command *U99*. Indeed, by the beginning of 1940, Kretschmer's accomplishments were relatively modest in terms of tonnage sunk or prestigious raids such as that mounted in Scapa Flow.

With a high degree of efficiency demanded of its crew, *U23* spent the least amount of time possible in the shipyard between patrols, putting to sea once more on 18 January, bound again for the Shetlands. Over the course of ten days Kretschmer found himself frustrated by enemy nets, patrolling armed trawlers, gyrocompass failure and, perhaps most crucially, torpedo failure. Two days from port an attempted surface attack on an estimated 1,000-ton steamer failed, the torpedo with magnetic pistol arcing into the darkness with no observable result. The following morning, at 0542 hrs, another attack was made against a second freighter, Tiesenhausen firing the 'eel' in Tube I at a range of only 300 metres but, yet again, showing no visible result. Both attacks had been made at close range and almost perfect right angles, and their failure was both galling and unexplained.

> We had the worst torpedoes in the world, which simply did not work. The firing device, which was magnetic, you had to shoot under the target and then it was supposed to break the keel plate and so [the target would] go down immediately. This, they just would not do. They would not explode that deep, 50 per cent of them were duds that did not explode at all. Some exploded earlier or later, at the end of the run; all sorts of things, but just not what they were supposed to do. This was a very unhappy time at the beginning of the war and also when we were ordered not to use

the magnetic firing mechanism but to fire on impact, then we found out that our torpedoes were running too deep and there was no impact, at least not for destroyers . . . maybe for a deep-draught tanker or large ships, but not for destroyers.[4]

Unbeknownst to Kretschmer and the crew aboard *U23*, in Wilhelms-haven Dönitz had called an urgent meeting with members of the Torpedo Inspectorate to discuss the burgeoning crisis of German torpedo failure. The year had begun with newly appointed Torpedo Inspector Vizeadmiral Oskar Kummetz conducting numerous emergency tests at Eckernförde under difficult conditions. These resulted in an 8 per cent rate of premature detonation and an additional 6.5 per cent in which there was a danger of premature detonation. Thus, the fact that German torpedoes were potential defective was at last officially proven. However, Dönitz's primary concern, as recorded on 17 January, was to examine the possibility that the *Magnetzündung* (MZ – magnetic trigger) was faulty.

The main matter under discussion was the suspicion held by BdU for some time now that MZ could fail to operate, even if aimed under [a target ship]. There have been repeated cases of shots fired at close range with good firing data which have not brought results and the reasons have been obscure even to the Torpedo Inspectorate (*U47*). These cases have increased particularly recently (*U24, U15, U20, U59, U60*). The Director of the Torpedo Experimental Command reports that *U20*'s shots cannot be explained. Even if the speed had been wrongly estimated, at least one shot should have hit. The only possible explanation for the failure of the three torpedoes to detonate would be the fact that the size of the ship had been very much over-estimated. The Commanding Officer of the boat denies this possibility. I have reached the following conclusions regarding these and similar failures.

All the Torpedo Experimental Command's analyses of shots are possible for the particular case under consideration and possibly correct in some cases. But I cannot believe that, with a whole series of failures of this kind, there are other reasons in every case. I am convinced that there is a connection between all these so-called unexplained shots and there is a common cause for their failure which has not yet been discovered. Up to now I have believed that in many cases boats have fired past, due to misinterpretation of the firing data or aiming mistakes. In individual cases I have sent the boat for further training. But now, with these failures of shots fired under the simplest conditions by a series of the best-trained commanding officers and torpedo men, I cannot accept this explanation any longer. Some of these commanding officers have undergone two years of training in peacetime and all of them, when re-examined, were found to have good or very good skill in firing. From now on, I shall regard all such shots at closest range, where a detailed examination of the circumstances and the firing data exclude the possibility of a miss, and which so far have been regarded as unexplained, as failures of the firing unit. It has happened again and again in these cases that the Torpedo Inspectorate has held the view that the boats have missed or made incorrect observations, only because the reason for the possible failure was not known and could not therefore be made to apply and that afterwards their view has turned out to be incorrect. See, for instance, premature detonations, detonations half-way through the run, firing under with impact firing. The attitude to be adopted to this problem is therefore, other unknown causes of failures are possible. Otherwise we shall never get anywhere.[5]

A fresh set of instructions regarding the use of the MZ was transmitted to every U-boat at sea. Against targets of less than 4,000 tons – such as Tiesenhausen's last target – all U-boats were now to adapt a depth setting of four metres as opposed to the previous six. Against targets under 1,000 tons it was simply to be accepted that there was a good chance that the torpedo would not detonate at all. Against all other targets, U-boat commanders were instructed to fire the torpedo with a depth setting of the ship's estimated draught plus one metre.

East of the Orkneys, Kretschmer ordered his boat dived at 0750 hrs on the 21st as dawn streaked the sky. A single tanker was approaching on a southerly course while the steamer that he had previously attacked doubled back to sail alongside the new arrival. Kretschmer immediately smelled a trap, suspecting the apparently innocuous freighter potentially to be a Q-ship, loitering in the area most likely to attract enemy attack rather than heading at all speed for the safety of harbour. With only a single torpedo loaded, Kretschmer took the boat down to a depth of fifty metres to free the two reserve torpedoes from their storage and load tubes one and three. The process was arduous and time-consuming and Kretschmer fully intended to return to the attack in daylight though the distant sound of depth charges – estimated to be at least five nautical miles away – gave him pause. The explosions began to creep nearer as *U23* cruised at listening speed towards the east and abandoned any attempt at closing the potential targets again. At nightfall Kretschmer surfaced and resumed his course northwards to the Shetland Islands.

U23 was suffering problems with both compasses: the gyrocompass was providing doubtful readings and the magnetic compass was unreliable due to the northerly latitude. Testament to Petersen's navigation, the boat made landfall precisely at the entrance to Yell Sound as planned. However, only two days from a full moon, the clear bright night made surface travel perilous, the U-boat's low silhouette being starkly outlined against the snow-covered shoreline to any watching vessel to seaward. Kretschmer submerged frequently and found his path frustratingly barred by anchored patrol vessels and new net barrages. The defences of both the Orkneys and Shetlands had begun to be strengthened significantly and obviously, primed by growing fears in Whitehall of a potential German seaborne attack on the most northerly British islands, either with the purpose of invading or perhaps to destroy the seaplane base that had been established at Sullom Voe.

However, not all of the newly deployed barriers were effective and Kretschmer actually found that the net defences before Sullom Voe itself were located in such deep water that he noted recommendations within his war diary that the British entrance channels could probably be blocked with future careful positioning of U-boat mines.

Nonetheless, he sighted no targets of opportunity until he departed the Shetlands, diving at 2020 hrs for a submerged attack on what he estimated to be a 1,000-ton steamer; the torpedo now set to run at a depth of four metres rather than the previously accepted six following BdU's newest recommendations. Tube III was prepared for firing as Kretschmer lined his target squarely in the crosshairs of the attack periscope. At close range he gave the familiar '*Lohs!*' and the firing handle for the G7e torpedo was hammered downward. Unfortunately, nothing happened. The torpedo had been loaded too forcibly, which had pushed the weapon hard against the tube restraining bolt and resulted in the 'eel' being 'pinched'. It was *Rohrversager*, a 'hang-fire' where the torpedo failed to leave the tube after firing. Increasingly frustrated at his lack of success – and this time the fault lying with human error during loading – Kretschmer retreated and surfaced to prepare a second shot, while the restraining bolt was changed on Tube III and the torpedo cleared.

Racing at full speed on a path running almost parallel to the steamer's predicted course, *U23* was able to position ahead of the ship for a second submerged attempt, the moonlight too bright to allow Kretschmer to attack while remaining surfaced. At 2156 hrs Tube II was fired at a range of only 400 metres, once again almost at perfect right angles and providing a textbook target. Infuriatingly, this torpedo also failed: a *Kreislaufer*, or 'circle-runner', as the torpedo's own delicate gyroscope failed and the weapon turned in a lazy circle and missed the freighter entirely, endangering the firing U-boat instead and forcing a hurried dive to greater depths.

Kretschmer opted to leave the scene before swinging back towards the Shetlands with his remaining torpedoes, frequently travelling submerged rather than be silhouetted against the snow-covered land illuminated under what was now full moonlight. At 1850 hrs on 24 January he mounted yet another submerged attack on a steamer that he estimated to be 1,500 tons, possibly the same ship that he had already twice failed to sink. Another torpedo was fired at only 240 metres distance against the slow-moving target and finally, Kretschmer was rewarded with a tangible hit. Captain David Sjurson Humlebrekk, a 43-year-old native of Voss, Norway, was taking his 1,086-ton SS *Varild* from Horten to Southend in ballast, due to collect coal for return to neutral Norway. The single torpedo hit the ship's port side amidships and it went down in only 45 seconds, the blast wave shaking *U23* as it coursed through the water. From the freighter's entire complement of fifteen men there were no survivors.

Kretschmer continued to stalk the steamer tracks that he knew lay off the Shetlands' south-east coast with his one remaining torpedo, until water was discovered inside its small control compartment during maintenance, rendering it inoperable, and *U23* began its return home. Directed by FdU West to Wilhelmshaven away from the hazardous ice-strewn Baltic, *U23* was escorted into harbour by a *Sperrbrecher* and the tug *Geier*, making fast at the U-boat base at 2045 hrs on 29 January.

From the war diary of FdU West:

> 29 January 1940: *U23* into Wilhelmshaven after its Shetlands trip. Sullom Voe secured by web barrier without discernible gap. In the numerous bays searched, no ships sighted. The operation was strongly hindered by especially bright nights (full moon, shining snow slopes). A steamer 1,500 tons sunk, one circle runner, two failures by non-ignition. Both failures were fired before new orders had been issued on the pistol adjustment.

The following afternoon the faulty torpedo was removed from *U23* and the boat moved into the West Werft to begin cleaning and complete overhaul for the next patrol. After days of shipyard repairs, last-minute work on the forward trim tanks was finished on 8 February and the boat moved back to moor alongside the *Donau* depot ship that served as crew quarters for the 1st U-Flotilla. The U-boat already had its full complement of five torpedoes aboard – three in the tubes and two reloads under the forward compartment floor, but took on a sixth G7e as Kretschmer received his orders for sailing to Heligoland the following morning, at 0825 hrs on 9 February. He and his officers were determined to increase the ammunition load aboard the small boat, the extra torpedo crowding an already uncomfortably small bow room yet further.

U23 slipped from the *Donau* and rendezvoused with Sperrbrecher VII *Sauerland* which would escort the boat into the Jade basin as both protection and icebreaker. *U23* had been fitted with an *Eisschutz* – ice protector – a metal protective cover over the bow. This shielded the delicate doors of the bow torpedo tubes and was held in place by connecting rods across the top and over the bow-decking, while the space between the hull of the U-boat and the ice protector was filled in with wood which afforded greater shock resistance. The boat made the eight-hour voyage to the German island bastion where Kretschmer and his men spent their last night ashore in barracks before sailing the following day. The opportunity was also taken to ventilate the two electric torpedoes stored in the forward compartment. This routine procedure was a by-product of recharging the electric torpedo's batteries, a process that released highly flammable hydrogen gas, which had to be evacuated from the mechanical spaces of the weapon to prevent explosions caused by sparks from the electrical motor. This process, too, would later prove to be responsible for one of the final flaws in Germany's torpedoes, but not discovered until 1942 by chance aboard *U94* on an Atlantic patrol.

At 1215 hrs on 10 February, after the *Eisschutz* had been removed, Kretschmer took his boat out to sea and followed the path designated *Weg Grün* ('Green Route') towards the operational area east of the line between the Moray Firth and Shetlands that had been allocated to him as part of Operation *Nordmark*. Alongside Kretschmer, *U13*, *U18*, *U19*, *U22*, *U57*, *U60*, *U61*, *U62* and *U63* had been committed to the operation, in which they were acting as support for the battleships *Scharnhorst* and *Gneisenau*, the heavy cruiser *Admiral Hipper* and eight escorting destroyers.[6] The Kriegsmarine had received Luftwaffe reconnaissance reports of convoy traffic between Norway and Scotland, the ON/HN series of convoys between the Inner Leads off Bergen and Methil that had begun in November 1939. Fish, butter, meat, timber, pulp, aluminium, ferrous alloys, minerals and other commodities were gathered in the ports of Narvik, Trondheim, Bergen and Gothenburg and loaded aboard ships for transport to the United Kingdom (HN), the ships then returning in ballast to collect more (ON). Initial convoys were small, composed of British ships, but their size swelled over the harsh winter that provided excellent protection from the Luftwaffe and potential cover from U-boat interception; there were later up to forty ships in each convoy including many chartered from neutral countries, while others just 'tacked themselves on' for the benefit provided by protection in numbers. Generally, each convoy was escorted by between four and seven Home Fleet destroyers, a C-Class anti-aircraft cruiser and/or a submarine, as well as a separate force of cruisers providing distant cover to the south.

Berlin issued a declaration to all neutral nations that any ships which joined the convoys between Scandinavia and the United Kingdom did so at their own peril while planning *Nordmark* as an interception of this valuable mercantile traffic. Postponements through ice-damage to *Gneisenau*'s propellers meant that the surface force did not sail until 18 February after Luftwaffe reconnaissance reported the Norwegian departure of the twenty-seven ships that comprised HN12 on 16 February and twenty-four ships of ON14 leaving Scotland the following day.

Commanding Admiral's plan: Surprise sortie with the battleships, the *Hipper* and three Type 36 destroyers against enemy convoy traffic between Norway and the Shetlands, destruction of merchant ships belonging to, or sailing for the enemy, also their escorts. Furthermore, the heavy ships' appearance in the northern North Sea should draw enemy home forces putting to sea towards our U-boats in waiting disposition.

Destroyers are to complement the heavy ships' sortie by carrying out operations against commercial shipping in the eastern Skagerrak. The battleships' advance proceeded according to plan on 18 February. Radio monitoring did not detect any striking radio traffic and it seems that the enemy has failed to notice anything. Naval Staff thinks that enemy situation and the expected convoy traffic afford good prospects for the operation.

Air reconnaissance by Commander, Naval Air, West and Luftflotte 10 as far as 61° North has not produced any reports on the enemy. Our own U-boats in the Orkneys–Shetlands area, which sent some reports on enemy ships and convoys, have been allocated new attack positions appropriate to the enemy movements detected.[7]

As events transpired, *Nordmark* was a complete failure. British reconnaissance had, in turn, detected the departure of the surface force and convoy ON14 which had already left Methil was ordered to divert to Kirkwall until a powerful covering force of heavy ships – HMS *Rodney*, *Hood* and *Warspite* – arrived in the area. Though Germany's naval signals intelligence service, B-Dienst, detected the new British orders they remained uncertain which convoy had actually been diverted to the Orkney anchorage and was now due to resail on 20 February and SKL still expected ON14 to be perfectly positioned for interception by *Nordmark* between the Shetlands and Norway. Even after the actual situation was recognised in Berlin, high hopes were maintained that by extending the *Nordmark* sortie by an extra day, a strong chance remained of intercepting significant enemy convoy traffic or even closing on Kirkwall and bombarding the gathered merchant ships in port. However, since shore commanders were unwilling to interfere with an operation in progress, unequivocal instructions were not issued, and the surface force was back in Wilhelmshaven by the afternoon of 20 February; the performance of the battle group was deemed 'unsatisfactory' by SKL in a lengthy written critique of this timid operation.

The sole victory against the Norwegian convoys achieved by any part of the *Nordmark* operation was made by Kretschmer. *U23*'s outward journey had sighted only a Swedish independently sailing freighter and suffered an alarm dive after two moving trails of fresh oil indicated a possible British submarine attack. As the boat reached trim following the sudden dive and quietly moved at slow speed underwater, the distinctive sound of a nearby submarine's propellers and electric engine switches being thrown was heard through the water as the enemy passed close by submerged, near enough to rock *U23* gently with its wake.

By 14 February Kretschmer was sailing submerged by day and searching for anchored warships in Lax and Cat Firths on Mainland Shetland's eastern coast. However, after creeping stealthily through four different inlets he sighted no worthwhile targets, only prowling patrol vessels and the occasional ancient reconnaissance aircraft above. As his role was primarily one of reconnaissance for the heavy surface units, Kretschmer was under strict instructions to attack only 'valuable targets' and so ignored Norwegian and Danish steamers that passed him by and was redirected to head at speed for the Fair Isle passage at midnight on 17 February. At 0927 hrs that morning he sighted the unmistakeable silhouette of a *Norfolk*-class cruiser at a distance of six nautical miles. However, pinned to his slow submerged speed, any attack was impossible and he could only watch in frustration as the ship disappeared to the north-east. All he could do was transmit a radio message of the sighting later using his periscope aerial, while also collecting information of enemy ship sightings transmitted by the other U-boats.

On 17 February 1940, D-class destroyer HMS *Daring* had been ordered to join convoy HN12 carrying iron ore from Bergen to Methil. Twenty merchant ships were deployed in three columns with an escorting destroyer on each quarter and the submarine HMS *Thistle* trailing astern. HMS *Daring* and *Delight* flanked the port side of the convoy with HMS *Ilex* and *Inglefield* to starboard. By the early hours of 18 February, HN12 was forty-five miles east of Wick and making seven and a half knots, the foremost destroyers (*Delight* and *Inglefield*) zig-zagging, but the stern escorts sailing a straight line as dictated by standing orders for all trailing destroyers, a tactic that was to lead to disaster.

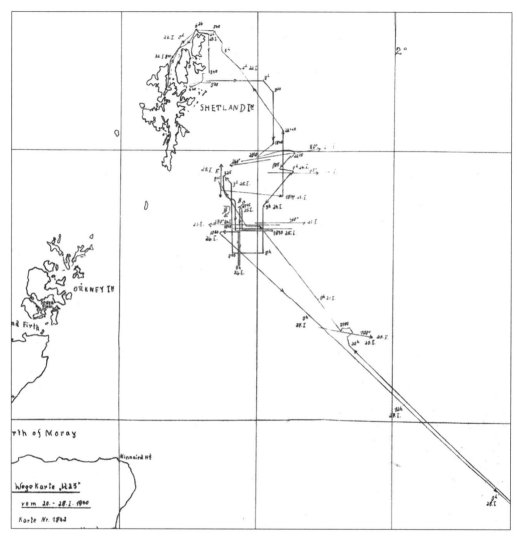

Kretschmer's seventh, and last, patrol in *U23*.

The convoy's position had already been reported by Joachim Schepke in *U19* a few hours before and Kretschmer moved towards its predicted course though, before he found HN12, he finally sighted what could be fairly described as a valuable and worthwhile target. At 2130 hrs on the 17th a single heavily laden freighter of a type operated by J. & C. Harrison Shipping Line, London, estimated at 5,000 tons, was seen by lookouts on *U23*'s conning tower as the boat ran surfaced by night. Kretschmer approached the unsuspecting merchant ship at moderate speed and Tiesenhausen fired from a range of only 300 metres. The electric torpedo disappeared without trace, another failure.

Despondent at the waste of precious ammunition, Kretschmer took *U23* south to his new operational zone where he sighted the first ships of HN12 a little after midnight, his war diary recording what happened as he prepared to mount a surfaced attack:

> 0000–0107 Grid square [AN]1832. Two destroyers sighted heading south-west. Must relate to earlier W/T transmission from *U19* [053/0015/18/1: Enemy convoy sighted Square 1494, enemy steering southerly course.] I steer in this direction.
>
> 0305. Convoy heaves into sight at bearing 0 degrees. I manoeuvre ahead of it to eastward in order to have the dark horizon at my back and avoid the unwanted attentions of the moon. The convoy, comprising twenty ships, is sailing in three columns with a destroyer at each corner; those on the port and starboard bows are zigzagging to and fro ahead of the wings of the convoy. The rear destroyers are maintaining a steady course.
>
> Astern of and between these two is an L-class submarine. While attempting to penetrate the convoy from the east and fire a shot at one of the steamers sailing in the middle I get caught between the two portside destroyers so decide to attack the one in the rear of the convoy.

The destroyer was so close that Kretschmer could see the blue glow of shaded lights on deck and at 0354 hrs he fired a single torpedo towards HMS *Daring* at a range of only 800 metres. The 'eel' struck the ship on its port side aft, an initial explosion recorded by observers aboard HMS *Thistle* as a 'dull red glow', but followed by a second more violent explosion that immediately blew the hull apart and broke the ship in two, the stern towering out of the water and sinking until only a small section broke the surface of the sea, while the forepart capsized and sank within half an hour. The convoy steamed onward.

Six minutes later Kretschmer fired a second torpedo at HMS *Thistle*, but missed. After intercepted reports named the destroyer as HMS *Daring*, Kretschmer reported his attack and the convoy course position before leaving the scene, followed by HMS *Ilex*, though the destroyer had obviously failed to detect the U-boat and made no effort to engage Kretschmer. After hours of surface speed, Kretschmer dived at 0755 hrs while the sun rose; five powerful depth charge detonations were then felt within *U23*, but no damage was sustained as they were distant enough to indicate that they were being dropped by guess-work and the U-boat had not actually been detected.

Meanwhile, HMS *Ilex* signalled *Thistle* to rescue survivors while it swept ahead to attempt to locate the attacking U-boat. The submarine commander, Lieutenant-Commander W. F. Haselfoot, was somewhat confused by the instructions and he requested *Ilex* lower a boat to assist, though his message was never received aboard the hunting destroyer. Oblivious to Kretschmer's attempted attack on his submarine, Haselfoot took *Thistle* close to the drifting wreckage, sighting three men. The first of the three soon disappeared from view and sank into the North Sea while Lieutenant R. P. N. Ennor dived from the submarine deck into the frigid water with a line attached to attempt to rescue the second man who clung to a floating raft and had evidently broken his arm. The panicked survivor gripped the young officer as he attempted to fasten the line around his body, dragging them both underwater where, slick with oil, the injured rating also soon disappeared into the depths. A lone survivor clinging to what protruded of the stern was finally rescued with the assistance of two whalers lowered from a returned HMS *Ilex*. In total, only four other survivors had been rescued; the captain, Commander Sydney Alan Cooper, RN, and 156 men were killed in the sinking. The tragedy of HMS *Daring* prompted the C-in-C Home Fleet, Admiral Sir Charles Forbes, immediately to alter standing orders that forbade escorts stationed astern of a convoy from zigzagging.

Kretschmer had continued south-east, entering grid square AN4141 a little after midday by Petersen's reckoning, when five destroyers approached at high speed and stopped nearby, beginning to drop depth charges. Two barrages followed, exploding in *U23*'s proximity but causing no damage as a biplane also began circling overhead to join the hunt. In mid-afternoon a line of ASW trawlers approached and Kretschmer took his boat to eighty-six metres at dead slow speed. A U-boat's greatest chance of attack and defence was while surfaced and moving at speed to take advantage of the small silhouette and capabilities of the diesels. However, without the blanket of night to cover him he was forced to remain in the depths, vulnerable to ASDIC detection and robbed of high speed and manoeuvrability. Fortunately, his luck held and the Royal Navy failed to find his slowly moving boat as *U23* crept away.

At 1630 hrs he rose to periscope depth once more as hydrophones reported the steady throb of merchant ship screws. Once the periscope head cleared the surface, Kretschmer saw another convoy steaming steadily north. Escorted by ASW trawlers, an S-class submarine and five destroyers, at least twenty-two steamers sailed in two columns while above them four Avro Ansons flew patrol patterns, one leading the procession and three in loose formation astern. It was ON14, an impressive sight and an impressive target.

Surfacing once the convoy had passed from visual range, Kretschmer reported ON14, later that night receiving a radio message from BdU that two British cruisers had departed Kirkwall and were likely heading towards his position. While the merchant ship train was a worthy target, the opportunity to attack one of the Royal Navy heavies was too good to miss and *U23* travelled slowly along a course that ran parallel with the convoy track on a gentle swell beneath a partially covered moon. At 0235 hrs on 19 February, Schepke's *U19* was sighted by lookouts and approached Kretschmer's boat, the two commanders exchanging information and good-natured banter as Schepke joined the wait for the expected cruisers. However, less than one hour later, a 5,000-ton steamer was sighted dead ahead and the two U-boats separated, Kretschmer diving to make a submerged attack lest the glittering moonlight betray his presence. It was a textbook attack. At 0405 hrs Kretschmer fired a single torpedo which hit 5,225-ton British steamer SS *Tiberton* and broke the ship in two, both halves sinking within thirty seconds. Master Hugh Mason was taking his ship unescorted from Narvik to Humberside with a load of iron ore and neither he nor any of his 33-crew survived the sudden destruction of their ship, which was at first officially posted as missing by *Lloyd's Register*, eventually marked as a 'presumed war loss' when it could no longer be assumed only overdue. Less than twenty minutes later Kretschmer had resurfaced and was once again sailing alongside *U19*, as another boat, Kaptlt. Karl-Heinrich Jenisch's *U22*, passed nearby.

With the dawn, Kretschmer dived once more and proceeded at periscope depth; a single patrol ship was sighted which dropped apparently random depth charges, once again near but causing no damage. The day passed unremarkably with no sign of the expected heavy ships. After nightfall, and *U23* once again surfaced and proceeding slowly, flares and signal rockets were periodically sighted, *U19* reporting a successful attack on the unescorted Royal Fleet Auxiliary tanker SS *Daghestan* south of the Shetlands, though if he had stayed long enough to confirm his kill he would have realised that he had missed and the torpedo exploded prematurely at some distance from the hull.[8]

Kretschmer began trailing a large and clearly lit freighter that left Kirkwall on 21 February but that evening was directed to rendezvous with Kaptlt. Claus Korth in *U57* who had hit and disabled the 4,996-ton freighter SS *Loch Maddy* twenty miles south-southeast of Copinsay, Orkney Islands. Korth torpedoed the unescorted ship, which had straggled from convoy HX19, with a single hit amidships to starboard. The torpedo exploded in the engine room, and the merchant's second engineer (Ian McLean), a donkeyman (Anthony McAllister), and two firemen and trimmers (Mathew Murphy and Herbert Phipps) on watch below were killed while the remaining survivors abandoned ship.

> We were in the boats four hours before we were landed. There were thirty-five of us, and we lost all our belongings. After we got away from the ship there were two heavy explosions. A warship which we had previously sighted in the distance [HMS *Diana*] came and picked us up.[9]

Once he had located the derelict but still floating *Loch Maddy*, Kretschmer was unwilling to risk exposing his men in dinghies by sending a boarding party with explosives to finish the large merchant ship off. It had already been over six hours since Korth had disabled it and there was no way of knowing how far away enemy forces could be as they potentially sought to salvage the ship and its valuable cargo of 2,000 tons of wheat, 6,000 tons of timber and stored aircraft. Instead he opted to use his final torpedo at a range of only 330 metres and hit *Loch Maddy* squarely amidships. The ship broke in two almost immediately.

> The bow stands up and down. Turns and sinks very slowly. Stern also sinks very slowly. The two wreck parts are separated. The gun on the stern is intact. Steamer is about 7,000 tons (six hatches). At a distance of about four nautical miles a patrol ship with lights heading on a north-easterly course takes no notice of the detonation.
> Within hailing distance of *U57*.

Since all the torpedoes have been fired, return journey started.
Both pieces of wreckage still afloat.[10]

Though the bow would eventually sink, the stern section remained
buoyant due to its cargo of timber. Later, this section was taken in tow
by the tug HMS *St Mellons* and beached in Inganess Bay, from where its
sodden cargo was salvaged.

Kretschmer reached Wilhelmshaven on the morning of 25 February
after letting his crew have a practice shoot of fourteen rounds from the
boat's 20 mm C/30 deck gun. It had been *U23*'s longest single patrol,
lasting for seventeen days, and they passed through the Nordschleuse
and tied up alongside the depot ship *Donau* on the Brügge Mole at
1155 hrs. As always, his crew were immaculate upon their return. While
the popular convention was for U-boat crews to remain unshaven on
patrol and return looking like dangerous warriors of the sea, Kretschmer
maintained his independent opinion and military discipline throughout,
a trait he would take into the Atlantic aboard *U99*.

> We were told by Dönitz that a submariner must look like a pirate,
> unshaved and dirty. I didn't like this. I asked 'Why? We are people
> like everybody else. So why should we look like anything we don't
> believe in? We are not pirates.' Coming from the Baltic to the
> North Sea, from Kiel to Wilhelmshaven for instance, we were not
> to shave. And those who shaved were not real submariners, and
> they were looked at, well . . . like they should go somewhere else
> and not be in the submarine service.[11]

Kretschmer presented his report – Petersen was awarded the Iron
Cross First Class for his performance at sea – and the crew were able
to return to the relative comfort of the *Donau*, though the boat would
not stay long in Wilhelmshaven. The following morning *U23* made
way for Kiel, spending that night and the following day in Brunsbüttel
awaiting transit of the Kaiser Wilhelm Canal. Seven crewmen spent
the nights ashore in barracks until *U23* travelled with the tug *Norder*
on 28 February through the Schleswig-Holstein waterway, towed part
way as bearing trouble had brought the U-boat to a temporary halt. At
1800 hrs, *U23* was made fast in Kiel's Deutsche Werke where it would
undergo more extensive repairs and refitting.

From the war diary of FdU West:

U57, *U23* and *U22* into Wilhelmshaven from operation (*Nordmark*). *U23* has sunk the destroyer *Daring* and a 5,000-ton steamer and given the coup de grâce to a steamer damaged by *U57*. The cooperation between *U57* and *U23* is particularly noteworthy; the success was only possible by the exact location of *U57* and *U23* in relation to the 7,000-ton steamer. Another meeting between *U22*, *U23*, *U19* in Square 1623 was arranged by radio as a control point for a potential operation against two enemy cruisers.

Kretschmer's period in command of *U23* had reached its end. He had sailed on eight war patrols totalling ninety-seven days at sea and sunk 27,624 tons of enemy shipping, plus a destroyer. Though he had unintentionally over-claimed several of the ships that he had sent to the bottom, Kretschmer's was still an impressive quantity of ships destroyed; an equally grim tally of 236 lives were lost from his victims, two of which left no survivors at all. Sadly, such was the nature of war at sea.

Coupled with his torpedo sinkings, Kretschmer had displayed a cast-iron nerve in the course of inshore minelaying and reconnoitring of the bays and inlets among the Orkney and Shetland Islands. His crew had reached a level of high efficiency as a result of his relentless quest for perfection, and some would serve later with him aboard *U99*. His watch officers Schnee and Tiesenhausen would also both go on to be successful commanders of their own boats, and would both survive the war. On 4 March, the 1st U-Flotilla commander, Korvettenkapitän Hans Eckermann, provided a confidential character assessment of Kretschmer for Dönitz and onward transmission to SKL.

Kapitänleutnant Kretschmer is a very quiet and reserved, but able and energetic officer. Talented, clear in his judgement, safe and sure in his aim, he shows favourable characteristics for his post. Kretschmer is very popular among his subordinates and colleagues, who are quick to recognise his true merits despite his reserve.

I can fully confirm the very favourable report which my predecessor made on Kretschmer's work and duties.

During three further successful war patrols, Kretschmer attacked unceasingly and brought out the best efforts from himself and his crew. He was always full of ideas on how to shorten time in harbour and how to increase the number of torpedoes that could be carried.

His great ability, calm and decisiveness made it possible for him to go on especially difficult assignments several times without pause. Kapitänleutnant Kretschmer is eminently suited to be the commander of a large boat.[12]

Chapter Four

Into the Atlantic with U99

Kretschmer was granted leave during March 1940 as were most of his crew. The decision had already been taken that he was to move on to a larger boat in which he could fully reach his potential as an excellent tactician and torpedo shot. *U23* was handed over to 32-year-old Kaptlt. Heinz Beduhn on 8 April. Beduhn would later take the boat on a single unsuccessful patrol before transferring to command the temperamental Type I, *U25*. It was aboard this unwieldy U-boat that he was killed on 2 August 1940, *U25* being destroyed by a mine with all forty-nine hands lost. *U23* itself was relegated to training duties after Beduhn's tenure and would not see action again until 1943 when the boat was one of six transferred by road, river and canal to the Black Sea to combat the Soviet Navy as part of 30th U-Flotilla. Kretschmer, for his part, took command of a brand-new Type VIIB U-boat in construction at Friedrich Krupp Germaniawerft AG, Kiel. The boat had been ordered on 15 December 1937, its keel finally laid down at the end of March 1939. A little less than a year later the completed hull of *U99* was launched and its fitting out began within the dockyard.

Many of the crew had already joined the boat during its construction as part of the *Baubelehrung* process, the Engineer Officer, Oberleutnant (Ing.) Gottfried Schröder, the first to arrive after transferring from Oblt.z.S. Herbert Wohlfarth's *U14*. Schröder had enlisted in the Reichsmarine in 1934 and served in U-boats since the beginning of 1938. Kretschmer had managed to secure the transfer of his trusted navigator and IIIWO Stabsobersteuermann Heinrich Petersen from *U23* to *U99*, and his new IIWO was Leutnant Horst Elfe. A native of Allenstein, East Prussia, Elfe had been an active member of the Hitler

Youth, in which he attained the rank of *Stammführer* and had learned to sail on the Wannsee Lakes near Berlin. He joined the Kriegsmarine at the age of eighteen in 1936 and had been promoted to *Leutnant zur See* on 1 October 1938. Before the outbreak of war, he had spent a summer near Bath and in Oxford where his already good grasp of the English language improved considerably. From September 1939 until transfer to the crew of *U99* he had served as adjutant to the commander of the 1st U-Flotilla *Weddigen*.

The post of IWO was taken by 28-year-old Oblt.z.S. Klaus Heinrich Bargsten. He had been born on 31 October 1911 in Bad Oldesloe, his mother an aristocrat whose father had made a fortune in farm machinery and banking, though she had married a man of 'peasant stock' according to his interrogation report by the US Navy in 1943. After completing his schooling, Bargsten trained as a merchant marine officer and was later employed by the North German Lloyd Steamship Company, serving mostly aboard freighters but also on the transatlantic liner SS *Europa*. Distracted by Germany's internal political strife, he joined the Nazi Party but received such adverse criticism from his family that he later resigned, entering the Kriegsmarine in 1935. As a *Fähnrich* Bargsten served for a brief period aboard the state yacht *Grille*, though his contact with Hitler and the cream of Nazi society was limited. Nonetheless, he did recount a few anecdotes to his captors in 1943 about his time near the personalities at the centre of German political power:

> While he was serving as a midshipman on the yacht *Grille*, Bargsten had occasion to see many of the leading members of the Nazi Party. Once, he said, when a group of these Olympians was aboard, an orchestra was playing for their entertainment, but the ship's ventilators were making so much noise that the music could scarcely be heard. Goebbels complained to the captain in his usual high-handed manner, ordering him to do something about it. The captain, while engaging Goebbels in conversation, managed to back him into position in front of one of the ventilators. When he gave the order for the ventilators to be shut off, the shutter gave Goebbels a resounding whack on the back side.
>
> Bargsten also spoke somewhat heretically about the alcoholic habits of the Nazi great. Hitler, he said, objected strenuously to

drinking and often gave his staff violent temperance lectures. Shortly after having been subjected to one such harangue on board the *Grille*, the staff gathered in the saloon to soothe their frayed nerves with a bottle of champagne. Suddenly Hitler appeared in the doorway and the bottle, which had just been opened, was discreetly hidden beneath a table. Hitler strode into the room, kicked the bottle, spilling its contents, turned on his heel, and walked out without uttering a word.[1]

Additionally, the Allied interrogation provides an insight into the character of this young officer:

[Bargsten] has an extremely pleasant personality, is enthusiastic and carefree, and gives the impression of being an excellent officer. He was greatly admired by his crew for these qualities. Although he is an ardent patriot, Bargsten is in no way a typical Nazi and, in fact, hinted that he was not altogether in sympathy with the Nazi regime.[2]

Shortly before the outbreak of war he entered the U-boat service and was assigned as a watch officer to Kaptlt. Joachim Matz's *U6*, aboard which he made a single war patrol between 24 August and 13 September 1939, monitoring shipping passing through the Kattegat. After leaving *U6* following its return to training duties in October, Bargsten served for a time as adjutant to Korvkpt. Ibbeken, then commanding officer of the U-boat School at Pillau. During this time, he married and established his home in Bremen before being added to Kretschmer's new crew of *U99*.

The Type VIIB boat was a major improvement on Kretschmer's last: a genuine ocean-going craft capable of taking the fight into the Atlantic, which Dönitz had declared the centre of gravity of his war against the Allies. Kretschmer's previous experience aboard the Type VII *U35* already placed him in great stead for command of a Type VIIB, which boasted a number of important improvements over its predecessor. The underwater turning radius had been greatly improved by the use of twin rudders, one behind each screw, rather than the single rudder design that had gone before. This also allowed the installation of an internal stern torpedo tube that fired from between the screws rather than the single external tube that had previously been mounted protruding atop the stern decking and therefore vulnerable to the effect of the elements. Torpedo storage was also increased by allowing a stern reload to be carried under the floor plating of the motor room, and another in an external pressure-tight container between the wooden decking and pressure hull. One more such external container was carried beneath the forward decking and with all four bow tubes loaded, reloads under the floor of the bow room and also stored on the deck amongst the crew, the total number of torpedoes that could be carried into action numbered fourteen.

The Type VII's range had also been increased through lengthening the hull by two metres to 66.5 metres – increasing internal bunkerage slightly – and also by additional 'saddle tanks'; each side of the hull was given an added self-compensating fuel bunker that lay between the existing bulge of the ballast tanks and the pressure hull. The term 'self-compensating' alludes to the fact that the tanks were open at the bottom. As diesel oil is lighter than water, it floats on seawater that enters a tank and as the fuel is consumed, its volume is replaced by seawater entering from below eliminating potential air pockets that can affect stability. Though these additional bunkers also required extension of the existing ballast tanks both in length and beam, the Type VIIB U-boat was capable of a range of 6,500 nautical miles at a surfaced speed of 12 knots and 90 nautical miles at 4 knots submerged. Maximum surface speed was increased from 16 to 17.2 knots by adding superchargers to the MAN diesels. The deck gun was an impressive 88 mm naval cannon and a single 20 mm flak gun was carried atop the aft portion of the conning tower.

Internally, the boat was cramped though must have appeared spacious compared to the Type IIB *U23*. The pressure hull was divided into three separate compartments by two pressure-proof bulkheads, watertight bulkheads further subdividing the internal space into six rooms. From stern to bow, Compartment 1 began with the stern torpedo and electric motor room. Here were housed the single stern tube, electric motors, converters, switchboards, air compressors, driving motors for the main rudders and after dive planes, torpedo compensating tank and after trim tank. There was also one oxygen flask and a single emergency fresh-water tank as well as the emergency helm that was locked in place to the hull wall, but could be swung into action if required. Beneath the decking there was stowage for a single reserve torpedo and three distilled water containers. Room 2 was the diesel engine room which also contained auxiliary machinery, two starting air flasks, two oxygen flasks and whatever workshop facilities could be created, with a large vice and small work table to the port of the forward door. Room 3 was the petty officers' accommodation (*Unteroffizierraum*), with eight bunks, the tiny aft WC, the small galley that was the domain of the *Smutje* (ship's cook), as well as stowage for provisions, refrigeration plant and high-pressure air bank number 3. Under the floor were tanks for fresh and waste water, fuel oil and the first bank of batteries.

Compartment 2 comprised the central control room, which included the drive for the aft (attack) periscope, control station for the main rudder and dive planes and gyro compass. The IIIWO also had his navigation station to port of the attack periscope well. Above the control room, the conning tower was ellipsoid in its aft section and the arc of a circle in the lateral and forward sections. These parts were joined together without flat spots, which served to decrease drag during submerged travel. This tower structure was enclosed within an outer casing. The top of the tower was crowned by a bridge deck fabricated from 30 mm thick steel plate, welded to the conning tower walls. Within the pressure hull portion of the conning tower were the aft (attack) periscope with hydraulic driving motor, which was used for submerged attacks, the main rudder steering station and torpedo fire control installation. Externally, the bridge was manned by four lookouts, each watching his own ninety-degree quadrant, and a watch officer who kept an overview. During torpedo attacks, the IWO would man the UZO while Kretschmer maintained his overall control of events. The stern section of the tower – known as a 'bandstand' to the Allies, and *Wintergarten* to German crews – hosted the 20 mm flak weapon.

Compartment 3 began with the tiny commander's 'cabin' to port, separated from the rest of the boat by a simple green curtain. Kretschmer's bunk lay opposite the information nerve centre: the small radio/telegraphy and hydrophone rooms. The officers' and chief petty officers' quarters (*Oberfeldwebelraum*) were next, then the forward WC and more fresh-water tanks. Stored here, beneath the floor plating, were explosive charges, and the munitions magazine, alongside more water and fuel tanks. Finally, the forward torpedo room also doubled as enlisted men's quarters. This room housed the four forward torpedo tubes, two reloads above deck and a great quantity of torpedo loading and maintenance gear. It was also where the majority of the crew slept, 'hotbunking' between twelve bunks, one man rolling into the cot to sleep as its previous occupant rose to go on watch. Three tables could be erected for meal times, though only after enough stored torpedoes had been fired to make room. Each man had a small wooden locker in which to store his few personal belongings aboard the boat. Beneath the decking was stowage for four reserve torpedoes or mines.

It was a spartan, functional weapon of war and, at that stage of military development, extremely effective in the right hands. Some of the most famous submarines of the Second World War – Prien's *U47*, Schultze's *U48*, Schepke's *U100*, and Kretschmer's *U99* – were all Type VIIBs of which only twenty-four were built before the improved Type VIIC design came into production, subsequently becoming the mainstay of Dönitz's U-boat force.

Kretschmer and his crew oversaw the final stages of construction and fitting out before commissioning the U-boat into the Kriegsmarine in a ceremony in Kiel's military harbour on 8 April 1940. From there they took the new boat into the Baltic for testing, at around the same time as Schepke took his freshly built *U100* for the same exercises. Preliminary trials were made under the auspices of *the* Unterseeboots-Abnahme-Kommando (U-boat acceptance commission – UAK) within Kiel Bay and included timed surfaced runs, pressure dock tests, submerging and trimming exercises, while Kretschmer established the boat's manoeuvrability. After this first series of shakedown sailings in the company of senior dockyard officials, *U99* was officially handed over to the U-boat training flotilla (U-Ausbildungsflottille) on 21 May 1940. Exercises took place within the Baltic Sea from Memel and torpedo practice was conducted off Gotenhafen. As well as the familiar doctrine of submerged attacks that Kretschmer made, surface torpedo-firing practice was also conducted by Kretschmer and Bargsten as his IWO, and artillery firing as part of Elfe's responsibilities as IIWO alongside further maximum speed and mileage tests. Finally, *U99* joined in tactical training against simulated convoy targets. Here Kretschmer put into practice his theoretical preference for surfaced attacks even against a protected convoy and one that was, in this case, actively searching for him and forewarned of impending attack. During the course of these exercises *U99* successfully penetrated the defensive screen of destroyers and simulated attacks on the two steamers that comprised the 'convoy', sailing undetected close alongside both before shining the searchlight used to indicate a torpedo attack. He had finally proved his theory to himself that a U-boat should attack under cover of darkness and remain surfaced at all costs: to submerge was to lose mobility, speed and – somewhat ironically – cover, as the probing fingers of ASDIC were more advanced at that stage of the war than surface radar detection.

Towards the end of this working-up period, *U99* received its iconic symbol which would later adorn the conning tower. On raising the anchor in Kiel harbour, a crewman was surprised to find two horseshoes hooked on the flukes and claimed it a positive omen for the new U-boat. Though he was no more susceptible to superstition than most mariners, the inference of good luck was obvious, and Kretschmer readily agreed to adopt the horseshoes as the boat's *Wappen*, a chosen symbol that had become popular amongst U-boat crews since Fritz-Julius Lemp had his radioman Georg Högel paint a picture of his dog 'Schnurzel' on the tower of *U30*. Prien had adopted the 'Snorting Bull' – that would later become the emblem of the entire 7th U-Flotilla – and Schepke's *U100* would show a dramatic symbol of a crouching panther. Kretschmer arranged for the two horseshoes to be painted gold and one welded on each side of the conning tower for luck, the open ends facing downward in the same manner in which German farmers would hang them in barns. The significance of that fact to a British observer would only be pointed out to Kretschmer in 1941.

U99 went back into the shipyard on 9 June for a week of refitting, though no major alteration work was required after the trials had been completed. Prepared for the inaugural patrol, Kretschmer was finally ready to take *U99* into the Atlantic from Kiel on 18 June 1940, the same day that France requested an armistice with Germany after the stunning feats of arms performed by the Wehrmacht had brought the country to defeat in less than six weeks. *U99* passed through the Kaiser Wilhelm Canal and reached Brunsbüttel just as the Royal Air Force began bombing oil storage targets and railway marshalling yards near Hamburg as well as naval installations on Norderney, Langeoog and Oldenburg. Several light bombs fell near the western end of the canal and Kretschmer's crew could see heavy flak exploding in the sky over Cuxhaven and Hamburg as *U99* rendezvoused with its escort, Sperrbrecher IX *Lüneburg* which would shepherd the boat across the mouth of the Elbe. As Kretschmer headed north-west, the *Sperrbrecher* was replaced by V205 *Hermann Bösch* of the 2nd Vorpostenboot Flotilla. These converted trawlers had become invaluable for U-boat escort, providing flak cover for traversing coastal waters and moving within the vulnerable choke points of waterways' entrances and exits.

However, not even a day into his voyage and Kretschmer was forced to divert to Norway to land a sick crewman. Stabsobermaschinist Edmund Prochnow was suffering from severe rheumatism, complaining of sharp pains in the joints of his right shoulder and elbow. Since he was incapacitated, and unlikely to improve in the damp confines of a combat U-boat, Kretschmer had no alternative but to land him for hospitalisation. Prochnow was a veteran of the U-boat service who had joined the Reichsmarine in 1932 and served for three years aboard cruisers until transferring to the U-boat service and the *Weddigen* Flotilla. Robertson's book *The Golden Horseshoe* states that Kretschmer was convinced Prochnow's medical complaint was born of fear rather than a genuine health issue, but there appears no real evidence to sustain that idea and Kretschmer was given permission by BdU to unload Prochnow in recently conquered Norway.

The fighting in Norway that had begun in April had only recently finished. Though Bergen and other centres in the south were occupied within twenty-four hours of the invasion beginning, in the north the battle for Narvik had swayed backwards and forwards until the final Norwegian surrender of 10 June. Amongst the Kriegsmarine operations mounted in support of the German invasion had been a sortie codenamed Operation *Juno* by the battleships *Gneisenau* and *Scharnhorst*, supported by the heavy cruiser *Admiral Hipper* and four destroyers. Their purpose had been to disrupt the Royal Navy's backing of Allied forces in Narvik and attempt to relieve pressure on the hard-pressed Wehrmacht troops ashore who had been forced to retreat from the town and were desperately attempting to wrest it back from Allied hands. While *Juno* had succeeded in sinking the carrier HMS *Glorious*, two destroyers, one minesweeper, one troopship and an oil tanker, *Scharnhorst* had taken heavy damage from a torpedo hit fired by one of its victims, destroyer HMS *Acasta*. A hole fourteen by six metres was torn in the battleship's hull, allowing severe flooding that caused a list and killed forty-eight men. The battleship, hounded by British aircraft that were only just kept at bay, headed first for Norway for emergency repairs, and then south towards Kiel's shipyards. The journey was fraught with danger, as

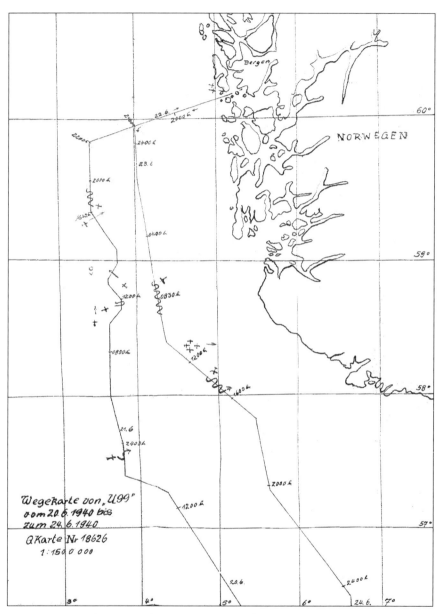

Kretschmer's rather unsuccessful first mission with *U99*.

not only were frequent aircraft attacks a menace, but up to five British submarines had been reported in the German Bight and surrounding waters and strong surface forces appeared to be attempting to intercept the damaged behemoth. The battleship's Arado 196 aircraft were flown in continuous combined reconnaissance and anti-submarine patrols; all U-boats were instructed to avoid the area through which the battleship would pass.

Kretschmer was considerably seaward of the prescribed area, travelling surfaced at economical speed to reach Bergen before passing north of Scotland and into the Atlantic Ocean. Regular sightings of aircraft, both British and German, forced repeated alarm dives until at 1240 hrs on 21 June, Bargsten sighted a 'large surfaced submarine', Kretschmer diving and giving the enemy craft a wide berth. Radio instructions were also received for both *U99* and the outward bound *U26* to attempt to intercept incoming Royal Navy heavy forces, thereby acting as cover for the retiring *Scharnhorst*. Unwittingly, *U99* strayed into the search radius of the *Scharnhorst*'s aircraft and, from seemingly out of nowhere, came under aerial attack.

> Diving before – apparently our own – floatplane (monoplane). As the boat reaches 20 metres, a bomb detonates over the conning tower. Further bombs follow after a few minutes and then in intervals of about a quarter of an hour until 1830 hrs, always quite close despite course change after the diving. I suspect we have an oil leak, because the contact aircraft stops and then what seem to be other aircraft participate. Minor damage in the boat (light bulbs, fuses, depth gauges, ammeters, and for a short time also the manometer in the control room, rudder position indicators and similar).
>
> Surface. It is found that the attack periscope has failed. The lens glass has burst. No light reaches the eyepiece. Starboard diesel bunker leaking, thus there actually is an oil leak.[3]

Kretschmer headed again for Bergen, passing Børnestangen light in the early morning darkness of 22 June. Prochnow was unloaded onto the locally commandeered vessel *Stör* and hospitalised. He would not return to Kretschmer's crew but was reassigned to the 3rd U-Flotilla for a recovery period until 1941 and a return to the 7th U-Flotilla in France. It was some time before he went to sea in a different combat boat, *U93*, and he survived the boat's sinking by HMS *Hesperus* on the early morning of 15 January 1942.

Meanwhile, the damaged *U99* returned to Germany, bombed with several near misses again during the following day, betrayed even while submerged by the trickling oil slick behind it. Finally, at 1620 hrs on 24 June, *U99* met escorting Vorpostenboot V1503 *Wiking 10* in drifting fog and was shepherded into Heligoland harbour, from where Kretschmer followed in the wake of Sperrbrecher IX *Lüneburg* to Wilhelmshaven, arriving a little before midnight. Once again, the boat sailed into the sound of exploding bombs and answering flak as the Royal Air Force attacked the port town during raids that dotted the country between Hamburg and Mannheim. Kretschmer anchored in the centre of the bay until the attack had ended, whereupon *U99* was docked for repairs, estimated to take two and a half days. It was an inauspicious start to the new U-boat's career.

Work was completed on schedule and *U99* sailed once more, with the minimum delay possible, at 0900 hrs on 27 June. Again, the familiar escort ships accompanied Kretschmer outbound, numerous minesweepers and patrol ships passing as the U-boat made speed towards the north. Engine trouble in the port diesel caused a temporary delay, Kretschmer recording 'faulty work in the shipyard' in his war diary as Schröder's engineering crew laboured to rectify a major oil leak. Dornier Do 18 flying boats were seen with relative regularity and Kretschmer passed *U25* inbound to Wilhelmshaven, which reported by Morse the sighting of an enemy submarine to the north-west. During the early hours on 29 June, Kretschmer's voyage was nearly curtailed once more by German aircraft; this time a Luftwaffe bomber based in Stavanger narrowly missed the boat with three bombs as it frantically submerged, too late to reach the safety of depth despite forward hydroplanes thrown to full down angle. Fortunately, it was a botched attack as the boat's stern was still above water when the explosions rocked the hull. There was relatively minor and temporary damage though the glass was ruptured in many dials and the boat's porcelain plates were strewn across the floor, many smashed, as the hard-pressed *Smutje* attempted to save his galley contents. The insulator through which the radio aerial passed into the hull was later found to be chipped and so there was a temporary failure in transmitting once they had eventually resurfaced. To compound their problems both compasses were also out of commission. Though the gyrocompass was soon repaired, the magnetic compass remained faulty and unreliable for the remainder of the patrol. Determining on a period of calm in which to get *U99* back into fighting trim, Kretschmer had the boat descend to eighty-one metres to touch the seafloor, where he settled it on an even keel so that repairs could be taken care of in peace.

The bombing attack had taken place well outside of the prescribed Luftwaffe anti-submarine patrol area, Petersen's faultless navigation putting *U99* clearly within declared transit channels and forty-five nautical miles from the border of the submarine-hunting area. Therefore, Kretschmer angrily noted in his war diary, the aircraft could not claim his own faulty positioning as an excuse. Indeed, when Kretschmer later resurfaced with his transmitting gear repaired he reported this to BdU. Dönitz was immediately aware of a Luftwaffe report, noted within his own KTB, that a Stavanger aircraft had attacked a British submarine at the same time, but in a position claimed as approximately forty miles from Kretschmer's location. Doubt was immediately placed on the Luftwaffe's version of events as nautical navigation frequently confounded Luftwaffe pilots; this was one of many reasons that effective Luftwaffe–Kriegsmarine cooperation in support of the U-boat war was never satisfactorily achieved.

By mid-morning, *U99* was surfaced again and running for the Fair Isle passage. However, loud noises were heard from the starboard diesel, creating strong vibrations that were found to have sheared off seven out of eight retaining bolts holding the large engine in place. A similar issue had been reported by Kaptlt. Max-Herman Bauer in *U50* during February, forcing him to abort a successful maiden patrol in which he sank four ships (mistakenly claiming six). Bauer had been compelled to return to Kiel for nearly a month of shipyard work, but Kretschmer was determined that he would not have to end his mission prematurely for the second time running. The bolts were unshielded and vulnerable to breakage; this was clearly a design flaw that needdd to be reported to BdU. The mechanical crew replaced all seven bolts as the boat carried on, for the moment using the port diesel only. All reserve stocks of the weighty bolts were now exhausted and Kretschmer hoped that the existing bolts securing the port diesel would hold for the duration of the voyage, Schröder's men ensuring that they were as tight as possible to eliminate as much destructive vibration as they could.

Both diesels were operable once more as *U99* passed Fair Isle around midnight and ploughed onward into increasingly heavy seas. Royal Navy patrol boats were sighted more frequently, one sailing from the Minch close enough probably to have sighted *U99* but unable to use artillery in the wildly pitching seas. Kretschmer dived for a time to allow his crew to rest as the boat travelled onward for eight nautical miles, surfacing once more to use diesels to push past the St Kilda group on 1 July.

Dönitz was concentrating his available Atlantic boats in the Western Approaches in an attempt to locate incoming convoy traffic and at 0800 hrs on 4 July, Kretschmer reported *U99* in position in grid square AL7978, south-west of Ireland. The weather had not improved and despite recent successes in the area reported by Prien in *U47*, Kretschmer was not confident of his ability to use his weapons, the boat having to dive for torpedo maintenance as it proved impossible while pitching and rolling on the surface.

Despite a miserable night during which nothing was sighted, dawn heralded a slight moderation in the weather and improved visibility and at 0925 hrs the smoke plume of a merchant ship headed east was sighted by sharp-eyed lookouts. Kretschmer moved to intercept, sailing a perpendicular course in preparation for a submerged attack. Straggling from convoy HX52, the 2,053-ton Canadian SS *Magog* wallowed low in the water with a full cargo of 512 standards of timber from Halifax to Preston when *U99* attacked. Having moved 800 metres past the steamer's anticipated line of travel, Kretschmer fired a single torpedo from the stern tube; this ran true but with no visible result. A full thirteen minutes later the loud explosion of the so-called 'end of run' detonation was heard. The *Magog* was apparently damaged by the explosion – recorded as 'near' within Kretschmer's war diary – but at a range of 800 metres, the expected torpedo run was less than one minute, leading Bargsten to surmise that the torpedo's propulsion unit was defective, possibly because of evaporation of the stored water used to generate the required steam.

Regardless, *Magog* sailed slowly on and Kretschmer brought *U99* to the surface for gun action, the 88 mm deck gun opening fire under the direction of IIWO Elfe and bringing the Canadian to a sudden halt with shells that hit forward. Radioed messages giving the ship's name and position were soon silenced as the entire crew of twenty-three men took to their lifeboats. The freighter burned but stubbornly refused to sink and, once the lifeboats were clear, *U99* submerged for a second underwater attack. This time the electric torpedo arced from Tube IV for a 600-metre run that lasted only thirty seconds. The warhead exploded

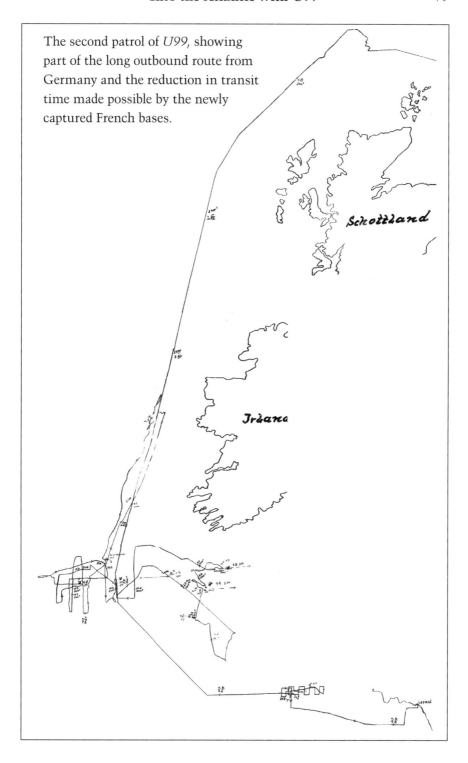

The second patrol of *U99*, showing part of the long outbound route from Germany and the reduction in transit time made possible by the newly captured French bases.

slightly aft of midships, blasting water and debris eighty metres into the sky and splitting the hull in two. Kretschmer surfaced, to see the ship's forepart already having sunk while the stern remained afloat because of its timber cargo and a large trapped air bubble. Three rounds from the 88 mm deck gun failed to sink it and, after questioning Master T. Swales Doughty and providing the survivors with directions to Ireland and a bottle of brandy, *U99* departed. The survivors were later rescued by the Swedish merchant ship SS *Fidra* and landed at Queenstown, Cork, while the stern part of *Magog* finally sank after three days of bobbing in the Atlantic Ocean.

The new boat had achieved its first victory, though not without complications. An hour after leaving the scene, *U99* dived to avoid patrolling British aircraft and allow the tubes to be reloaded. Upon resurfacing Kretschmer received instructions from BdU to head south-west to where a convoy had been reported. *U99* travelled in company with *U34* for several hours after the other Type VII had sailed into view destined for the same area of the ocean.

Not long into the dark morning of the new day a lone merchant ship was sighted travelling westbound from British waters. The 1,964-ton SS *Sea Glory* was carrying china clay from Cornwall to Philadelphia and was only two days into its voyage when encountered by *U99*. The conditions were perfect for a surfaced attack and under Kretschmer's command Bargsten took his place at the UZO; tubes one and three were both readied for use. The ship was only a matter of 480 metres distant when Bargsten ordered his first G7e away. However, although the second tube had actually been loaded for possible use as a finishing shot (*Fangschuss*) if one torpedo proved insufficient, a mistake in communication led to both tubes being fired virtually simultaneously; both torpedoes impacted just forward of the merchant's bridge on its port side, a column of water shooting 100 metres into the air as *Sea Glory* broke apart and began to sink immediately. Within two minutes it was gone and nothing left to mark its passing but sparse floating debris. There were no survivors: Master Stanley Winston Harvey and his entire crew of twenty-seven men and one eighteen-year-old gunner were lost to the depths with their ship.

At 1240 hrs another solo steamer was sighted heading east and steering a pronounced zig-zagging course. *U99* was forced to submerge by the distant appearance of an Allied aircraft on ASW patrol and so

Kretschmer, unable to close the ship, prepared to mount a submerged attack at a distance of 2,500 metres. The ship was the large 5,360-ton SS *Manistee* of the Elders & Fyffes Shipping Company, built to ply the passenger and banana route from the Caribbean to the United Kingdom. Captain George Llewellyn Jones was taking his steamer into British waters when *U99* fired a single G7e torpedo from Tube II. A failure in the firing system held the torpedo for several seconds before it was released manually in the bow room and sped on its way, though due to the errant launch it was something of a forlorn hope, and missed the target. Kretschmer later reasoned that he had probably underestimated the target's speed in any case as his firing solution was largely guesswork.

Unwilling to let such a large ship escape and knowing that he needed to close the distance, Kretschmer brought *U99* to the surface to prepare for gun action. As the artillery crew tumbled from the conning tower and began firing the 88 mm deck gun, *U99* headed on an interception course. The German firing was accurate despite a strong swell, but return fire from two guns began to land close to *U99*, and Kretschmer turned away after ten minutes of trading fire, with a final few shots sent towards *Manistee* before the reappearance of enemy aircraft forced *U99* below, where the crew reloaded torpedo tube two. The ship had been identified by intercepted radio messages and Kretschmer was loath to let go such a large target, but his options were limited. Submerged they could not hope to catch it; surfaced they were vulnerable to artillery and air attack. Aboard the merchant ship there was jubilation that they had bested the enemy in their first encounter with a U-boat. Captain Jones was amongst fifteen men later commended in the *London Gazette* on 8 October 1940, for 'good services when their ships encountered enemy submarines, ships or aircraft'.[4]

Two hours later *U99* surfaced once again and, despite sighting an Avro Anson in the distance, Kretschmer resumed the hunt for fresh targets, rewarded at 2033 hrs with the sighting of smoke from an approaching steamer moving at speed. The ship was large – estimated at 8,400 tons – with four visible masts and Kretschmer identified it as the same type as the Harrison shipping line's SS *Astronomer*. A British aircraft was visible circling above and Kretschmer began to suspect that he had encountered a possible 'U-boat trap', a Q-ship. Although the effectiveness of the Q-ships perhaps exceeded their reputation, they were still a prickly proposition for a U-boat to engage. However, the steamer was heading directly in front of *U99*'s position and Kretschmer submerged once more to prepare for a surprise torpedo attack. At 2312 hrs a single G7e was fired from Tube IV at a range of only 600 metres and after a run of 40 seconds the contact-fused torpedo exploded just forward of amidships. It transpired that Kretschmer had misidentified his target by quite a large margin. It was the Swedish merchant ship SS *Bissen*, a 1,514-ton steamer carrying pulp wood and pit props from Canada to Ridham Dock, Kent. The explosion threw water and debris high into the air, scattering parts of the deck cargo all over the ship and blowing a liferaft overboard. Immediately the *Bissen* began to settle by the head, Kretschmer recording in his war diary that the 'steamer breaks apart forward, stern stands obliquely high'.

The Swedish crew immediately abandoned ship in two lifeboats, but noticed once clear of their stricken vessel that the second officer had been left aboard. The engines of the sinking merchant ship were still running and what remained afloat of *Bissen* steamed in slow lazy circles as it settled into the water, difficult to reboard as the merchant's crew determined to look for their missing officer. Eventually, after much perseverance, the lifeboat under the command of the master, E. Svensson, managed to get near enough to rescue the stranded officer. All twenty crewmen survived the sinking, picked up an hour later by the approaching destroyer HMS *Broke* of the 6th Escort Group. The destroyer already carried fifteen rescued survivors from the Estonian merchant ship *Vapper* that had been sunk the day before by *U34* south of Cape Clear.

The appearance of HMS *Broke* prompted Kretschmer to dive. ASDIC beams were heard probing through the water but no depth charges were forthcoming as *U99* crept away from the sinking Swedish ship, Kretschmer having realised that his Q-ship assumption was incorrect.

0013 hrs: Surfaced; steamer apparently sunk, destroyer still in sight. Immediately dived again due to the brightness of the night.

0057 hrs: Dived and resurfaced. Destroyer is still standing near my shooting position, moving to and fro.

0256 hrs: Bearing 340° a convoy; about twenty steamers with destroyer escorts. Moving forward. Contact signal sent.

Kretschmer had chanced upon HX53; a forty-four-ship convoy from Halifax bound for Liverpool and steering a zig-zagging course whose mean direction was almost due east. He spent the next four hours racing ahead of the projected convoy path until, with daybreak, there came British air cover and *U99* dived, lying in the convoy's path as destroyers prowled relentlessly along the flanks of the merchant ships. Audible ASDIC probed the water around *U99* and a destroyer passed directly before Kretschmer's stern tube, tempting him to shoot, before appearing to pinpoint *U99* and changing course to head straight for Kretschmer's periscope. The U-boat was forced to descend, reaching only twenty metres before the escort ship thundered overhead, its fast-turning screws a notably higher pitch than the low rumble of approaching freighter propellers. However, there were no depth charges and all Kretschmer could do was to lament the time and speed he was losing while being pinned below the surface. Frustrated, with the nearest merchant ships only 300 metres distant, he opted for the difficult but tested and approved attack method of steering a parallel course to HX53 and firing torpedoes with a 90° deflection angle.

If during an approach to target the U-boat was deemed too close, the captain could opt for a gyro-angled attack. Ordering a ninety-degree gyro-setting on the torpedo, he would alter the U-boat's course to run parallel to the target and once the target ship reached the traverse line of the U-boat, the torpedo would be launched. At 0752 hrs, Kretschmer ordered Tube V fired. However, his initial attack using this stern tube failed after the correct information was not transmitted to the tube operator; the shot never fired as the tube was unready. Undeterred, he fired Tube I to starboard, a single G7e leaving the boat and making a dramatic turn, running for only twenty seconds before hitting 5,758-ton SS *Humber Arm* in the bow. The heavily laden steamer was transporting 5,450 tons of newsprint, 1,000 tons of steel, 450 tons of pulp and 300 tons of lumber from Halifax to Ellesmere Port and though Kretschmer had identified it as a 10,000-ton ship of the Union Castle Line, the freighter was still a valuable target and the only vessel lost from convoy HX53. Master Jack Rowland Morbey and his entire crew of forty-one, plus a single passenger, successfully abandoned ship; they were later rescued by HMS *Scimitar* and *Vanquisher* and landed at Milford Haven.

However, Kretschmer was not to escape retribution. Unable to observe the merchant ship going down nor able to detect the sound of cracking bulkheads as it headed for the Atlantic floor, the strong detonation alone led Kretschmer to assume it sunk. *U99* fell behind the convoy body as escorting destroyers began hunting him, the first depth charges falling at 0806 hrs as Kretschmer took his boat down to a depth of 90 metres. There then followed fourteen hours of alternating ASDIC pings through the water and depth-charge salvos. In total, 107 depth charges were dropped, thirty-seven of them dangerously close to the U-boat's hull.

The crew of *U99* were receiving their baptismal depth-charge attack and it would test their nerves and stamina to the maximum. The conduct of a boat's captain could have a profound effect on the reactions of his men under such extreme pressure and in Kretschmer the men of *U99* had a perfect example of how to endure the hours of terrifying bombardment. Alternating between sleep and feigned nonchalance, Kretschmer closely watched his crew to support them with his calm sense of authority. Terence Robertson recounts a story of this attack given to him by Funkmaat Josef Kassel, the hydrophone operator.

> At the hydrophones nearby, Kassel looked in amazement at his commander sitting on the control room deck reading a book. It was a detective thriller, and Kretschmer seemed thoroughly engrossed in it, showing no signs of emotion as the depth charges blasted them with the horrible grating of a thousand chisels on steel and rolled them around the decks. But after another hour had passed, Kassel found there was something wrong in the picture of Kretschmer reading a book. A few more glances over his shoulder and he became suddenly aware that his commander was not turning the pages; in fact he had been looking at the same page since first opening the covers. A further lingering look and he saw the book was being held upside down. A lasting affection for Kretschmer was born in Kassel at that moment. It is still there today, and Kassel recalls the incident as one of the finest examples any U-boat commander ever showed his crew.[5]

The hunt for *U99* pushed not only the crew but also their boat to its limit of endurance. An Achilles heel of the U-boats remained the limited storage capacity of their battery packs held beneath the floor plating. Once these were exhausted, the electric motors would no longer be able to turn the screws and the U-boat would be helpless. If that point were reached the only alternative would be to use any available compressed air to blow the U-boat's ballast tanks and bring it to the surface for the last time, probably directly under the enemy's guns. It was a danger in the forefront of every U-boat skipper's mind when faced with a prolonged hunt.

> 2000 hrs: Since the battery is quite empty, I can only proceed with alternating slow speed and stopped motors for creeping speed. Everything turned off except for listening gear (GHG) with emergency transmitter and gyro compass, since the magnetic compass has failed. The crew is equipped with emergency breathing gear connected to Alkeli cartridges. Lighting out except only the most necessary lamps. While I'm running on course, two destroyers are hard on our heels. By hooking around by 90 degrees it is possible to peel them off temporarily; but after only one hour they are back on us. Since I have the impression that I have been accurately located, I now put the next destroyer astern. The depth charge salvos are now getting worse. Once a destroyer runs straight above our boat, but he does not seem to be aware of this fact. Around 2030 I get the impression that they have lost me. The thick darkness observed after we had surfaced appears to have made their work very difficult for them.
>
> 2228 hrs: 107th and last depth charge.
>
> 2400 hrs: I continue on my course and will only surface in complete darkness at about one o'clock.
>
> 0102 hrs: Surfaced, no enemy in sight.[6]

In the early morning darkness of 9 July, the diesels were ignited once more and *U99* got under way, fresh air coursing through the boat as the sickly green column of foul and fetid air dissipated from the conning tower hatch. Contrary to written accounts, the crew did not race onto the U-boat's deck to gulp lungfuls of fresh Atlantic air; Kretschmer led his bridge watch on to the conning tower in preparation for a silently waiting enemy, though the sea remained mercifully empty. The diesels pushed the boat through the moderately running sea, charging the depleted batteries as they did so and taking *U99* north-west into the

Western Approaches while the re-energised crew set about repairing damaged equipment and squaring away their boat, which had withstood the onslaught without serious damage.

Later that afternoon the U-boat was briefly dived once more to allow the reloading of torpedoes without *U99* pitching and rolling in the Atlantic swell. Otherwise they ploughed through the seas at good speed surfaced until the morning of 10 July when a fast-moving destroyer appeared over the horizon on the starboard bow. With no choice, Kretschmer took *U99* below once again where hydrophones detected other destroyer propellers and the sound of distant depth charges were heard within the boat even without the aid of hydrophones. Through his periscope Kretschmer saw traces of a distant water column thrown into the sky just beyond the horizon, probably the spume of a depth charge detonation as the Royal Navy hunted *U34* following its sinking of the Finnish ship *Petsamo*.

Kretschmer did not make his next attack until the early hours of 12 July. During the course of the previous evening lookouts had sighted a lone steamer on the port bow headed towards Ireland and an intercept course was plotted by Petersen. After nearly two hours of high-speed travel along an interception route the steamer was close enough to be identified as Greek and, as it was within the declared blockade zone, *U99* prepared for a surface attack. At a range of 750 metres a single G7a steam torpedo was fired, running true for fifty seconds before the contact pistol exploded against the hull just aft of midships. The 4,860-ton SS *Ia* was travelling unescorted, carrying 6,666 tons of wheat and a quantity of timber products from La Plata to Cork. Three men were killed in the blast and the remaining twenty-seven, including the ship's master, took to two lifeboats as *Ia* slumped lower in the water.

Though the merchant ship was clearly heavily damaged, it showed no signs of sinking after forty minutes and required a finishing shot. Bargsten fired Tube I once the lifeboats had pulled clear and within seven minutes the freighter was gone. There was time to close the lifeboats and confirm the ship's identity, cargo and route before *U99* disappeared once more, the survivors eventually landing on the Scilly Isles after five days adrift.

Later that day two more solo-sailing steamers were sighted, a two-master and a single master. Distant, they appeared at first beyond Kretschmer's reach until the masts of the first steamer were seen repeatedly, indicating a zig-zagging parallel course, the hull just beyond the horizon and out of sight. Kretschmer ordered full speed to intercept and prepared to attack the unsuspecting freighter. After five and a half hours of manoeuvring, *U99* was in position, though conditions had worsened and the sea was running high with wave tops whipped by strong winds. Kretschmer submerged as the freighter approached, struggling to maintain depth in the difficult heaving sea. At 2231 hrs, a stern shot at a range of only 500 metres was made, though in the steep waves the torpedo veered off course and missed. The ship's neutral markings were now visible and it was identified as the Estonian SS *Merisaar*. Kretschmer brought *U99* to the surface and ordering his 20 mm flak weapon manned and shots fired across the steamer's bow. *Merisaar* wallowed to a halt and two boats were swung out as the entire crew abandoned ship, though Kassel reported no radio transmissions sent from the freighter. *U99* approached the boats, whereupon the master was able to present papers showing that his ship was carrying lumber from New Orleans to Cork. Though neutral it was nevertheless within the prescribed blockade area and Kretschmer fired a second torpedo intending to sink the stationary ship, though this too failed in the rough seas. Unwilling to waste a third, Kretschmer ordered the ship reboarded and sailed to Bordeaux as a prize of war, cautioning the master that *U99* would follow and any use of the radio, except in distress, would result in his ship being sunk without warning. It was, of course, bluff. As soon as the Estonian ship had passed beyond view *U99* resumed its previous patrol in search of fresh targets.

It was quite a coup for a U-boat to capture a ship as a prize, but Kretschmer would be robbed of the achievement by the Luftwaffe. Two days after the ship set course for Bordeaux, on the evening of 14 July, SS *Merisaar* was strafed by a Luftwaffe Heinkel He 111 bomber belonging to KG26. The twenty-six crewmen abandoned ship in the same lifeboats they had used before, rowing away from the vessel as fast as they could while the Heinkel made a second attack run and dropped a bomb which hit the engine room whereupon *Merisaar* caught fire and sank. The entire crew, headed by Master August Schmidt, survived, and began rowing for land, a French fishing trawler finding them two days later and taking them to Lorient, where they were interned for three months before being released to return to Estonia.

During the following days, *U99* rode increasingly heavy seas and sighted occasional ships, most of which were out of range. An attack against a 'Clan-Line Type' freighter of 10,400 tons was thwarted by a tube malfunction, another by the target ship zig-zagging out of range as *U99* lay submerged by daylight and struggled to keep pace. With the target periodically disappearing into strong squalls that swept across the Atlantic, *U99* gave chase, diving at intervals when the target ship was obscured to ensure that they had the correct interception course by tracking the low rhythmic thud of merchant propellers with the hydrophone. By 0203 hrs the following morning *U99* was in position for a surfaced attack from 900 metres. A G7e torpedo was fired from Tube I that hit the ship aft of midships, bringing it to a halt as it sank lower into the water stern first and the crew abandoned ship. By 0250 hrs the 4,434-ton British freighter SS *Woodbury* was gone, taking 3,000 tons of tinned meat, 2,500 tons of wheat and 2,500 tons of general cargo bound for Manchester from Argentina with it to the bottom. Master Norman Rice and all thirty-four men aboard survived, Rice and eighteen others making landfall in County Cork, and the sixteen remaining crew members at Cahiriveen, County Kerry, on 19 July. The ship's radio officer, Harry Weightman, later recalled the sinking and its aftermath:

> I was awakened by the explosion of the torpedo striking the ship on the starboard side aft. The radio room was located on the aft end of the boat deck. After throwing the secret code books in the weighted canvas bag overboard, I sent out the distress call, using the war time secret call sign. Unfortunately, midway through this transmission, it terminated as the external aerial collapsed. I reported this event to the Captain. At this time, the ship was taking on a list to starboard but still moving forward.
>
> The two launched lifeboats were at a safe distance from the ship, waiting for the remaining crew. Myself, Captain Rice and three others climbed down the Jacob's ladder to the Jolly boat [dinghy] which was unfortunately waterlogged. We held on to the sides until one of the lifeboats came over to pick us up. At this time, the *U99* came alongside the other lifeboat and gave the course and distance to the nearest land as northeast, approximately 165 nautical miles. It was wartime practice for U-boat captains to take the Captain and Engineer Officer prisoner, but *U99* did

not. [This only became standard practice later after Dönitz gave orders to do so in an attempt to deprive the merchant navies of experienced officers.]

The *Woodbury* was now about three-quarters of a mile away and went down stern first. Without a doubt, the nature of the cargo restricted the inflow of sea water into the rear holds. There were nineteen in the Captain's boat, including myself and sixteen in the Chief Officer's boat. One life raft had been deployed but was eventually abandoned. On the evening of the fourth day at sea, July 22, we made landfall. As the coastline was foreboding and rocky, we 'hove to' for the night.

At daylight, we proceeded towards the small break in the coastline. A motor launch came out and towed us into the small port of Castletown Berehaven, Eire. We were greeted by a member of the National Union of Seamen, who arranged accommodation and clothing as required. We spent two to three days there and then went by train to Dublin, ferry to Holyhead and then dispersed to our various destinations, mine being Bournemouth . . . On arrival at my parents' home, they told me that they had received a telegram from the ship's owners that the ship had been torpedoed and sunk and that there was no further information.[7]

Kretschmer had now used all of the torpedoes stored below decks and there only remained the two in external stowage canisters; impossible to load into the boat's interior due to the harsh weather conditions. A radioed request to replenish in Lorient was transmitted and BdU acquiesced. *U99* expected to make landfall alongside *U56* within three days but Dönitz would demand an immediate turn-round as a new Halifax convoy had been reported and there were few U-boats available in the Atlantic to intercept it.

Briefly diverted on an unsuccessful search for a downed Luftwaffe bomber crew, and despite occasional rapid dives to avoid aircraft, *U99* rendezvoused with Oblt.z.S. Otto Harms's Type IIC *U56* the following evening and at 0500 hrs on 21 July Isle de Groix was in sight. Both Kaptlt. Otto Salman's Type VIIB *U52* and the small *U56* accompanied Kretschmer into Lorient, under escort by three small minesweeping *Räumboote* of the 2nd R-Flotilla. *U99* made fast alongside the hulk of the *Isère* in Lorient's naval arsenal that the Kriegsmarine had inherited from the conquered French Navy. A reception committee of officers and men from the newly installed 2nd and 7th U-boat Flotillas as well as an advance party for BdU, who was about to establish his own headquarters at Kernevel on the outskirts of Lorient, were on hand to welcome the victorious crew of the 'Golden Horseshoe' boat that had claimed the sinking of six ships and capture of a seventh for a combined claimed tonnage of 35,461 tons. The port was still months away from bunker construction, so the boats lay under camouflage netting while work began immediately on refitting them for action. Repair facilities were not yet fully operational, Brest harbour to the north being more suitable for any kind of extensive repair work to be undertaken. Meanwhile, several Iron Crosses were awarded, including the Second Class to both Klaus Bargsten and Horst Elfe.

Off-duty crew-members were accommodated within the Hotel Pigeon Blanc on Rue de Clisson, while officers were billeted nearby in the Hotel Beauséjour that looked out over the Place Alsace-Lorraine, both requisitioned for German usage earlier that month. One of Kretschmer's immediate concerns was the provision of clean clothes for his crew, their own uniforms reeking of diesel, sweat and hours of turgid putrid air from a boat under sustained depth charging. Lorient's new naval commander provided Kretschmer, and other commanders, with access to stocks of captured battledress uniforms; at first Kretschmer obtained dark blue French clothing before replacing it with khaki summer uniforms that had been left by the retreating British Expeditionary Force evacuated from the port in Operation *Aerial* a month before. The freshly issued clothing was augmented with German rank patches to prevent any possible misidentification of the men as not Kriegsmarine personnel.

For those men ashore, Lorient offered comparative freedom to relax and unwind in what was now the westernmost reach of the Third Reich. Military discipline was rigorously enforced in order to maintain cordial relations with local inhabitants, but there remained considerable latitude in what the young Kriegsmarine men could do. Celebrations at having cheated death in the Atlantic for the first time stretched late into the nights as *U99*'s men investigated the back streets and alleys of the French naval town. Resistance movements had yet to gain traction within the area and there was little hazard for the crew of *U99* as they mixed relatively freely with other German servicemen and French civilians. Kretschmer himself was not a man to sit with his crew in a bar and he is reputed to have given his crew a dressing down when he saw some of them reeling back to barracks after copious quantities of alcohol. He maintained a distance from his men in social situations, but was never considered aloof or arrogant. Instead, his quiet authority and coolness under pressure had earned their respect and admiration. Horst Elfe later remarked that Kretschmer 'wasn't someone who gave big encouraging speeches, he was always very matter of fact, very unemotional, but was not without a heart'.[8]

This patrol marked the beginning for Kretschmer of what has now come to be known as the 'Happy Time' for U-boats in the Atlantic. Lorient in particular would soon become the 'Port of Aces' as those U-boat captains already highly esteemed in public, such as Prien and Herbert Schultze (*U48*), began to frequent the port as part of the 7th U-Flotilla, while those about to make a name for themselves, such as Kretschmer and Schepke, also shared the harbour. However, the phrase is considered by many a complete misnomer, as Kretschmer himself was later at pains to point out.

> The 'Happy Time'. I don't like this term. We were the first ones to probe the defences of the enemy and this was not a happy time, because fifty per cent of our forces perished. I remember when I was with *U99* and went into the Atlantic for the first time, I found out that before me there were six submarines sent to the Atlantic and three were sunk. Fifty per cent losses. So, this is called the happy time? I don't know why. And, of course, we had been trained during peacetime and we had to discover whether the peacetime tactics were any good for war, which they were not at all times. We had been sent with *U23* into the Firth of Forth and were laying mines at the harbour entrances, so that was not a happy time. I also remember with *U23*, for instance, when I had to drop to the bottom, my engineer came to me and showed me [faulty] parts out of the motor of the diesel engines! Only fifty metres of water, and with this sort of thing, we had to go to war? So, this was not a happy time at all. The 'Happy Time' had been invented by the Propaganda Kompanie in Germany; they were the first to speak about it.[9]

Chapter Five

Lorient

It was only a matter of days before Kretschmer was ordered to sea once more. Dönitz needed every boat he could get in the Atlantic Ocean where he knew his war on Allied commercial shipping would be either won or lost. *U99* sailed from port on the evening of 25 July under escort by R-boats and in the company of *U56*; Kretschmer for the North Channel and Harms's smaller boat for the Western Approaches and the St George's Channel. German signals intelligence had deduced that incoming Halifax convoys were likely being routed through the North Channel whenever possible rather than coming within striking distance of the French bases by using the Western Approaches and *U99* sailed at speed for the waters off the north-western coast of Ireland. Within two days *U99* was heading for the known steamer tracks near St Kilda and actively searching for targets and, at 0455 hrs on 28 July, Kretschmer found one.

In near perfect conditions of a gentle northerly breeze and slight sea, an unescorted freighter was sighted steering a zig-zag course north-northeast. At 0557 hrs Bargsten fired a G7e from Tube I at a range of 1,800 metres and it took nearly two minutes of travel before the contact-fused torpedo exploded against the ship's stern. The ship's master, New Zealander David Rattray MacFarlane, was taking his 13,212-ton MV *Auckland Star* from Townsville, Australia, to Liverpool via the Panama Canal. The ship had been at sea since 25 May, hauling 10,700 tons of general cargo that included lead, steel, hides, refrigerated goods and wheat and was eighty miles west of Dingle Bay, only days short of completing the journey at full speed of 16½ knots, when *U99*'s torpedo struck below the waterline. The torpedo exploded on the port side abreast of Number 5 and 6 holds and *Auckland Star* started to settle low in the water at once as distress messages were transmitted from the radio room. Within half an hour, MacFarlane was forced to give orders for the ship to be abandoned using all four lifeboats, telling the officers they were to stand off near the ship until it sank; MacFarlane himself left the ship in the second officer's boat with no casualties suffered amongst the sizeable crew.

Meanwhile, Kretschmer watched as the light of dawn tinged the eastern skyline. The large freighter was stubbornly refusing to sink and he decided to finish it with a second torpedo, submerging and approaching to within 600 metres before firing a G7e at 0653 hrs that hit *Auckland Star* in the engine room after a minute's run and hurled a black column of water and debris 100 metres into the air. Still the tenacious motor vessel refused to go down and a third torpedo was fired eighteen minutes later that exploded abreast of Number 2 hatch. Finally, a little over twenty minutes later, *Auckland Star* rolled over to port and sank by the stern. None of the seventy-four men from the merchant ship sighted *U99* during the attack until Kretschmer surfaced and approached the lifeboats to interrogate the survivors and confirm the identity of his victim while also providing a course for the nearest land.

One crew member, Cadet Robert Taylor, had taken the time to rescue his camera before abandoning ship and took two photographs as *Auckland Star* went down that were later published by the *Evening Standard* newspaper along with a story entitled 'Pets were saved too':

> Ship's lifeboats pull away as a merchantman, sunk by enemy action, slides beneath the waves . . . and in one of those boats were the three pets of the crew – as you see below: 'Jacko' the monkey held by the mate at the tiller, 'Peter' the Chief Steward's canary and 'Cobber' the ship's cat. 'Peter' was saved in a cigarette tin, 'caged' when he reached the lifeboat. At night, a life-jacket was wrapped around his cage to keep him warm. 'His singing kept our spirits up' said one of the crew. And after three days at sea the crew and pets all reached port safely.[1]

The survivors sailed for the Irish coast, one boat coming ashore on 30 July at Slyne Head lighthouse, County Galway, while the remainder reached to within twelve miles of Dingle, County Kerry, the following day and were towed ashore by a local fishing boat.[2]

U99 departed the area at speed on the surface for fear of aircraft responding to *Auckland Star*'s distress signals, although that was far from their only danger. At 0904 hrs a periscope was sighted 2,000 metres distant and Kretschmer threw his boat into high-speed evasive manoeuvres while diving to avoid attack. While surfaced the U-boat was vulnerable to torpedoes; however, once submerged it was a game of blind man's bluff and the chances of a successful underwater torpedo attack using the weapons systems of the time were virtually nil. In fact, the only confirmed sinking of a submerged submarine by another submerged submarine was on 9 February 1945 when HMS *Venturer* sank *U864* west of Bergen after hours of stalking. Ten minutes after *U99* had dived, two explosions were heard in the distance indicating possible end-of-run detonations of torpedoes, and Kassel soon detected the sound of enemy propellers. Kretschmer took *U99* west away from the enemy's position for over an hour before surfacing and running a gradually looping track back to his previous plotted course towards the North Channel. Twice more they were forced to dive by the appearance of British aircraft, until darkness fell and at 2109 hrs lookouts sighted the unmistakeable silhouette of another solo-sailing steamer headed towards the north-east. Bargsten and Kretschmer studied the ship through binoculars and identified the heavy loading gear of a Clan Line steamer.

The Clan Line had become the world's largest cargo-ship business by the 1930s; its ships were either requisitioned or used to convoy supplies during both world wars and known with some affection as the 'Scots Navy'. This particular ship was the 7,336-ton SS *Clan Menzies* sailing unescorted and zig-zagging towards Liverpool with 4,000 tons of wheat and grain, 2,000 tons of dried fruit, 1,500 tons of zinc and 840 tons of general cargo that had originated in Australia. Master William John Hughes pushed his ship at high speed as he knew that he was within the declared blockade zone and a legitimate and valuable target for the Germans.

For Kretschmer the difficulty lay in his ability to get ahead of the ship into a suitable firing position as *U99*'s top speed barely exceeded that of his quarry. Ironically, the zig-zag course steered by Hughes allowed *U99* to draw ahead by following a straight path that matched the mean direction in which the merchant ship sailed between the Porcupine Bank and the Irish mainland. At 0203 hrs on 29 July Kretschmer fired

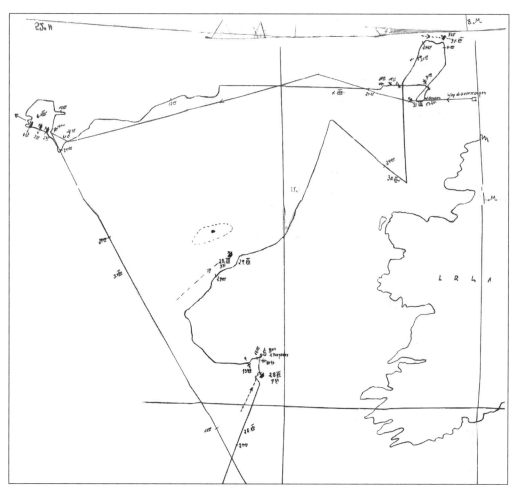

U99's successful third war patrol.

his first torpedo but this passed in front of the steamer which was then nearly 700 metres distant. Twelve minutes later a second shot left Tube I and, though the range had increased over the intervening minutes, after a run of seventy seconds the torpedo exploded on the ship's starboard side, just aft of midships, throwing a column of water fifty metres into the air. The warhead detonated in the ship's engine room killing two British engineers – William McCartney, fourth engineer, and Francis Joseph Hamilton Currie, fifth engineer – and four Indian crewmen – Abu Mian Tindal (bosun's mate), Ali Ahmad, oiler, Aziz Ullah, oiler, and Rustam Ali, trimmer. The blast also damaged the starboard lifeboats beyond use and rendered the radio gear inoperable, eliminating the possibility of any distress signal being sent. Hughes ordered the ship abandoned and in total eighty-eight survivors crowded into the two remaining lifeboats: fifty-two in one, and thirty-six in the other.

The ship settled low in the water by the stern but, as before, failed to sink. Unwilling to use another torpedo, Kretschmer ordered Elfe to break out some explosives from the U-boat's stores. While Elfe began preparing the scuttling charge, Kretschmer brought *U99* close to the lifeboats and interrogated Hughes as to his ship's identity, cargo and destination. On being told the ship's name, Kretschmer apparently remarked 'One of my Clan friends' to the shocked survivors. After requesting information on the cargo and destination, Kretschmer ensured that the lifeboats were adequately provisioned and the men aboard aware of the correct course to the nearest coast. Kretschmer then went astern with *U99* and turned very quickly alongside *Clan Menzies* in order to fix an explosive charge on to a midships ladder on the port side. Five minutes later the steamer blew up and gradually sank after about twenty-five minutes. Kretschmer also warned Hughes that if any of the men aboard the lifeboats showed lights while *U99* was still nearby they would be fired on, an empty threat, but one that nonetheless registered with the merchant crew. The two lifeboats became separated later that night, long after *U99*'s departure; Captain Hughes successfully navigated his boat into Enniscrone, County Sligo, while the other was picked up by passing Irish steamship *Kyleclare* off the Mayo coast during the day after their sinking.

Sailing onward, Kretschmer took advantage of the slight seas and cover of darkness to load the two external torpedoes into the hull, a time-consuming job during which the U-boat would be vulnerable and unable to dive until complete. However, by doing so early in his patrol he avoided the situation that he had faced previously when he had been unable to use external reloads that remained trapped in their containers above the pressure hull by heavy weather. Despite having fired three torpedoes, the bow room remained nearly as crowded as before, much to the chagrin of the 'Lords' who resided there. Cramped conditions were alleviated enormously once the first two 'eels' that were stored above the deck had been fired. Though one was now gone, there still remained a single torpedo cluttering the bow room floor prolonging the relative discomfort of the bow-room crew until they could make their next attack.

By mid-afternoon *U99* was cruising slowly north of Ireland along the entrance routes into the North Channel. A Royal Navy ship identified as a *Kingfisher*-class sloop forced a dive on 30 July as it sailed rapidly towards Lough Swilly, moving too fast to be attacked in what was otherwise an uneventful day of sweeping the barren skies and ocean with binoculars. Not until 0106 hrs the following morning was another merchant ship sighted directly to starboard travelling at 14 knots. This time *U99* was able to haul ahead and within half an hour Tube II was fired at a range of 900 metres and hit just aft of midships, flames bursting from the single smokestack and a large oil slick forming around the ruptured hull. The damage was considerable: the ship's stern had been practically blown off, the main deck on the port side was intact, but on the starboard side it was cracked; the shaft in the engine room was broken, both masts were split, and the main and auxiliary aerials were brought down. As the hull sagged into the water, radioed distress messages gave the steamer's name as SS *Jamaica Progress*, a 5,475-ton refrigerated cargo ship sailing independently from Kingston, Jamaica, to Holyhead with a cargo of 2,179 tons of fruit, predominantly bananas. Five crew members, one gunner and one Jamaican passenger were killed in the attack and one further man badly wounded but successfully helped into a lifeboat as the remaining forty-seven survivors abandoned ship, some swimming for their lives away from the shattered hull. At 0244 hrs a finishing G7e hit squarely amidships and sent the steamer under stern first.

U99 closed the chief officer's boat and a survivor of the ship, whom the German crew attempted to pull from the water, was dragged under by the suction of the U-boat and drowned. Kretschmer ordered the lifeboat to come alongside and questioned the survivors as to whether anybody remained aboard the freighter. Apparently satisfied with their answer *U99* moved away and submerged to fire a finishing shot after which the steamer rapidly sank. *U99* surfaced and again closed the chief officer's boat. Kretschmer, on hearing that the survivors had a compass and knew their position, wishing them a pleasant trip as he departed the scene. The master, Alfred McColm, and twenty-four crew members, one gunner and four passengers were later picked up by the British trawler *Newland* and landed at Fleetwood, while the chief officer and sixteen other crew members landed at Barra, Hebrides.

After *U99* moved away Kretschmer was forced to dive some hours later by the appearance of a British flying boat. However, Kretschmer used the time to reload all torpedo tubes and allow the crew some brief relaxation. In the small wardroom Kretschmer noted the events within his war diary, Horst Elfe expressing surprise that at this stage of the battle Atlantic steamers were still willing to sail independently rather than seek the protection of a convoy. Not long afterwards the hydrophone operator reported the distant sound of massed propellers: convoy OB191 comprising twenty-eight merchant ships under the weak escort of two warships, destroyer HMS *Walker* and corvette HMS *Periwinkle*. Kretschmer took *U99* to periscope depth.

> 1200 hrs: Quadrant 5285. Fifteen steamers in a three-line formation with weak destroyer protection; to the starboard side a destroyer. The convoy tacks. I'm in an unfavourable position, but with the starboard destroyer position and the convoy course change I am put on a collision course, forcing me to dive under the outer column. I can only aim for the last ship in the central column and not for the tanker that I was hoping for. Fire once from 800 metres; on target.
>
> 1324 hrs: Single shot at 800 metres; hit.
> It is a large, old freighter of at least 8,000 tons. The entire convoy consists of fifteen to twenty large ships, with tankers among them. Most freighters are heavily laden, some to their loading lines. A destroyer starts searching for us with listening gear.

Kretschmer had been confronted with the unnerving sight of a wall of painted steel as the convoy was unexpectedly close, hydrophone reception apparently rather poor as *U99* slipped under the convoy column and returned to periscope depth to prepare a firing solution. A G7e was fired from Tube IV and ran for fifty-three seconds before impacting against the hull of the 6,322-ton British freighter SS *Jersey City* travelling in ballast from Newport to Baltimore. The torpedo had exploded on the starboard side at the after end of the engine room and the merchant ship at once buckled at the point of the explosion, cracking badly amidships. The strong detonation was heard clearly by all the men in *U99* as the U-boat dived to prepare for depth-charge retaliation. Above them, two men had been killed – Third Engineer John Green and Able Seaman Wybert Rowland Gwyther – while the master, Frank Jameson Stirling, and his forty-two surviving crew were picked up after abandoning ship by the British merchantman SS *Gloucester City* and later transferred to HMS *Walker* for return to Liverpool. Twenty depth charges were fired from the escorts, but badly aimed and inaccurate as *U99* had obviously escaped detection. Throughout the quietly running U-boat the sound of exploding boilers, cracking bulkheads and collapsing metal plates could be clearly heard transmitted through the dense water, the death throes of the merchant ship as it plunged to the seafloor 300 metres below.

Kretschmer stayed submerged until the sound of propellers had faded and at 1614 hrs surfaced to an empty sea. Though the convoy had disappeared, he planned to follow its westerly course and regain contact. *U99* raced at speed to overtake OB191, passing the site of the *Jersey City*'s destruction that was still marked by two abandoned lifeboats. In less than an hour the smudge of smoke generated by numerous funnels was sighted to the west, though the appearance of a flying boat circling overhead resulted in an unwelcome emergency dive and time lost in pursuit. A stick of bombs chased *U99* below, reminding Kretschmer of the danger posed by escorting aircraft alert to the presence of a U-boat, a pattern repeated twice more that day with bombs exploding close enough to shake the diving U-boat severely at least once. By the time *U99* had surfaced once more, the aircraft had departed into the darkness and the convoy was out of visual range. However, faint traces of propeller noise promised that OB191 was continuing its course and Kretschmer resolved to continue the chase, Petersen plotting an expected interception point for the following morning.

Dawn of the first day of August revealed no trace of OB191, though a quick dive to sweep the sea with hydrophones placed the distant convoy due south, Kretschmer altering his course in a bid to overtake the merchant ships and lie in wait for another attack. No aircraft were seen and *U99* ploughed through deteriorating weather, the sea turning rough and the Atlantic winds freshening, before once again catching sight of the smoke trail left by OB191. A periscope was sighted at 2218 hrs about 1,000 metres distant, but *U99* simply increased speed with evasive zig-zagging and left the potential enemy behind. Kretschmer was determined to attempt a surfaced night attack from within the convoy itself rather than rely on the orthodox method of firing a fan-shot from outside the convoy body into the mass of merchant shipping. His torpedoes were precious and he had long believed the principle of the fan shot that remained a cornerstone of training instruction to be wasteful of valuable – and expensive – ammunition. He had become a vocal advocate of the 'one torpedo for one ship' principle and OB191 presented an opportunity to prove its viability. Kretschmer was also aware that outbound escorts generally departed from a convoy once it had reached the 20th meridian which was rapidly approaching.

His assumption was correct and at 0050 hrs on 2 August, blue Morse lamps began flashing from the distant escorts signalling their departure to the convoy body. The pair were due to leave and make speed to a rendezvous with SL40, inbound from Freetown, Sierra Leone, and now the ranks of OB191 were undefended apart from whatever guns were carried aboard the freighters. Kretschmer moved *U99* into the attack.

> 0050 hrs: The anticipated has arrived. What will now follow will resemble the havoc of a wolf amongst a herd of sheep; four torpedoes are still available.

Kretschmer conned his surfaced boat at speed through a gap in the assembled ships and into the body of the convoy itself, racing between the merchant ships which had ceased to zig-zag as they entered the oceanic phase of their North Atlantic crossing. Both Bargsten and Elfe were also atop the tower alongside the lookouts and he and Kretschmer were initially terrified of the spectacle of enemy shipping passing so close on either side of the low-trimmed U-boat. Though the warships had departed, defensively armed merchant ships were still capable of inflicting a grievous wound to the fragile pressure hull, which would then rob *U99* of the safety of the depths should it be required. However, as Kretschmer cold-bloodedly raced his boat between rows of ships and prepared to attack, the genius of their commander became apparent. The last place that an attack would be expected was from within the boundary of the convoy itself. Locating the U-boat would be difficult, depressing a gun low enough to fire at it equally tricky. If escort ships had still been present, their ability to hunt actually within the merchant columns would be hugely reduced. With his new approach to torpedo attacks, Kretschmer was using every advantage that the U-boat possessed: a low silhouette, speed on the surface and excellent fire control.

At 0251 hrs a G7e electric 'eel' left Tube III, aimed at the largest tanker visible only 500 metres distant, the third ship in the second column. Identified by Elfe from the book of tanker silhouettes as a Dutch *Barondrecht* type of approximately 9,385 tons, the torpedo hit 10,973-ton Norwegian MT *Strinda* amidships on the port side in the Number 9 wing tank and bunker oil tank. All power was suddenly lost because the explosion had stopped the engines and, with one of the port lifeboats destroyed in the blast, the crew hurriedly abandoned ship in the remaining boats, standing by near the wallowing tanker. Kretschmer watched the crew depart *Strinda*, which lost way and slumped low in the water, while signal lamps frantically flashed amongst the remaining merchants. The convoy began to scatter in obvious confusion, Kretschmer remarking within his war diary that what had started as ordered columns of shipping rapidly devolved into a 'hopeless mess'.

Deliberately hunting out the most valuable targets, at 0340 hrs *U99* shot at a second tanker from 450 metres and hit it amidships. This time there was no ambiguity over its identity as distress signals were immediately picked up from the 6,556-ton British tanker MT *Lucerna* which was hit directly under the bridge and gradually shuddered to a halt. The track of the incoming torpedo had been spotted by lookouts aboard the tanker, and the wheel put hard to starboard though *Lucerna*'s bow had barely started to swing when the torpedo exploded amidships on the port side. The explosion punched a hole and the impact passed right through the cavernous ship, tearing a gap on the port side below the waterline approximately thirty-five feet long and eighteen feet deep, and another on the starboard side that was about two feet in diameter. The *Lucerna* was travelling in ballast, like the remainder of OB191, and the crew abandoned the vessel, the boats remaining close by in case they could reboard and attempt to rescue their damaged ship. In due course this is exactly what they managed to do, the badly holed tanker eventually limping to Greenock where it docked on 8 August.

Meanwhile, Kretschmer was surrounded by twisting merchant ships in a welter of confusion as they attempted evasive action from an enemy they could not see, the air alive with frantic radio messages from all quarters. He had hit two tankers so far, believing them both in the process of sinking, and now sought another. With Bargsten at the UZO a third torpedo was fired at a ship wrongly identified as a steamer, 8,016-ton British tanker MT *Alexia*, which was hit and fell out of convoy, its radioed distress calls confirming the ship's identity and tonnage. The tanker had taken an immediate list to port, and the Chinese crew rapidly abandoned ship in lifeboats. However, by a systematic opening of internal valves, the captain managed to get his vessel back onto an even keel, and, although it had sunk about four feet into the water, it was saved and would also later return to port for repairs. To starboard, two ships collided and lost way as *U99* hunted for a final target on which to use its last torpedo. Kretschmer selected one at last, an unidentified tanker of between 5,000 and 6,000 tons, and at 0501 hrs Bargsten fired their final G7e from Tube II at a range of only 500 metres. Stopwatches ticked away the seconds of the torpedo run within *U99*, its track clearly visible in the strong moonlight but disappointment followed swiftly as the 'eel' exploded prematurely after covering only 100 metres.

U99 was now bereft of torpedoes and returned to find *Alexia* still lying stopped though refusing to sink. Kretschmer ordered the deck gun manned and Elfe opened fire as *U99* slowly approached the tanker. Thirty shots were fired, of which up to twenty hit; impacting between the waterline, engine room, upper deck and the ship's bridge. The British tanker appeared to be sinking by the stern, though hardy gunners still aboard had begun to return fire from the defensive weapon, the first shots going wide but becoming increasingly accurate and landing a bare fifty metres from *U99* before Kretschmer broke off the action and departed at full speed. Dawn was spreading across the sky and the radioed calls for help were likely to be answered soon; at 0652 hrs the superstructure of an approaching destroyer was sighted and *U99* headed north directly away from the oncoming enemy. Later that day, at 1330 hrs, *U99* passed the position in which they had hit MT *Strinda*, finding wreckage and a strong oil sick and believing this to be evidence of its sinking, though in reality the Norwegian ship had simply drifted out of sight and remained afloat.

It had been a tremendous attack launched by Kretschmer in which he believed three tankers sunk or sinking.

> *U99* reported the sinking of independently routed steamers, totalling 24,211 tons, and one freighter and three tankers from a convoy totalling 31,957 tons. It appears (radio intelligence)

that three of the vessels reported sunk were only damaged and returned to Britain. But it may be that the British aircraft making the report confused these with other ships.[3]

The B-Dienst intercepts were, however, correct and all three would later return to port under their own steam despite significant damage. The crew of the *Strinda* had waited nearby, the master and some men reboarding the tanker after four hours, bringing the listing ship back to an even keel by shifting the ballast and managing to restart the engines. The courage of these men cannot be overstated as they laboured aboard a disabled ship which remained a priority target for German attack. They had no way of knowing whether any U-boats remained in their vicinity as they lay motionless on the Atlantic swell. The rest of the crew were taken back on board and the lifeboats recovered once power was restored and the ship returned to port under its own power, arriving with the other two damaged tankers on the evening of 4 August. On 21 October, the *Strinda* was taken to Cardiff for repairs and returned to service in March 1941. The skippers of all three tankers later expressed surprise – and no doubt relief – at what they observed to be the poor destructive power of German torpedoes even after scoring a direct hit.

Both the G7a and G7e torpedoes carried a warhead of 280 kg of Schießwolle 36, a composite explosive comprised of 67 per cent TNT, 8 per cent hexanitrodiphenylamine (more powerful than TNT) and 25 per cent powdered aluminium, though the ratios varied at times during the war. The aluminium component extended the explosive pulse underwater which, in turn, increased the destructive power of the explosive. By contrast, the Mark VIII torpedo with which British submarines were equipped from 1927 onwards, initially carried 340 kg of TNT but was modified to the Mark VIII** type, which packed 327 kg of the far more potent Torpex explosive within its warhead (42 per cent RDX, 40 per cent TNT and 18 per cent powdered aluminium). This was the principal Royal Navy submarine torpedo of World War Two and variants were still in use in 1982 when HMS *Conqueror* sank the Argentinian cruiser ARA *General Belgrano*.

Nevertheless, despite his torpedoes failing to sink the trio of valuable tankers, all three ships were out of action for some period of repair at least – the SKL war diary stating that 'empty tankers are probably very hard to sink' – and *U99* made way for Lorient at the end of a successful patrol in which all torpedoes had been used within nine days at sea. On 3 August Kretschmer was mentioned in the *Wehrmachtberichte* for the first time: this was the daily Wehrmacht High Command mass-media communiqué, produced by the Propaganda Department of the OKW, headed by General Hasso von Wedel, and broadcast by the Reich Broadcasting Corporation.

> A U-boat under the command of Kapitänleutnant Kretschmer has during one patrol sunk seven armed enemy merchant ships totalling 56,118 grt, three of them tankers sailing in convoy. Thus, this U-boat has sunk 117,367 grt of enemy merchant shipping plus the British destroyer *Daring*.

While commander of both *U23* and *U99*, Kretschmer had actually accounted for 79,177 tons of commercial shipping destroyed, another 2,136 tons as a prize (later sunk in error by the Luftwaffe), and 25,545 tons of damaged tankers a total of 106,858 tons altogether, and the destroyer HMS *Daring*. The following day it was confirmed that Kretschmer was to be awarded the Knight's Cross for passing 100,000 tons of claimed sinkings. He was the twenty-third member of the Kriegsmarine to receive the prestigious award. At 0748 hrs on 5 August *U99* rendezvoused with its minesweeper escort and was brought into Lorient where it tied up alongside Lemp's recently returned *U30*. When docked, Kretschmer duly submitted his report, explaining his tactics and decisions during the patrol that he had just completed. Dönitz subsequently noted in *U99*'s war diary:

> 28 July: 0904 hrs. Diving after sighting a periscope is not recommended, especially if, as in this case, you could expect a counter attack on the surface. It is more correct to put the periscope astern and take off at high speed, as happened on 1 August at 2218 hrs.
>
> 2 Aug.:   With courage and deliberation, a very well executed attack.
>
> Short, particularly successful mission.

On 8 August, at 1730 hrs, Grossadmiral Erich Raeder presented Kretschmer with his Knight's Cross in a ceremony held on the cobbled dockside before the hulk *Isère* with *U99* moored alongside. Kretschmer and his crew were drawn to attention in their clean British battledress and Raeder presented Kretschmer with his medal in a brief ceremony during which he congratulated each crew-member of the Reich's newest successful U-boat. Once the formalities were over, the entire crew of *U99* boarded their boat and drank a celebratory beer with their captain as Kretschmer smoked one of his familiar black cigars.

Otto Kretschmer had joined the pantheon of bona-fide U-boat heroes with his award and subsequently began to receive the attention of the German military propaganda machine on a scale that he had hitherto managed to avoid. Kretschmer's dislike of propaganda is well documented and, as his fame grew with greater success in action, he steadfastly refused to partake in many of the activities that men in his position frequently found part and parcel of being a military icon. For example, he declined requests to make public speeches such as that during February 1941 at the Berlin Sportspalast given by his friend Joachim Schepke before thousands of schoolchildren, shaping the U-boat volunteers of the future.

Alongside the public events, Schepke also, like many of his contemporaries, wrote and illustrated a book about his experiences as a U-boat officer entitled *U-Boot Fahrer von Heute* ('U-boat Men of Today') that was published in 1940. However, the term 'wrote' is perhaps overly simplistic as no such official publication was the product of the named 'author' alone. Like Günther Prien's similar book (*Mein Weg nach Scapa Flow*), it was 'ghosted' by an authorised writer from Goebbels's propaganda ministry – Prien was reputedly horrified after reading what was supposedly his own autobiography. Books attributed to Hartmann, Prien, Lüth, Korth and Schepke were all published, giving what was often a thinly disguised politically motivated account of the U-boat war at sea. This goes some way to explain the overt political phrasing and occasional disparagement of Jews found within the pages of Schepke's book, for example, and the glowing references to National Socialism within both Prien's and Schepke's works that would later result in the two being frequently referred to as 'hard-core Nazis'. Though they were undoubtedly patriotic and nationalistic, it is arguable whether these characteristics were particularly political in motivation. Indeed, Kretschmer's relentlessly cold-blooded and ruthlessly analytical approach to U-boat warfare resulted in the same label being attached to his name. To many, any German soldier dedicated to his combat role was unarguably a Nazi. It is true that Prien had actually enrolled in the

Nazi Party before being accepted for the Kriegsmarine, but that was probably fuelled more by pragmatic employment reasons than ideological fervour, whatever measure of approval he and others harboured for their *Führer* who – to many Germans around this time – appeared to have delivered Germany from the chaos of the interwar period.

Nonetheless, when approached to write a book during late 1940 recounting his U-boat experiences – or at least provide enough material for text to be prepared without him – Kretschmer, once again, refused. For a brief period of time he had reluctantly agreed to the suggestion, but only after mistakenly believing it to have been a direct order from Dönitz. Clearly annoyed at the order, Kretschmer complained in person to Dönitz, whereupon he discovered that he had been deliberately misled: no such order existed. To his credit, Dönitz did not at any stage order any of his men to take part in such propaganda exercises and when his star captain complained about it to him, he remonstrated with the Berlin publisher and got the book 'torpedoed', never to be brought up again.

Kretschmer did indeed take reporters aboard his U-boat as was a relatively frequent norm at that time. At least one identifiable reporter of the naval Propaganda Company, Hans Kreis, travelled aboard *U99* and filmed the young captain and his crew at work in the Atlantic on the boat's sixth war patrol during November 1940, a patrol during which Kretschmer was awarded the Oak Leaves to his Knight's Cross and Petersen his own Knight's Cross. The film that Kreis accumulated was compiled with existing library footage from the Kriegsmarine propaganda company archive and aired as *U-Boot Feindfahrt: Herbst 1940* from the weekly *Deutsche Wochenschau* ('German Weekly Review') cinema newsreel narrated by Harry Giese.

Kretschmer's aversion to interviews is also well-known, though it is inaccurate to say that he never gave them. He undoubtedly detested the nature of propaganda, particularly the mixture of news and flagrant invention that both denigrated the enemy and perpetuated the warrior mythology deemed necessary to maintain the morale of a nation at war. He also had no love at all for National Socialism and could not bring himself to venture anywhere near a politically motivated broadcast. Though a fiercely nationalistic German, he harboured a strong disapproval of Hitler's ruling party and railed against any perceived intrusion of politics into the U-boat service. In order to prevent having to deal with reporters as much as possible, he had assigned Funkmaat Josef Kassel the task of becoming spokesman for *U99* in all matters relating to the press and its insatiable appetite for stories with which to regale the hero-worshipping German public.

It had become obvious that Kretschmer possessed a purely military mindset, unfettered by the desire for undue publicity, and his distaste at the distortion of reality that became the staple of war reporting was profound and continued past the end of the war. Arguably the most famous German war correspondent of the Second World War was Lothar-Günther Buchheim, an amateur artist and journalist who volunteered for the Kriegsmarine during 1940. Buchheim was designated a *Sonderführer* in the Kriegsmarine Propaganda Company and contributed numerous articles, photographs and drawings of life aboard minesweepers and destroyers, later going to sea aboard Kaptlt. Heinrich Lehmann-Willenbrock's *U96* in the autumn of 1941.[4] While his words and selected photographs appeared in *Signal* magazine and were verbosely nationalistic and pro-military, it was post-war that he published a more complete photographic record of that patrol aboard *U96* in what is, frankly, a stunning collection of images entitled 'U-boat War'. The patrol also formed the basis from which he wrote *Das Boot*, an acclaimed piece of fiction that was made into a highly regarded and commercially successful film long after the war. However, the aggressively outspoken Buchheim himself became a contentious character within the community of U-boat veterans; some such as Erich Topp and Jürgen Oesten supported his work, albeit with some reservations, while others such as Friedrich Merten and Otto Kretschmer became outspoken critics.

> He was a war reporter who had been on board *U96* during a single patrol which was completely unsuccessful. That means that Buchheim had experienced neither a single depth charge nor the torpedoing of a single ship. When I had read the first chapter (Bar Royal) of his book *Das Boot* I threw it away because that world he described was unknown to me. And the stress in a submarine on patrol is so immense that there is no time . . . for porno-talks, which in our current time are a MUST for a bestseller. The crews of submarines on patrol had only time for watches (twelve hours), meals and sleep. A journalist–tourist like Buchheim, on

the other hand, had plenty of time to dream of his experiences and future adventures ashore. Buchheim had already written a book on submarines during the war and had dedicated it to Admiral Dönitz. You can imagine the difference between the two publications. That war propaganda of his he nowadays tries to have forgotten. The film [*Das Boot*] is better because Buchheim was constantly overruled by the director.[5]

Nevertheless, in August 1940 following Kretschmer's award of the Knight's Cross, the reporter Herbert Kühn approached him for an interview for the magazine *Ran an den Feind! – Kampfberichte von unserer Kriegsmarine* ('Charge at the Enemy – Combat Reports from our Kriegsmarine'). Needless to say, it was Kassel's colourful account of the patrol that finally graced its pages:

Horseshoe as a Symbol of Victory
Successful Breakthrough of a British Convoy.
We never have the feeling that anything could 'happen' to us, and we would go through fire for our 'old man'. Thus, our conversation began with the young *Funkmaat*, a Cologne boy, who has just returned from a war cruise against Britain in Kapitänleutnant Kretschmer's U-boat. A *Funkmaat* has numerous duties on board a U-boat and so he is in a way a 'universal' *Maat*; he is *Funkmaat*, Sick Bay *Maat*, Supply Assistant and also No. 1 at the gun. 'We were operating in the Atlantic,' this man, on whose breast the ribbon of the Iron Cross is fastened, told us. 'We had only been three days at sea. We had had aircraft alarms on various occasions, and then we dived, for aircraft are an infernally unpleasant affair for us. Then, during the night, we sighted the first morsel. We pursued it and were soon able to fire our first round. It was a heavily armed British steamer, the *Auckland Star*, 11,400 grt. It didn't take long to sink. The next day the 7,336 grt British steamer *Clan Menzies*, which was on the way from Australia to England with general cargo, came across our bows; it also was dispatched in a few minutes.

'Two days later. We followed a steamer, and when we submerged to periscope depth, the C.O. found that we had a convoy ahead of us. There wasn't much beating about the bush, and quickly No. 3, the 5,475 grt banana ship *Jamaica Progress* was prevented from

The austere formal portrait of Kretschmer with his Knight's Cross and Oak Leaves.
This kind of photo is most often associated with Otto Kretschmer, though it is not
particularly indicative of his studious and shy nature nor his often dry sense of humour.

Above left: Sail training was an integral part of Kretschmer's early experience as an officer cadet in 1930.

Above: The *Niobe* on which Kretschmer sailed. The loss of this ship to a freak accident on 26 July 1932 had a profound effect on the Kriegsmarine and the career of Kretschmer's contemporary Günther Prien.

Left: The light cruiser *Emden* built by the Reichsmarine in the early 1920s and used extensively as a training ship. Kretschmer was posted aboard on 10 October 1930.

Right: Kapitänleutnant Hermann Michahelles, commander of *U35* (*left*) and Kretschmer in *U35*'s conning tower.

U35 pictured here before the outbreak of war with harbour rails attached.
Kretschmer's service as a watch officer board this U-boat included patrols as part
of the international naval presence maintained during the Spanish Civil War
and the first Kriegsmarine U-boat foray into the Atlantic.

Kapitänleutnant Michahelles of *U35* pictured here in his conning tower at manoeuvring stations in harbour.

When *U35* sailed to the Azores, veteran officer Hans-Rudolf Rösing (*left*) was placed in temporary command. Here he is pictured later in the war as FdU West with Adalbert Schnee, who had served as Kretschmer's IWO and had later become a U-boat ace in his own right.

U-boats of the *Weddigen*, *Satlzwedel* and *Lohs* Flotillas in Kiel before the outbreak of war. On the opposite side of the pier are the depot ships *Saar*, *Donau* and *Weichsel*.

The *Weddigen* Flotilla in the Baltic. The U-boat is at anchor, evidenced by the round mooring buoy marker suspended before the conning tower.

An early model Type II U-boat. Kretschmer's first command was *U23*, a Type IIB. It sported this metal eagle screwed to the conning tower front, although the outbreak of war in 1939 led to the 'bird being taken off its perch' on all boats.

Adalbert 'Adi' Schnee who began the Second World War as Kretschmer's IWO and left to take his captain's course in January 1940.

Prewar coffee on the forward deck of a Type II.

Grossadmiral Erich Raeder, chief of the Kriegsmarine until 1943. Though Raeder was rooted in surface naval tradition he understood the importance of the U-boat fleet and chose the perfect man to become BdU in Karl Dönitz. With Raeder is U-boat commander Karl-Friedrich Merten (*right*) who began in the surface fleet before distinguishing himself in the U-boat service.

Right: A torpedo with dummy warhead – signified by its striped paint job – is loaded for firing practice.

Left: The diminutive boats of the *Weddigen* Flotilla moored in Kiel. The prewar establishment of this and other flotillas allowed extensive training of captains and crews aboard a limited number of U-boats. During frequent Baltic exercises, Kretschmer emerged as one of the best torpedo marksmen in the Kriegsmarine.

Left: The calm before the storm for the men of this Type II (possibly *U4*). Each time Hitler attempted a new gamble at expanding the borders of the Reich, such as into Memel and Czechoslovakia, Dönitz ordered his U-boats to sea lest the adventure misfire and provoke hostilities. In September 1939, the *Führer* took one gamble too many and war was declared with the Kriegsmarine's most dangerous adversary, the Royal Navy.

Below left: Latvian born Hans-Diedrich Freiherr von Tiesenhausen, who replaced Schnee as IWO aboard *U23*. He is pictured here after winning the Knight's Cross as commander of *U331*. He was captured in November 1942 when his U-boat was sunk north of Algiers.

Below: Victory pennants flying from the raised attack periscope on Kretschmer's return to port. This symbol of victory became a tradition amongst Dönitz's men.

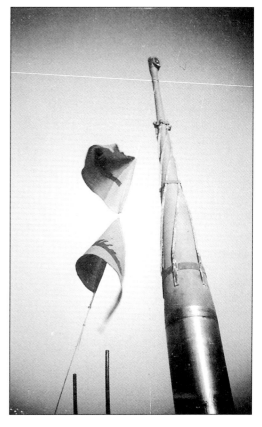

Above: An officers' meeting in Wilhelmshaven on 11 March 1940 (predominantly members of the 1st U-Boat Flotilla): 1. Kretschmer (*U23*), 2. Dietrich Knorr (*U51*), 3. Wolfgang Lüth (*U9*), 4. Harald Jurst (*U59*) 5. Otto Harms (*U56*) 6. Harro von Klot-Heydenfeld (*U20*), 7. Herbert Kuppisch (*U58*), 8. Werner Hartmann (*U37*), 9. ObltzS. Hans Heidtmann (*U2*), 10. Hans Eckerman (commander, 1st U-Flotilla), 11. Wolf-Harro Stiebler (*U21*), 12. Günther Prien (*U47*), 13. Claus Korth (*U57*), 14. Karl-Heinrich Jenisch (*U22*), 15. Herbert Sohler (*U46*),16. Rudolf Franzius (training commander, 24th U-flotilla), 17. Wilhelm Ambrosius (*U43*).

Left: Günther Prien (*left*), after returning to port aboard *U47*. A complex character, Prien became one of the original new generation of U-boat aces after his attack on Scapa Flow and sinking of HMS *Royal Oak.* He and Kretschmer maintained a relatively close relationship until March 1941.

One of the two golden horseshoes welded to the conning tower flanks of *U99*. British tradition would have placed the horseshoe facing upwards, lest the luck 'run out of the shoe' from its open ends.

The photograph is frequently reproduced as an image showing the attachment of the horseshoes to *U99*. However, this is not the case. Somewhat ironically, this shows the crew of Type VIIC *U570* attaching a horseshoe to the front of their conning tower. At least seven U-boats included a horseshoe somewhere within their chosen *Wappen*, but *U570* was to have a particular impact on Kretschmer's later life.

Joachim Schepke, Kretschmer's close friend and peer, aboard *U100*, which sported the crouching panther *Wappen*.

A combat U-boat putting to sea amid the fanfare and ceremony usual during the early years of war.

Kretschmer issuing instructions to his crew as *U99* leaves port. Flying from the commander's staff in the background is the boat's commissioning pennant.

Kretschmer is welcomed to Lorient. Cameramen were frequently present at the departure and arrival of U-boats during the early years of war.

U-boat commanders were summoned by Dönitz to report in person incidents and decisions that had taken place during their patrol. This allowed Dönitz not only to gain a first-hand account of events but also to offer critique and advice or, in extreme cases, remove men unsuitable for U-boat command. Here Heinrich Liebe (*U38*) makes his after-action report to Dönitz (*left*).

Kretschmer (*right*) is amongst the welcoming committee for Günther Prien (in white cap) as he returned to Lorient in *U47*.

Konteradmiral Eberhardt Godt, former U-boat commander (including of *U23* between September 1936 and January 1938), who was Chief of the Operations Staff (*Operationsabteilung*) at BdU , which held tactical command of all Atlantic, North Sea and Indian Ocean U-boats.

Otto Kretschmer pictured on his successful return to Lorient from a patrol aboard *U99*.

Raeder presents Kretschmer with his Knight's Cross in Lorient on 8 August 1940. The entire crew are dressed in captured British summer battledress, their German uniforms not yet having arrived in Lorient from Wilhelmshaven. The event was photographed by propaganda reporter Mannewitz of the Propaganda Kompanie Atlantik.

Klaus Bargsten secures the medal ribbon around Kretschmer's neck.

Raeder shook hands with the entire crew of U99 during the Knight's Cross ceremony. Though he lacked Dönitz's approachability, he still cared deeply for the welfare of his men.

Kretschmer and his IIIWO, Stabsobersteuermann Heinrich Petersen, posing for a photographer on *U99*'s conning tower in Lorient.

The Hotel Beauséjour on Lorient's Alsace-Lorraine square where Kretschmer and his officers were billeted.

Captured on film for the weekly *Deutsche Wochenschau* newsreel.

Obermaschinist Edmund Prochnow's family medical card. Prochnow was put ashore in Norway on *U99*'s first patrol because of illness. He later transferred to *U93* and survived the boat's sinking by HMS *Hesperus* on 15 January 1942 to be taken prisoner.

Left: Following the Knight's Cross ceremony, Kretschmer and his crew retired to the foredeck of *U99* for a well-carned bottle of beer each.

U99 (*right*) in a Lorient dry dock. The netting used to camouflage the boats from aerial reconnaissance and attack is obvious. So is the need for reinforced concrete bunkers that eventually protected U-boats after U99 had been lost in action.

Dönitz and members of the BdU staff outside their Kernevel headquarters. Kretschmer and his fellow captains no longer had to travel to Paris to make their after-action reports after BdU relocated to villas near Lorient in October 1940.

Before the interview . . .

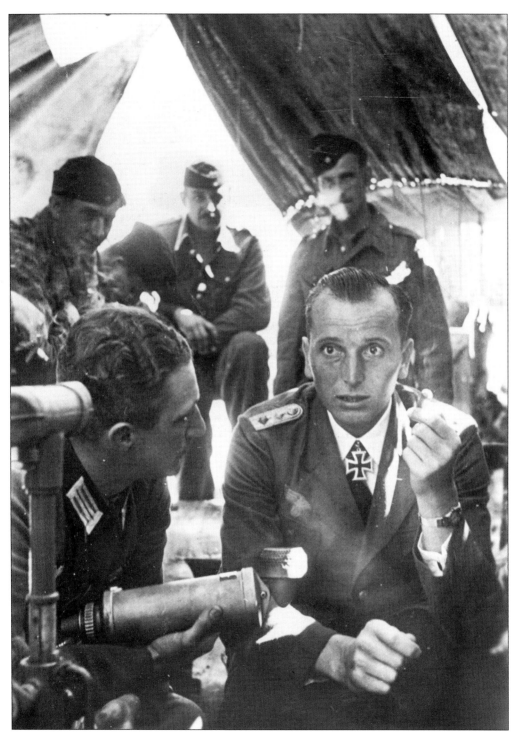

. . . and during. Kretschmer answers questions from an Army reporter in Lorient in the summer of 1940. Photographed by Karl-Heinz Fremke of Army Propaganda Company 689, the reporter is holding a 'Neumann Bottle' microphone.

Heavy seas in the Atlantic.

Italian Commander Primo Langobardo (*left*) who guested aboard *U99* during September 1940. Langobardo is pictured here with Hans-Rudolf Rösing, FdU West, while captain of the BETASOM boat *Pietro Calvi* in which he was killed on 14 July 1942.

Joachim Schepke speaking in Berlin during a state-sponsored recruitment drive.

HALF SUNK BENEATH THE WAVES

The 5,000-ton Glasgow steamer 'Loch Maddy' was torpedoed by a U-boat on February 22, 1940. The photographs above show: left, the bow half of the 'Loch Maddy' sinking beneath the waves; right, the stern half of the vessel taken in tow by another ship.

A British newspaper report of the sinking of SS *Loch Maddy*, hit by torpedoes from *U99* on 22 February 1940, after already having been damaged by *U57*.

An illustration 'by the author' from Schepke's book *U-Boot Fahrer von Heute* ('U-Boat Men of Today') published in 1940. Though Schepke was credited as author, these kinds of books were largely ghost-written by the Propaganda Ministry. Kretschmer refused repeated requests to add his own to the library of books 'written' by U-boat captains.

Seven victory pennants fly from the extended attack periscope of *U99* after return to Lorient, 22 October 1940.

In Lorient Kretschmer joined the dockside greeting party for any U-boats returning from patrol whenever possible.

Kretschmer at his navigation periscope during the November 1940 patrol in which he won the Oak Leaves.

Kretschmer meets Adolf Hitler for his award of the Oak Leaves to his Knight's Cross, 12 November 1940.

A slightly less formal portrait from among the official photos of Otto Kretschmer after the Oak Leaves award.

A member of the technical crew (identifiable by his collarless leather jacket) takes an opportunity for fresh air at sea.

Particularly bad Atlantic weather dominated the winter of 1940/41, rendering convoy locating difficult and using weapons frequently impossible.

The typically clean-shaven crew of *U99* return from patrol, 8 November 1940. The photographer who took this image was named Hermann Tölle of the Marine Propaganda Kompanie. Tölle captured one of his fellow reporters, Hans Kreis, already aboard *U99*, filming from the *Wintergarten* platform.

Klaus Bargsten (*right*) was IWO aboard *U99* until January 1941 when he transferred to *U563* after his commander's course. Subsequently taking charge of *U521*, he was captured as the boat's sole survivor after being sunk in the western Atlantic on 2 June 1943. Here he is pictured talking to Lieutenant Commander Sherman B. Wetmore aboard USS *Pilot* the day after his capture.

Left: Kretschmer receiving his copy of 'The Kretschmer March', while the crew of *U99* look on. The story is often told that Kretschmer refused access to the press for this event, although not only do we have cinema film of it, but the movie camera that captured it is plainly visible in the foreground of this photograph.

Below: The sheet music for 'The Kretschmer March'; this copy was published after his capture by the Royal Navy.

Above left: Another view of the ceremony, during which Kretschmer was given a copy of the music written in his honour: 'The Kretschmer March'.

Left: Kretschmer speaking to Army officers during the presentation of the life-ring from 'ghost ship' MV *Conch*; this is a still captured from a cinema recording of the event.

Otto Kretschmer comes ashore at the Prince's Landing Stage in Liverpool and into captivity.

Commander Donald Macintyre (*right*) pictured aboard HMS *Bickerton*. Macintyre's first action as Senior Officer Escort aboard HMS *Walker* resulted in the sinking of both *U99* and *U100*.

A portrait of Otto Kretschmer, taken in Lorient during 1940 but retouched to show the
Oak Leaves and Swords to his Knight's Cross.

reaching its destination. There was space for a million bananas in this vessel! The British ladies and gentlemen will have to curb their appetite for bananas I expect!

'Then on the next day we were right in the middle of a strongly guarded convoy. Destroyers and flying boats were acting as escort, and we were forced below the surface over and over again. About twenty depth charges were dropped, some of them close to the boat. But they did us no harm and we hung on to the convoy's heels. During the night we surfaced again and found ourselves like the wolf among the sheep, right between the fattest morsels. We attacked the largest one on the surface. It was the *Alexia*, 8,016 grt; the second followed, the 6,556 grt *Lucerna* and yet a third ship, a 9,400 grt freighter, whose name is not known to us, was sent to the bottom.

'During this time messages were being continuously despatched by the destroyers. Again and again flying boats and destroyers passed over us and dropped bombs and depth charges on our estimated position. We returned later to the scene and ascertained that the *Alexia* had not yet been completely destroyed. We were soon to have the satisfaction of sinking this obstinate opponent. The *Alexia* fired at us like mad, and we were forced to turn away in order not to be caught by the gunfire. Moreover, our torpedo was not intended for the *Alexia* at all, but for a tanker which was proceeding next to her. But the latter had spotted the torpedo track in the strongly phosphorescent water and turned away. The torpedo understood this and struck the *Alexia* We also managed to cut an 8,000 grt unknown freighter out of another convoy and it quickly sank.'

In short, dry words, without any embellishment, this brave U-boat man related the events of the cruise. One noticed from his words that the dangers which this war cruise brought in its train were long forgotten and only the proud successes remained clearly in his mind. Again and again he talked about his CO, Kapitänleutnant Kretschmer. His coolness and confident control of the boat gave the whole crew a feeling of absolute security. When Kapitänleutnant Kretschmer was decorated with the Knight's Cross of the Iron Cross by the C-in-C of the German Navy, the whole crew was overjoyed. The boat lay for a long time in her home port, and the men were looking forward more and more to another trip against Britain. At last the time came and this war cruise was so successful that Kapitänleutnant Kretschmer became celebrated far and wide. The succeeding cruise was still more successful. All U-boat men want their boat to be the 'record' boat of the fleet.

Names such as that of Prien, Kretschmer, Schultze, Rollmann, Hartmann, Schuhart, are known to every German, and the British also know very well that they cannot easily escape the German U-boats. Their defence is becoming more and more intensive; but against the spirit, daring, dash and, above all, the capability of our U-boat men there is no antidote.

Two horseshoes decorate the conning tower of Kapitänleutnant Kretschmer's U-boat. According to the log, both these horseshoes were found adhering to the anchor when it was being weighed in Kiel harbour. It sounds almost incredible, but it is a fact. The horseshoe has become the device of this U-boat. The white pennants which the boat flies on its return from war cruises all carry the horseshoe. It is to be hoped that they may continue to bring the boat good luck.[6]

The day following a rowdy night of celebration by the crew in Lorient, their boat was moved to the arsenal repair yards, which had been operational for a week already. The first half of the crew and their commander were granted leave in Germany and would return on 18 August as the second wave of men departed for ten days' leave using the special train laid on by Dönitz for his men returning to the Fatherland. *U99* was not ready for its first test run outside Lorient harbour until the end of August, escorted by two R-boats of the 2nd Flotilla. The boat also carried a guest: Italian Commander Primo Langobardo. The 38-year-old Langobardo had been born in La Maddalena, joining the Regia Marina (Italian Navy) as a teenager in 1915 but did not see action in the First World War. Rising through the ranks after years of academy and onboard ship training, in 1929 he was sent to Tianjin, China, as deputy commander of the Regia Marina battalion at the Italian Legation, a post that he held until 1932. He then attended the Italian Naval Command School as commander of the coastal submarine *H4*, being promoted to *capitano di corvetta* in 1933. Langobardo next commanded submarines

Fratelli Bandiera, *Galileo Galilei*, *Pietro Calvi* and *Galileo Ferraris*, aboard which he participated in several covert operations during the Spanish Civil War, earning the Medaglia d'argento al valor militare (Silver Star for Valour). Promoted to *capitano di fregata* in 1938, he was assigned to the Submarine Office of the Naval Ministry and then to command the Tobruk Submarine Group where he remained until April 1939.

In accordance with an agreement reached between the Kriegsmarine and Regia Marina, an Italian presence was requested in the Atlantic Ocean to assist in the convoy war. Italian submarines were considerably larger and more unwieldy than their German counterparts, crew comfort being of greater concern within the Regia Marina than the Kriegsmarine, and so their forces would be tasked with patrolling the less heavily defended area south of Lisbon, while the Germans remained responsible for the seas north of the Portuguese capital. This dividing line not only suited the craft concerned, but avoided potential complication of coordinating fully the activities of the two navies and favoured the Italian vessels in terms of climatic conditions.

After a tour of the Atlantic ports by an Italian military commission, the Regia Marina chose to base their forces in the inland port of Bordeaux on the Gironde estuary, which was also being established as a major Kriegsmarine base in the southern reaches of the Bay of Biscay. The river was connected to a sophisticated system of navigable canals which led to the Mediterranean, though Italian submarines managed to break through the Straits of Gibraltar to reach their new Atlantic battleground. The designation for the new Italian base was to be 'BETASOM'; a telegraphic address that comprised 'B' (Beta) standing for Bordeaux and 'SOM' as an abbreviation for *sommergibile* (submarine). The Italian base occupied a constant-level basin that included two dry docks and was connected to the River Garonne by a pair of lock gates. It was officially opened on 30 August 1940 by Admiral Perona.

To acclimatise Italian officers to Atlantic conditions, several were sent out aboard combat U-boats to observe German practices at sea and generally get a sense of the differences in environment from the waters of the familiar Mediterranean. Langobardo was scheduled to take command of the *Luigi Torelli* which had left La Spezia on 31 August 1940 as part of the first group of BETASOM boats. It is fair to say that the taciturn Kretschmer was initially less than thrilled to be carrying a passenger on his next patrol. Introduced by Dönitz in the

Hotel Terminus, the pair's initial attempts at communicating in Italian and German proved fruitless, until they realised that they had a mutual knowledge of English, the language of their enemy.

Langobardo was installed aboard *U99*, quartered in Elfe's bunk for the duration of his stay, and when the initial test cruise was completed the boat rendezvoused with Schepke's *U100* which was due to return to port after a successful first Atlantic patrol, though Schepke's entry was delayed for a day and *U99* returned to harbour alone at 1950 hrs, moved into the dockyard for final repairs and refitting. By this time the Royal Air Force had begun to attack the dock installations of the Breton ports as well as minelaying to thicken minefields originally sown within the harbour approach channels by British submarines. Because of the increased danger of mines off Lorient, orders were restated to all U-boat commanders that they could only enter or depart harbour within two hours either side of high tide and then only under minesweeper escort. Sperrbrecher 19 *Rostock* was requested by Dönitz as a permanent fixture at Lorient, this large converted merchant ship being able to take over escort duties when bad weather conditions prevented the use of light-hulled R-boats.

Batteries of the Luftwaffe's Reserve-Flak-Abteilung 371 were already established within Lorient, but they were inadequate for the protection of a port that had begun to receive attention from the Royal Air Force. The battles raging in the skies above Britain prevented promised aircraft reinforcements from the Luftwaffe from giving cover, and Dönitz personally requested the additional batteries as 'necessary unless and until the Luftwaffe's successes in England eliminate the threat to Lorient base'.[7]

As if to prove Dönitz correct, the Royal Air Force attacked Lorient at 0130 hrs on 3 September, four small bombs landing near the moored U-boats within the Scorff River, though they caused no damage. That day Dönitz noted within the BdU war diary:

> I received the following impression from a short stay in Lorient:
> 1. The accommodation for the flotilla requires improvement; necessary work is in hand. Conditions for the ratings should be very good in Lorient, with the rest hostel in Quiberon.
> 2. Danger from mines and submarines is great and will require constant strong defence forces.

3. Flak defences must also be regarded as inadequate after the last attacks. 5 British aircraft were able to fly as low as 300 metres over the dockyard and drop 10 bombs which fell in the immediate vicinity of the U-boats. There is a distinct gap in the defences to the N and NE of Lorient which the British use to fly in. A third heavy flak battery will have to be stationed there. But above all there is a lack of light guns in the dockyard itself against low-flying aircraft. These conditions will have to be improved.

Taken as a whole, Lorient base is entirely suitable, and extremely valuable, but it will hardly be able to take more than 10–15 boats at a time for repairs. Even this number means accumulation which is a great disadvantage as long as air attacks can still be expected. It is necessary to obtain further bases on the Atlantic coast for the new U-boat flotillas.

U99 left Lorient.

As the boat made its first trim dive outside the harbour there was no sign of any oil leak, though the magnetic compass immediately malfunctioned. Furious that after four weeks of shipyard repairs they were still forced to return to port, Kretschmer followed the R-boat escort back into harbour whereupon the compass was replaced by one taken from *U38* which had returned earlier that day from patrol. His second attempt at departure was more successful and *U99* parted from the R-boats west of the Île de Groix as Kretschmer made his final test dive before beginning the surface trek towards the North Channel. Passing occasional French fishing vessels, Kretschmer fretted at the likelihood that any equipped with contraband radios could communicate their position to British forces, and was glad to have seen the last of them by the morning of 6 September.

Twice the boat was forced to dive due to the appearance of aircraft, though a third emergency dive at 1825 hrs on 8 September yielded an unexpected boon when Kassel detected on his hydrophone the distant sound of what Kretschmer deduced was an inbound Halifax convoy. Surfacing, *U99* battered through heavy seas until that evening lookouts sighted the smoke trail of convoy SC2 on the port bow. Prien in *U47* had already attacked the merchant ships repeatedly since the previous morning and sunk three. The onset of bad weather now coincided with

Kretschmer's arrival, the sea considerably rougher and dark clouds lying low on the horizon. Rain squalls periodically lashed the boat as *U99* ploughed through the troughs of a severe Atlantic swell.

A strong destroyer and corvette escort shepherded the remaining fifty ships that were headed from Canada to Liverpool. As well as Prien, *U65* and *U101* were already in contact with the slow-moving merchants, though the severe weather had prevented effective attacks more assuredly than any escort vessels could manage. With bad visibility and high seas whipped up by a Force 8 wind, there was nothing to be done by the U-boats except attempt to maintain contact. Despite the weather, aircraft were also frequently present, driving sighted boats underwater and away from their target. An engine defect forced *U101* to abort operations and head for Lorient, while Kretschmer made contact and attempted to gain firing position in the wildly pitching seas.

Running surfaced at the maximum speed possible, Kretschmer was sighted by an escorting destroyer during the early morning darkness and forced to make an emergency dive, swiftly followed by a sharp and accurate depth charging before the attacker returned to the convoy without an extended hunt. *U99* resurfaced and gradually managed to draw ahead of SC2, Kretschmer finally prepared to gamble on a surfaced attack at 0443 hrs when a torpedo was fired from Tube III, streaking towards a 6,000-ton freighter that wallowed heavily 700 metres distant. However, seconds after firing, the steam torpedo leapt into the air between wave peaks and veered erratically off course, completely missing the target and every other ship of the convoy. Furious, Kretschmer ordered a second shot prepared, Bargsten sending Tube I's electric G7e on its way towards the same target that was now only 650 metres away. This too failed dramatically as the 'eel' visibly broke surface and careered off course. The weather showed no signs of abating and Kretschmer faced a stark choice: abandon the hunt and continue to stalk the convoy with an eye to a later attack, or try his luck a third time. Perhaps piqued by the silent Italian officer also atop the bridge, who appeared to be amused by the German failure, Kretschmer chose the latter course and nearly an hour after the first shot Bargsten fired another G7e from Tube II. To his disbelief, this too crashed out of the water and shot away into the distance, far from the target ship.

Minutes later, three explosions were heard from the convoy's direction. While it was possible that the torpedoes had hit other unintended targets, they were more likely either to be end of run detonations as the torpedo motors stopped and the 'eels' sank, or an attack by another U-boat. Kretschmer was disappointed and angry at the outcome, pondering the cause as probable gyroscopic failure caused by the high sea in which the torpedoes were fired. Yet another defect to the U-boats' primary weapons, and three valuable 'eels' wasted. He had been tasked with showing his Italian guest how a decorated U-boat ace and his crew fought within the Atlantic; so far, he had only demonstrated how to fire three torpedoes and miss. For a perfectionist like Kretschmer it must have been a frustrating morning as *U47*, the original contact boat, lost touch with SC2 and in the spreading dawn Kretschmer too lost sight of the rear escort sweepers as they neared the entrance to the North Channel.

Bad weather had hampered Kretschmer's torpedo attacks in an unexpected way, by triggering an internal weapons malfunction, rather than it simply being too rough to mount an attack in the first place. As Horst Elfe later recalled, Atlantic conditions could render belligerents impotent as they struggled against the elements and were unable to wage war.

> We had to ride some pretty massive North Atlantic storms. It couldn't have been worse. Underwater we couldn't do anything; no U-boat could be controlled at periscope depth during a major storm – it either had to be above or well below sea level. So, underwater attacks were inconceivable. Surface attacks were unthinkable because nobody could see, move, aim or do anything. There were those occasions when you suddenly saw a single ship, which you would usually have attacked, but you couldn't. You'd steer a parallel course and neither party could do the other any harm. People thought only of their own survival in these seas.[8]

U99 dived into the depths to reload torpedoes. Far below the surface, the crew were able to relax and rest once their tasks were completed. The boat could be cleaned after the constant pitching and rolling had dislodged every possible object from personal spaces and the galley. For four hours they cruised slowly on electric motors, surfacing for fifteen minutes in mid-afternoon into gale force winds and towering waves. With visibility reduced to 500 metres maximum Kretschmer noted in his war diary that in such heavy weather no use of any weapons was

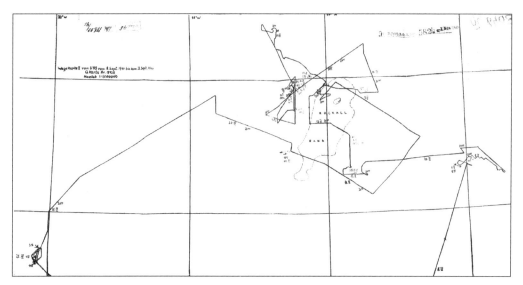

U99's operations around Rockall during its fourth war patrol.

possible, and dived once more. Below the surface they were at least able to sweep the surrounding sea with hydrophones, though there was no trace of anything to be found.

That night, Kretschmer surfaced once more. The seas were still running high but had abated at least a little. A fast-moving freighter was spotted a little past midnight and Kretschmer optimistically ordered *U99* on an interception course. However, this too was thwarted as the port diesel failed and required three hours of maintenance. With the freighter moving at 16 knots there was no way that Kretschmer could hope to match its pace on one engine and the chase was abandoned. Only two armed trawlers were sighted later that night to alleviate the routine, unsuitable for attacking despite the weather mercifully beginning to moderate. Not until 0555 hrs on 11 September did lookouts sight what they took to be a fully laden independently sailing 2,041-ton steamer of the Greek 'Virginia' type, headed on an east-northeasterly course towards Liverpool. Kretschmer moved his boat to firing position and at 0716 hrs a single torpedo was fired at a range of 1,200 metres. The 'eel' ran for one minute and twenty seconds before hitting British 2,468-ton merchant ship SS *Albionic* on its port side beneath the bridge. The blast threw a cloud of sparks into the air and within twenty seconds the ship and its cargo of 3,500 tons of iron ore were gone, two weak explosions heard as it plunged to the bottom two kilometres below. Neither Master Harry Thompson nor any of his twenty-four crewmen survived the rapid destruction of their ship.

The following few days remained frustrating. Amidst intermittent patches of deteriorating bad weather and dismal visibility, *U99* was bombed by a Short Sunderland that narrowly missed the crash-diving boat and generally swept a bare ocean with lookouts above surface and hydrophones below. Fast-moving refrigerated cargo ship MV *Waipawa* was briefly sighted and identified by radioed messages that it had observed a U-boat, but escaped unscathed at speed. A British aircraft carrier and occasionally its aircraft – probably HMS *Furious* – was also sighted, but without any hope of attacking. The war diary entries maintained a monotonous mantra:

> *Kein waffeneinsatz möglich* [No use of weapons possible].

Finally, on 15 September, the weather broke and *U99* surfaced into slight seas and good visibility. A little after midnight, a radio transmission from *U48* – recently taken over by Kaptlt. Heinrich Bleichrodt – reported an inbound convoy at the Rockall Bank. The convoy had been broken up by his first successful attack and contact lost but he was confident of the mean course and destination. Kretschmer was only seventy nautical miles to the northeast and he ordered full speed as the diesels sprung to life and pushed the boat towards the mass of SC3, a slow convoy from Halifax to Liverpool comprised of forty-seven merchant ships before *U48* had struck. At 0947 hrs the smoke trail became visible and just over an hour later a straggler detached from the convoy body came into view. *U99* had been forced to dive briefly by a circling Sunderland, but after observing the steamer and preparing a submerged torpedo attack, Kretschmer elected instead to use artillery on the ship, the flying boat no longer being visible and no weapons aboard the freighter being discernible through binoculars.

At midday, *U99* surfaced and the gun crew raced to remove the watertight tampion from the 88 mm cannon and open fire. A human chain handed shells up through the main hatch and into the small slide where they were manhandled by the gun crew into use. In total forty-nine shots were fired, at least forty of them hitting the 1,780-ton Canadian SS *Kenordoc*. The ship was carrying 2,000 tons of lumber, mainly pit props, from Quebec to Bristol and before long the fore-mounted bridge was ablaze and the stern engine room wrecked and billowing steam from fractured boilers. The gunfire killed the master, Charles Ernest Brown, along with six other men. Of these, twenty-year-old Geoffrey Tasman Barker, the radio officer aboard *Kenordoc*, was killed at his post as he frantically reported the attack and would later be posthumously awarded the Lloyd's War Medal for Bravery at Sea, honouring seafarers who performed acts of exceptional courage. Chief Officer Donald Kerr was also awarded the Lloyd's War Medal, as well as an OBE for his bravery under fire. The citation reads:

> When the ship was shelled at point-blank range by a submarine, a number of men, including the Master, were killed or injured. After staying behind to see all others off, the Chief Officer was pulled into the water by the suction from a shell and was not picked up until some two hours later. He showed great coolness and courage throughout.[9]

With the crew having abandoned ship and the freighter in flames, *U99* departed to continue the chase of the main body of SC3, briefly forced to make an emergency dive away from an oncoming Sunderland. In the meantime, *Kenordoc* stubbornly refused to sink and *U99*, which had drifted while submerged, passed the stricken ship once again while resuming the hunt, passed it once again, before destroyers HMS *Amazon* and HMCS *St Laurent* rescued the thirteen survivors and scuttled the shattered remains of the Canadian freighter.

Early the following morning *U99* sighted another straggler from SC3, reaching firing position at 0241 hrs and launching a close-range surfaced attack. The target was Norwegian 1,327-ton SS *Lotos* bound for the River Tyne with a cargo of 1,500 tons of lumber. The torpedo struck abaft of Hatch 2 on the starboard side, a green-white spume of water thrown as high as the mast tops, the bridge destroyed by the blast and the wheelhouse collapsing into the superstructure, though the helmsman was miraculously uninjured. Two lifeboats were immediately lowered, but the motorboat carried as deck cargo had been thrown across the winch by the explosion rendering it inoperable. Twenty minutes later *Lotos* was gone. It had been unable to keep pace with the main body of SC3 and had become separated days before, doggedly trailing the path set by the remainder of the convoy. Kretschmer hailed the lifeboats and provided them with a course to land before once again resuming the chase. Master Karl Hjellestad and all sixteen of his crew survived, though two men were wounded; one boat of nine men made landfall before the other eight survivors riding in the captain's lifeboat reached land at Castlebay, Barra, after almost five days at sea.

The night of 16 September was still plagued with occasional strong winds, but only a moderately running sea. A full moon hung in the sky brilliantly illuminating the Atlantic expanse for miles in every direction. At 2110 hrs a zig-zagging steamer was detected off the port bow and the diesels throbbed as Kretschmer raced to gain position. Sixteen minutes before midnight he tried a stern torpedo shot when the target was within 500 metres of his boat. The electric torpedo raced towards the steamer, but broke surface only 200 metres from *U99* and crashed off course into the night. Kretschmer and Bargsten had also both overestimated the target's speed and *U99* turned to make a second attack at midnight. However, now 2,000 metres distant from the steamer, *U99* was apparently spotted as the ship turned away and radio messages began to flash from it. It was the 2,372-ton British steamer SS *Crown Arun*, straggling from convoy HX71 with a cargo of 2,800 tons of pit props bound from Gaspé, Quebec, to Hull. The ship had actually begun life as German freighter *Hannah Böge* but had been captured by HMS *Somali* on the first day of war and taken as a prize to the Orkney Islands where the German crew were interned and the freighter renamed for British service. Master Hugh Laurence Leaske piled on every bit of speed that the ship's 4-cylinder compound steam engine could muster but at best – and in ballast – the maximum was 10 knots, and *U99* was more than a match for that.

Kretschmer knew he had been sighted, but was too far away for a reasonable chance of success using a torpedo and was reluctant to engage the ship in an artillery attack as lookouts identified two defensive weapons aboard the steamer. Instead he manoeuvred ahead in preparation for a submerged attack to rid the enemy's lookouts of the benefit of the bright moonlight. At 0400 hrs *U99* dived to prepare for a torpedo attack.

However, Kretschmer was unable to use the attack periscope as moisture had entered the sight tube and had misted the mirrors and lens, no amount of heating applied directly to the barrel having any remedial effect. Instead he took the shot using the larger-headed night attack periscope (*Nachtzielsehrohr*) from the control room, the large aperture giving excellent visibility in the bright moonlight. The boat attempted to maintain eleven metres depth but the tower broke the surface several times before and after firing the electric torpedo from Tube IV at 0444 hrs, and once more after the 'eel' had left the tube. The ship was only just over 500 metres distant and it was probably the briefly exposed conning tower that alerted British lookouts to their danger as the steamer turned hard away and Kretschmer's second torpedo also missed.

Kretschmer surfaced and raced ahead to try a second submerged attack in daylight. After nearly four hours of travel, *U99* was in position once again and at 0832 hrs, an electric torpedo leapt from Tube III and began a run of only forty-three seconds before hitting *Crown Arun* in the bow. The freighter slewed to a stop, its stem slumping low in the water, but it refused to sink, perhaps buoyed up by its wooden cargo. As Tube V was reloaded, Kretschmer watched the crew abandon ship, no casualties suffered from the twenty-five men aboard. Over an hour later, *U99* rose from the sea and the artillery crew began pumping shells into the ship's waterline in a bid to put it under. At least thirty shells landed on target from 102 fired, a mixture of high explosive and phosphorous. Eventually, after twenty-three minutes of shellfire the battered and burning freighter capsized and sank. Kretschmer approached the lifeboats and questioned the survivors as to their cargo and destination, confirming the identity of the ship already gleaned from radio transmissions. Lookouts then spotted HMS *Winchelsea* approaching over the horizon at speed and Kretschmer submerged and crept clear of the area while reloading torpedoes; the merchant ship survivors were rescued and later landed at Liverpool.

A little past midnight on 18 September, an earlier signal from *U65* was relayed and picked up by Kassel in the radio room: '1600 hrs: Enemy convoy sighted Quadrant AM1574. Southerly course, 8 knots; contact lost.' Kretschmer piled on high speed and attempted to make contact, searching north and east of Rockall Bank but finding nothing, the sea having risen once more and visibility decreased. Not until early on 20 September was another sighting reported, this time from Prien in *U47*: 'Enemy convoy in sight. Quadrant AL1968, easterly course, low speed.' In BdU headquarters, Dönitz immediately issued orders to all available boats as *U47* clung to the convoy as contact boat and an attempt was made to use the fledgling 'wolfpack' strategy.

U47 made contact with an inward-bound convoy. At the same time B-Dienst picked up enemy course instructions for a convoy coming from the west. It was first thought that these convoys were one and the same, because the course at first reported by the boat corresponded approximately to that given by B-Dienst. All boats in the vicinity were therefore ordered to attacking positions on the enemy's course which would give them a chance to contact the enemy in daylight. Later reports from *U47* showed clearly, however, that the convoy was making a detour to the south-east and the boats received orders to operate against it in accordance with shadowing reports from *U47*.[10]

Prien was low on ammunition at the end of a successful patrol in which he had sunk six ships, five of them from convoy SC2. Assigned the dreaded – and dull – task of Atlantic weather boat, providing meteorological information for the Wehrmacht, his duty was now to transmit occasional position reports as the other U-boats gathered. The convoy had already suffered the effects of a north-westerly gale that caused havoc amongst the ordered ranks of merchantmen. Station-keeping proved impossible, particularly for the larger ships, as towering waves crashed over their decks, frequently splintering lifeboats that had been swung out in readiness should the merchantmen come under attack. Some ships fell astern and began straggling as the convoy emerged into calmer weather. The oceanic escort, armed merchant cruiser HMS *Jervis Bay*, had departed and there was an anticipated twenty hours before the escort ships of Western Approaches Command were expected to reach the convoy during the afternoon of 21 September. The weather was also uncharacteristically mild with only a moderate south-westerly blowing across the Atlantic, isolated showers giving occasional cover while the nearly full moon shone brightly between cloud banks.

Of the boats summoned by Prien, *U99* was the nearest and reached the expected location first, followed soon thereafter by *U48* and then *U65*, *U38*, *U43*, *U32* and *U100*. By midnight, Kretschmer was in the area where he expected to find the heavily laden convoy, but there was nothing to be seen and he altered course to the south. At 0225 hrs on 21 September, Kretschmer's lookouts sighted the forty-two ships of convoy HX72 astern and to starboard and *U99* was immediately readied for action, though he was out of position for a smooth attack.

Boat stands on the unfavourable moonlit side. As the moon briefly concealed by a dark cloud, attacking the largest ship, a tanker. During the attack, the moon shows through again, so it must be a long-distance shot.[11]

Kretschmer knew that even the small silhouette of a Type VII U-boat trimmed down could be easily spotted if highlighted by moonlight behind it. Though that same excellent visibility had allowed Prien to shadow HX72 effortlessly and the other U-boats to make contact, it also provided hazards for the attacking U-boats. The night was obscenely bright with the moon in the east, the wind had dropped to the barest breeze and the surface of the Atlantic barely rippled. At 0312 hrs an electric torpedo was fired from Tube II, Bargsten at the UZO as Kretschmer maintained his overall view and cursed the presence of the bright moon. The range was 1,350 metres, further than Kretschmer would have hoped as he pined to be able to use his favoured attack technique of penetrating within the actual convoy itself. However, after ninety seconds were counted off on stop watches throughout the boat, the dull rumble of impact was heard, the tanker hit in the bow throwing a column of white and black spume thirty metres into the air. The large ship veered away from the convoy and began to sink by the bow almost immediately, though once the forward deck was lapped by the Atlantic water, the vessel hung motionless and refused to go any further. As surviving crewmen raced to abandon ship, radioed distress messages were intercepted, identifying the tanker as the 9,154-ton MT *Invershannon*, a British motor tanker hauling 13,241 tons of Admiralty fuel from Curaçao to Scapa Flow. Of special construction, the tanker had one hold forward for dry cargo and it was in this empty hold that the torpedo detonated. All forty-eight men aboard Master William Richardson Forsyth's ship – the majority of them Chinese – abandoned ship in three lifeboats. Kretschmer knew that a finishing shot would be required, but the ship was obviously not going to be moving so he planned to return later after he had pressed home his opening attack.

Creeping slowly around the convoy fringe, Kretschmer was surprised to find *U47* lying motionless in his path, even managing to approach to within hailing range and flashing a recognition signal twice with a small lamp before being spotted by an inattentive watch who were obviously distracted by the convoy's presence. *U47* immediately threw the rudder to starboard and began moving before Prien reached the bridge and calmed his lookouts. The startled crew would no doubt be berated by Prien for this lapse which could prove extremely costly in action and was unforgivable on an experienced boat. Robertson recounts that the two boats exchanged belated recognition signals before sailing near enough to exchange megaphone conversation.

> Prien called across: 'You wouldn't have got away with that if I had been on the bridge, Otto. You scared my watch stiff.'
> 'You need some look-outs,' Kretschmer replied tartly.[12]

As *Invershannon* fell out of position, Commodore H. H. Rogers aboard SS *Tregarthen* attempted to escape the danger by changing direction to port, abandoning the zig-zag and increasing speed to 10 knots. However, *U99* could outpace the merchants, though he noted that the remaining steamers were not all as large targets as the tanker had been, estimated mainly at 6,000 tons and smaller. He rapidly moved to the starboard flank of the convoy where the bright moon would not prove any handicap to a closer approach and at 0319 hrs he fired a single electric torpedo at a heavily laden freighter from 580 metres. After a direct hit amidships, the merchant ship broke in two and sank within forty seconds. It was the 3,668-ton British SS *Baron Blythswood*, dragged under quickly by its cargo of 5,450 tons of iron ore, so quickly that it is possible only a single man of the thirty-five aboard Master John Maclardy Robertson Davies's ship survived. Another shot followed:

> 0347 hrs: Single torpedo at the largest freighter of the convoy from 1,000 metres. Direct hit amidships. Ship veers away and stops with heavy list to starboard. It transmits its name and position by radio. It is the British steamer *Elmbank* 5,156 tons. Carrying wood.[13]

The ship's master, Harold Tyler Phillips, and a single crewman, helmsman Ali Hasan, were killed in the attack, while the fifty-four survivors took to their lifeboats. The ship once again stubbornly refused to sink, and Kretschmer decided to break out the gun crew once more and finish it off once the boats had drawn clear. Forty-one 88 mm shots were fired at the waterline, Prien's *U47* arriving to add the weight of its gunfire to the *coup de grâce*.

> I was firing at this ship and [Prien] asked me through the
> megaphone – he was very close – whether I would allow him
> to practise his gun crew with a few shots at the target. And of
> course, I said you can do that and they did; but without hitting
> the ship with one shell! I found out later that he was very
> angry and stopped shooting, then went on behind the Atlantic
> convoy.[14]

Kretschmer's gunners continued to hit *Elmbank* which had begun
to burn as mixed high explosive and phosphorous battered the hull
and cargo. Before long Prien's boat departed and Kretschmer decided
on a finishing shot from his stern tube, but it exploded prematurely
after breaking the surface repeatedly. All of the boat's below decks
ammunition had now been fired and, with no escort vessels present,
Kretschmer took advantage of the last dregs of darkness to unload the
two storage canisters under the decking and transfer torpedoes into the
hull. By 0700 hrs the task was complete and while tubes were reloaded
in the bow and stern, *U99* returned to the tanker *Invershannon* to
administer a *coup de grâce*. The main artillery piece was now bereft of
ammunition and a brief attempt at holing the waterline by use of the
20 mm flak gun failed, so Bargsten was ordered to break out the dinghy
and, together with an *Unteroffizier*, take scuttling charges aboard the
ship. However, soon after they entered the dinghy it was flooded by
the choppy sea and sank quickly, both occupants being pitched into
the water and then ignominiously fished back out by crewmen aboard
U99. Instead, the freshly loaded steam torpedo in the stern tube was
fired, breaking water several times before hitting the hull stern and
exploding, triggering further internal explosions as the masts collapsed
and the hull sank lower into the water. Though the battered tanker
still appeared reluctant to sink, Kretschmer had had enough. Its back
was broken and further sharp cracks could be plainly heard from the
hull, breaking apart behind the bridge. It was only a matter of time, but
Kretschmer wanted to return to the drifting *Elmbank* and make sure
that it too had gone down. A subsequent report to Royal Navy officers
made by the second officer of *Invershannon* described their interaction
with *U99* during the final destruction of his vessel.

> Ship sunk rapidly by head, and it was thought she was about
> to founder. Ship was abandoned, three boats getting away with

complete crew: first in the charge of Master; second in charge of Chief Officer and third in charge Third Officer. Nobody was injured. Boats pulled away from ship and made fast to each other during remainder of night. Second Officer states the possibility of returning to ship to try and pump out cargo from fore end of vessel was discussed, but valves which had to be opened were situated on fore deck and probably under water. In view of this, and the possibility of the submarine being in the vicinity the master agreed that it was best to await daylight.

By daylight boats had drifted about five miles easterly from ship, and they then proceeded to close their ship again. A short time after this, U-boat was sighted about four or five miles to westward of *Invershannon* steering towards. Passing along port side of *Invershannon* she subsequently contacted Chief Officer's boat. U-boat then disappeared from view of boats to port side of M/V *Invershannon*. U-boat was about half an hour out of sight of boats which had hoisted sail and proceeded in direction away from ship. During the latter part of this half hour a most violent explosion occurred in after part of vessel. The stern which had previously been high in the water, now began to sink until ship was on even keel, but very low in water. She remained like this, settling down bodily. Shortly after the explosion submarine was sighted steering away from ship, she submerged for a short period, then broke surface to contact Chief Officer's boat for the second time.

A man, who was found to be sole survivor of SS *Baron Blythswood* and had been rescued from a raft by submarine, was placed in Chief Officer's boat. The man had been given dry clothing while on board submarine, also a packet of American cigarettes. The Second Officer states that the cigarettes were the same as the stock on board M/V *Invershannon*. If this was transferred from U-boat on second contact it seems very definite that enemy boarded ship and made search. I find it impossible to establish whether this man was transferred to Chief Officer's boat on first or second contact with enemy submarine. Second Officer further states boats became separated three days later when, during night, weather deteriorated.[15]

There remains some debate about the identity of the sole survivor from *Baron Blythswood*. In Roberston's book he describes Kretschmer as having caught sight of the solitary figure while in the middle of his attack on *Elmbank* and being unwilling to pause and rescue the unfortunate survivor. Once *Invershannon* was settling into the sea Kretschmer then decided to find the unfortunate man who was brought aboard *U99* in a state of shock:

> We always acted with honour in the submarines against our enemies. We had only to do our job, do our duty and sink ships, not kill men. Several times we had the opportunity to save survivors from other ships but in our small submarine we couldn't have any extra people. So we put them in lifeboats and gave them food and whatever they needed and gave them at least a course to go home or Ireland.
>
> I remember that one ship from the convoy called *Baron Blythswood* went down immediately when the torpedo hit, broke in two and went down, which was very seldom the case. After I left the convoy in the morning to go back and find out whether the ship had sunk, which I could do then with gunfire, I saw, really far, a raft at the distance of a few miles. Well one man was standing with an oar erected and with his shirt or something waving from the top of the oar, just waving. It looked like a cartoon . . . So, I had done my job and sunk the ship and I went there and took him on board. He had a moderate concussion and didn't even know the name of his ship, which was very important for the war diary of course. And it was very difficult to extract from him, what is this, what is that. We had the thick bible of ship silhouettes and ship names from the *Lloyd's Register* . . . and all the time we were giving him food and drink and dry clothes and letting him sleep and everything. All the time I was trying to find a lifeboat, and saw people were there on the horizon so I went there and ordered them alongside. The look on the faces of the people in those boats. This lifeboat was manned by two white men in blue Merchant uniform, and manning the rudders were some yellow men, from Vietnam, Annamese as they were called back then, or something like that. When I gave orders to them via the megaphone to come alongside, they seemed a bit scared,

thinking now their end was near; they were full of war propaganda, that's what it looked like, they thought 'My God, we're going to be killed.' So they were mighty surprised when, instead, one of their own folks, wearing a German overall, carrying his own wet clothes in one hand and some provisions in the other hand, was to come aboard their boat. The Briton who was manning the helm was so impressed, he grabbed into his pocket and threw a pack of cigarettes onto our deck, as a sign of gratitude. I wished them well and that they may reach Ireland safe and sound, all this happened west of Ireland, and asked them if they knew the heading; 'Yes, yes, they knew', etc., so they set sail. The weather was pretty fine so they could well get back home. And the man who had been onboard, who was my guest, he didn't know all this time that he was on a German submarine. He thought it was a British one! He always told us, 'Well, my ship was sunk by the bloody Germans' and how lucky he was that a British submarine came and picked him up. Because we talked with him in English all the time, those of us that knew English.[16]

The man who came aboard was Irishman Joseph Byrne, a 35-year-old merchant mariner whose ignorance of his surroundings is corroborated by Kassel's later telling of the story. The crew were in featureless clothes, much of it British, Kretschmer and Langobardo were communicating in English atop the conning tower and Kassel himself was questioning him in flawless English. Whether there is some exaggeration in this unwitting belief that he was aboard a British submarine, or it reflected the general health of a man who would have been fortunate to have survived a rapidly sinking steamer, it appears that Byrne was warmed aboard the U-boat, and given dry clothes and some food and drink before Kretschmer approached the lifeboat controlled by *Invershannon*'s chief officer, Thomas Evans, and had him placed aboard.

The real confusion over Byrne's identity stems from the fact that, following the separation of the three lifeboats in the harsh Atlantic weather that overtook them, the one with Evans, fourteen Chinese crew members and the Royal Navy Able Seaman DEMS gunner were riding was never seen again, all of them lost at sea. However, it is likely that Byrne transferred to another lifeboat before their separation as he, no doubt, would have benefited from some medical attention. The master and a boat of sixteen men were later picked up by HMS *Flamingo* and landed at Londonderry, while the fifteen remaining survivors were rescued by HMS *Fandango* and landed at Belfast on 29 September.[17]

At 1607 hrs Kretschmer fired his last torpedo, a G7a that had been brought into the bow torpedo room from its external storage and launched from Tube I at over 1,000 metres range. The *Elmbank* stubbornly floated on its cargo of timber and finally went down by the stern so that only a metre or so of the bow remained above water when *U99* set course for home. Though the attack on HX72 would continue by the other boats, Kretschmer's ammunition was gone and he asked permission to return to Lorient.

> Radio transmission *U99* to BdU. 1610 hrs: Returning. Seven steamers for 25,498 tons, including one tanker and two freighters from convoy today. Little traffic in operations area, smallest steamers.

Kretschmer was briefly redirected to search for survivors of a Heinkel He 111 (TG+KA) of Brest's Luftwaffe meteorological squadron, Wettererkundungsstaffel 2, that had been shot down 400 kilometres from the Breton coast after encountering three Royal Air Force Coastal Command Blenheims of 236 Squadron. Leutnant Rudolf Prasse's Heinkel had been searching for the crew of another of the squadron's aircraft, Leutnant Horst Max Dümcke's He 111, that had ditched with technical problems earlier that day, landing on the sea near French fishing vessels, Dümcke and his crew were rescued and subsequently transferred to a German air–sea rescue plane. However, their distress calls had also attracted the Coastal Command Blenheims, which chanced upon Prasse and shot him down. The aircraft's observer, Major Dr Hans Reinhardt, was killed by the attack while the flight engineer, Unteroffizier Franz Liebl, later died of his wounds. Only Prasse and radio operator Unteroffizier Max Mrochen survived, though *U99* was unable to find the airmen in their small inflatable dinghy. *U99* encountered Bleichrodt's *U48* during their search and both boats scoured the area until breaking away for Lorient later that night. The two airmen were later rescued by a Breton fishing boat and returned to France after being adrift in a dinghy for two days.

An emergency dive prompted by the appearance of aircraft at 1333 hrs on 24 September left *U99* hanging at an almost uncontrollable forty-degree down angle. The stern external storage container had been left open for what Kretschmer describes as 'weight reasons', but as the boat began to descend it was too slow to drain of air, causing the boat to drive downwards at a steep angle that was only brought under control at fifty metres by the rapid blowing of ballast tanks. Nevertheless, following this last-minute reminder that there was never time for complacency, *U99* entered Lorient the following day under its familiar minesweeper escort. Seven pennants fluttered from the raised periscope, each hand-painted with the golden horseshoe insignia and the claimed tonnage of their victories. At 1600 hrs the crew were mustered for Dönitz, who congratulated them on their successes and delivered some decorations, including the Iron Cross First Class for Bargsten, before retiring to Kernevel – not yet operational as BdU headquarters but still inhabited by much of his advance staff – with Kretschmer to debrief him on his mission. Dönitz and the BdU headquarters were still quartered in Paris at 18 Boulevard Suchet, but he was frequently on hand in Lorient to greet returning boats, and commanders were generally required to travel to Paris for a full debriefing with their commander-in-chief in order to discuss their mission and decisions taken. This provided Dönitz with first-hand accounts that helped him gain a thorough appreciation of the reality of his battle in the Atlantic.

Langobardo accompanied Kretschmer to BdU headquarters. Despite the disappointments of imperfect weaponry and amusement of watching Bargsten and his NCO companion sink their own dinghy, the veteran Italian submarine officer had completed his first Atlantic patrol with a highly successful captain and crew and bonded significantly with Kretschmer regardless of the latter's earlier reluctance to carry a 'passenger' aboard his ship. Langobardo took command of *Luigi Torelli* and later the submarine *Enrico Toti*. In mid-1941 he was transferred to command the Submarine School in Pola before returning to active service aboard the BETASOM boat *Pietro Calvi*. On 14 July 1942, he was killed by gunfire from HMS *Lulworth* during the sinking of his submarine following an unsuccessful attack on convoy SL115.

The BdU war diary entry:

1. Tenaciously executed operation, no comments on the manner in which it was conducted.
2. Success is satisfactory, but it could have been greater if we had a torpedo which is also usable with a stronger sea.

Convoy HX72 lost eleven ships in total – three to Kretschmer, one to Bleichrodt in *U48* and seven to Schepke in *U100* – before reaching the safety of the Western Approaches escort that managed to drive Schepke away and prevent the other boats from making successful attacks. Kretschmer had managed to get close to the convoy body and Schepke penetrated the convoy itself; thus the two aces were leading the way in torpedo technique. However, their willingness to close the enemy and actually pass through any escort screen – if present – and attempt to attack from within the columns of ships was, as yet, unappreciated by the British Admiralty.

> The new enemy tactics seem to indicate that the U-boats work as surface torpedo boats, shadowing the convoy until dark or locating it in the dark, and then attacking by 'browning' from long range and escaping at high speed on the surface. This makes much more difficult the task of meagre escorting forces with the large convoys; they are separated from each other by long distances, sometimes so long that the escort is unaware that an attack has taken place . . . In these circumstance, if we can concentrate the necessary volume of anti-submarine forces in our trade approaches, and also find means of counteracting the new German method of long range attack, there is good reason to believe that the increased menace will be overcome.[18]

'Browning' was a Royal Navy term for a distant torpedo shot against a mass of shipping, either moving or stationary. By maintaining distance, the attacker did not require high-speed torpedoes or intense accuracy, but relied on the conglomeration of targets and adequate directional fire control. It dovetailed with Kriegsmarine orthodoxy that trained commanders in the fan-shot of torpedoes against enemy shipping, but was everything that Kretschmer in particular railed against. He continued to advocate penetration of the convoy body itself in order to attack at close range. Fast torpedoes, accurate shooting, cool nerve and quick-thinking decision-making were essential for the task, and Kretschmer proved the ultimate role model in all respects.

The First Lord of the Admiralty, A. V. Alexander, had issued his memorandum based on information supplied by Captain George Creasy, the recently appointed chief of staff to the First Sea Lord, Admiral of the Fleet Sir Dudley Pound. Creasy was a highly experienced ex-destroyer commander, who doubled as Director of Anti-Submarine Warfare. Creasy was correct in his estimation that U-boat captains' preferred method of operation was to attack at night, and the more successful U-boat skippers would certainly approach the convoy, fire a full bow salvo, turn about and fire the stern torpedo before retreating to reload. Correspondingly, general orders to merchant convoys were for the escorts to turn *outward* if attacked, with snowflake rockets fired into the sky, once again outward from the convoy body. These rockets deployed twenty-eight white star lights that turned night into day in the hope of illuminating a surfaced U-boat. In fact these very tactics played into Kretschmer's hands, as well as serving the purpose of aiding convoy location by nearby U-boats.

The day following their return to Lorient, ten of the crew began leave in Germany as the boat went into the yards for repairs. Another section of *U99*'s complement were taken by bus to Quiberon, where a hotel had been requisitioned for U-boat men, spending five days there at a time before rotating with others not lucky enough to have yet been granted leave in Germany. *U99* was moved into the drydock of Bassin No. 2 and was fortunate to suffer no more than some damaged wooden decking after Bomber Command carried out its first large-scale air raid on Lorient during the night of 27 September with thirty-five aircraft. The raid resulted in thirty-two French civilians killed and at least two bombs landed within thirty metres of the drydock basin containing *U99*. Flying chips of stone slashed through some of the deck planks, but otherwise the boat was unscathed.

While Kretschmer spent time dining with Schepke and Prien in the Hotel Beauséjour, he also took the opportunity to write a comprehensive set of his own standing orders for his crew in order to fine-tune the operation of his boat. Dönitz already had standing orders for the general prosecution of the war at sea, but it was a commander's prerogative to create his own supplementary rules and Kretschmer listed twelve detailed points, his first perhaps inspired by the ease with which he managed to surprise the veterans of *U47* during their last combat mission:

1. Of primary importance in all U-boat operations is an efficient lookout system. During sea operations, the finest possible organisation is the first precept of success. A weak link in the

system can mean the destruction of the ship and the death of its crew.

2. It is not enough that lookouts should sight every object that appears on the surface: they must sight in good time every object that appears in the sky. Aircraft are playing an increasingly important role in the enemy convoy organisation. They are a deadly menace to U-boats on the surface. We rely on lookouts to give us the time we need to dive and hide from detection or bombing at depths below twenty metres.

3. Lone ships not showing neutral flags or showing a red cross sign, and in every other way giving the appearance of behaving as a belligerent, should be sunk by gunfire if possible to conserve torpedoes for more difficult escorted targets. They may be torpedoed if gunfire is obviously impracticable.

4. Survivors are to be assisted if there is time and by doing so the U-boat is not exposed to undue danger. The crew should be made to realise that should *U99* be sinking and there is time to abandon ship they would expect to be rescued by the enemy. That is precisely what the enemy have a right to expect from us.

5. Only attack convoys by day if it is not convenient to wait for darkness. Day attacks on escorted convoys presuppose the necessity for taking a calculated risk, and should be made only after the most careful consideration of all the factors involved, particularly those concerning the question of whether the results to be achieved make the risk worthwhile.

6. In normal circumstances, *U99* will use daylight hours for shadowing a convoy and working up to a favourable attacking position by nightfall. A favourable attacking position is on the dark side of the convoy when there is moonlight, so that the convoy will be silhouetted to us, while our small bows-on silhouette will be almost impossible to detect.

7. When there is little or no moon, *U99* will always attack from the windward side of the convoy. Enemy lookouts peering into a wind and sometimes rain and spray are less efficient than those with their backs to the wind.

8. *U99* will abide by my principle that fans of torpedoes fired from long range are not guaranteed to succeed and are

actually wasteful. It should not be necessary to fire in the first instance more than one torpedo for one ship.

9. The principle stated above makes it necessary that we should fire at close range, and this can be done only by penetrating the escort's anti-U-boat screen and at times getting inside the convoy lanes. This should be the objective of all our attacks.

10. Once an attack has been opened under these conditions at night, we must not under any but the most desperate of circumstances submerge. As a general rule, I alone must decide when to dive. This instruction is based upon my belief that a surfaced U-boat can manoeuvre at high speed to avoid danger and, if necessary, can fight back with its speed and torpedo fire-power. If we are being chased, it is a general principle that once a U-boat submerges and loses the use of speed, it is at the mercy of the hunter.

11. Remember that at night on the surface, it is almost certain that you will see a surface vessel far sooner than it will see you. This applies to enemy destroyers and other anti-submarine vessels which might detect you with their ASDIC the moment that you dive, but would remain unaware of your presence if you ran away on the surface.

12. *U99* will dive for two hours just before dawn each day at sea. This purpose of this is twofold: first, it will avoid the risk of running into ships and aircraft that we have not seen during the night and which might see us first; and secondly, it gives us a chance to use the hydrophones to sweep for unsighted ships. Additionally, it gives the crew an opportunity to relax, clean up and have breakfast in peace.

Kretschmer was also harbouring grave misgivings about the amount of radio chatter that was taking place in action, particularly – though not solely – from less experienced U-boat commanders. He held a healthy respect for Allied radio direction finding and believed that careless use of transmissions in action could either attract anti-submarine forces, or cause the diversion of convoy traffic away from gathering U-boats. Due to the nature of Dönitz's 'wolfpack' theory, he required frequent updates from his U-boats at sea so as to coordinate the gathering of a patrol line for a concerted attack. Kretschmer was reluctant to provide more information by radio than absolutely required and had been admonished by Dönitz for his lack of contact, earning the nickname 'Silent Otto' amongst his peers, a soubriquet that fitted both his personal and professional demeanour. For example, during the period beginning at 0106 hrs on 18 October and ending at 2119 hrs on 19 October (encompassing attacks against convoys SC7 and HX79) Prien's *U47* and Schepke's *U100* sent eighty-two radio transmissions between them. During the same period, and in the same general location, Kretschmer sent two. Later, long after the war had ended, he would comment, 'I have the opinion today that much of the U-boat war's success was lost because of those damn radio transmissions.'

Kretschmer's was not the only voice expressing disquiet at the amount of radio traffic generated by combat U-boats. Within the SKL war diary of 23 January 1940 it was noted:

> The Chief of Naval Staff has called the attention of the BdU to the necessity for submarines to use radio as sparingly as possible, since the enemy direction-finding service works very quickly and accurately. BdU does not regard the danger as so great, since bearings also often show a substantial margin of error, and he emphasises that generally the boats only use their radio for the transmission of important shadowing reports and weather reports, or if their presence is known to the enemy in any case. The Chief of Naval Staff has ordered that weather reports are to be transmitted only when the boat incurs no risk by so doing.[19]

In his assessment of the situation, Dönitz would ultimately be proved wrong. Though his qualities as a manager of men within his U-boat service were beyond question, his limitations in the broader scope of the strategic U-boat struggle became increasingly obvious as the war progressed. His technical appreciation of enemy equipment and ability was sorely lacking, including an underestimation of code breaking and direction finding, which truly became two of the greatest threats soon to be faced by his boats in action. Instead Dönitz relied heavily on an *esprit de corps* to carry the day on the Atlantic battlefield. Indeed, Dönitz's 'personal touch' was admired by the men directly under his command, so much so that they probably overlooked his greater military shortcomings. Kretschmer later remembered:

Dönitz was the best naval commander I have ever met. He was a real leader of the U-boat service and also of the people, of the captains. I think that everybody always had in mind – it was certainly true for me when fighting the enemy – 'What would Dönitz say?' If you do something which is contrary to his way of thinking, you will have to explain it to him. I did quite a lot, I must say, which differed from peacetime tactics, but I was always successful in convincing him that this was the right way for me to do that.

But Dönitz had to switch over to a different sort of operational control, telling the boats from his control station more than he needed to tell us older submariners. But this was something difficult for us because we had to use more communications, asking questions and needing answers from submarines at sea. This, of course, was playing into the hands of British Intelligence. They could use their direction finder. They could also, which we did not know for certain, maybe read our signals etc. I, for myself, knew more about the Royal Navy because, as a midshipman, I took the interpreter's examination which was quite easy for me because before joining the Navy I had spent time in Britain, but I had to read in the Naval Academy, I had to read all books on World War I from British authors and there was one book which had told me that the British Intelligence knew everything about the movement of submarines in World War I. They could not read all the signals but there are some ways of how you put things in the short signals etc. etc. and I told myself as a midshipman, if I went to war, I would not use any communications myself; only when told to do so.[20]

U99 slipped from Lorient once more during the early afternoon of 13 October after test dives had been completed in the Rade de Lorient near Île Saint-Michel two days before. The boat carried only twelve torpedoes into action this time, Kretschmer opting to leave the external containers empty and avoid the problems associated with loading from them at sea. Harbour protection vessels and *U-Boot Jäger* escorted *U99* to sea, parting company close to Île de Groix as Kretschmer took his boat down into deeper water not only to check for any potential issues not discovered when in harbour but also to proceed south during the hours of daylight, resurfacing only once night fell. Immediately before submerging a message transmitted on behalf of the Commanding Admiral France was received announcing the immediate closure of the entrance to Lorient harbour due to mines and potential enemy submarine activity; *U99* had departed at just the right time.

At least one published book recounts the fanciful notion that the crew managed to 'manufacture' a mechanical fault so as not to sail on this 'Friday the 13th'. Though sailors are frequently prone to superstition – and this did happen to Erich Topp while in command of *U57* – in this case it is patently untrue: 13 October 1940 was a Sunday.

Once again, Kretschmer also carried a passenger, this time a prospective U-boat commander under instruction, known as a *Konfirmand*.

> Their official title was *Kommandantenschüler*, meaning, a student commanding officer. We knew them as *Konfirmand*, the name given to a boy of thirteen years who is being accepted by the Church as a full member in a special ceremony.[21]

At 2054 hrs the boat surfaced and began a long slow arc towards the north-west, beginning four days of transit interrupted twice for emergency dives to avoid Sunderland flying boats. During the previous evening Kaptlt. Claus Korth reported contact with an outbound convoy in the North Channel, soon joined in shadowing the ships by *U38*, and Kretschmer began plotting a potential intercept point within the North Atlantic. However, a message from *U48* was relayed to *U99* at 0900 hrs on 17 October of an inbound convoy's position and prompted an immediate change of course to the north-east as the diesels were pushed to high speed. Bleichrodt had identified what he took to be twenty-five merchant ships under escort by three warships and Dönitz immediately issued orders for available boats to operate against Bleichrodt's convoy. Kretschmer joined *U28*, *U46*, *U48*, *U100*, *U101* and *U123* in a hastily drawn-up patrol line stretching from Quadrant AM 2745 to AM 0125 north-east of Rockall Bank. *U48* made an initial attack and then appeared to lose contact as far as BdU was aware. The gathering of the boats including Kretschmer's was Dönitz's first proper attempt at forming a 'wolfpack'.

> I remember that there was a signal that a convoy was coming from America to England and that its position was not known.

Dönitz ordered all the submarines there to the west of Ireland to form a sort of 'recce line', a stationary 'recce line' to let the convoy pass through it. When the first submarine was sighted, the convoy made a contact signal and that 'recce line' was dissolved immediately and every submarine was free to go into the attack . . . This really was the first time that this tactic could be seen by all of us, and also by Dönitz himself who of course knew it only from our peacetime training.[22]

However, with the potential for intercepting either of two reported convoys, Dönitz and his Chief of Operations, Eberhard Godt, began nervously to reshuffle the boats in an attempt to find the enemy ships most likely to be located.

No further reports were received [from *U48*] and towards midday Operations gave the order 'Continue to operate against the convoy reported, general direction of advance 120°, 8 knots'. Towards 1800 a report was received from *U48* giving the last observed position of the convoy at 0930, which was further north, than hitherto reported, and its course which was also more northerly and could obviously only be steered for a time. This must have confused the boats. They were therefore ordered to form a patrol line by 0800 on the 18th which will be at right angles to the most probable direction of advance and should intercept the convoy in the morning. *U46*, *U100*, *U101* and *U123* can reach their positions but not *U28* and *U99*.[23]

It was a frustrating hunt for Kretschmer and his lookouts who tirelessly scanned the horizon for the slightest trace of the enemy shipping. A U-boat conning tower was spotted during the morning, the distant shape of Kaptlt. Engelbert Endrass's *U46* lying just visible in the distance at the extreme left of the patrol line, before disappearing from view. Frauenheim's *U101* was also sighted, but there was still no trace of the elusive merchant convoy as Kretschmer proceeded to sail up and down with the patrol line. Frustration boiled over in Paris where BdU Ops ordered the assembled boats to abandon their patrol line and instead operate independently against the outbound convoy shadowed by *U38*, Kretschmer was unhappy about the potential confusion that threatened to overtake them all.

1530 hrs: BdU Ops has assumed that *U99* is not in the patrol line. My reasoning for this assumption is that BdU Ops has not understood or confirmed that I am present in the patrol line from my short signals of this morning. By using the short signal 'On post', such misunderstandings are made.

I begin operating in an east-northeasterly direction.[24]

The U-boats had barely begun to turn towards the position of the convoy estimated by *U38* when *U101* made contact with the original inbound conglomeration of heavily laden merchant ships and began to shadow while transmitting position reports. The slow convoy SC7 had left Sydney, Nova Scotia, on 5 October and was bound initially for Liverpool before various ships made their onward journeys to other British ports. The convoy had been planned to make the crossing at a speed of 8 knots, but many of the older, smaller ships were incapable of this which brought a lowering of the pace. Thirty-five merchant ships departed Canada, but almost immediately some began to straggle and bad weather helped to separate several vessels from the main body, two of them subsequently being sunk. For three-quarters of the journey only the sloop HMS *Scarborough* was available for escort.

Just before Bleichrodt made contact on 17 October, *Scarborough* was joined by the sloop HMS *Fowey* and the new corvette HMS *Bluebell*, but within hours *U48* made its first attack and fired three torpedoes at three separate targets, sinking the largest ship in the convoy, the 9,512-ton tanker MT *Languedoc* (scuttled by gunfire from HMS *Bluebell*) and 3,843-ton SS *Scoresby*. *U48* was then attacked with depth charges that drove the U-boat deep and unable to report to BdU either their success or the convoy's position. However, HMS *Scarborough* spent so long hunting Bleichrodt that the sloop was later unable to catch up with the convoy, reducing the escort to two.

Kretschmer sighted an escort vessel first, running hard towards the east, before finally detecting the smoke from SC7 as a smear in the distant sky. It was already late afternoon and *U99* pounded through the short sea to reach a firing position when the unexpected sight of a westerly headed steamer appeared to starboard. Kretschmer dived to prepare a submerged attack as night had yet to fall and the projected

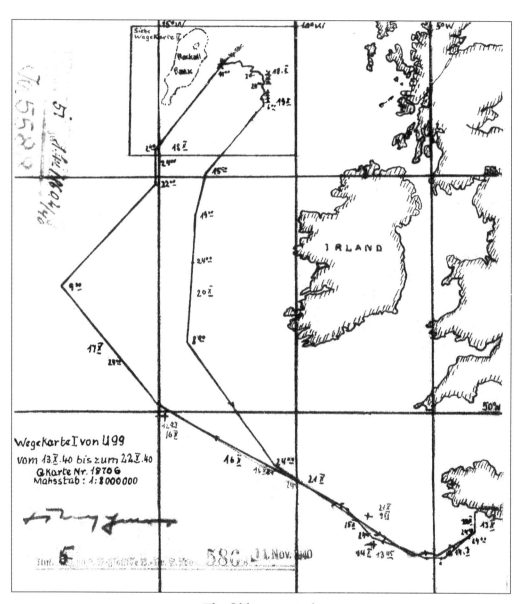

The fifth war patrol.

path of the merchant ship would lead it right before his bow. However, as suddenly as it had appeared, the steamer veered away to the east and disappeared, *U99* resurfacing to continue towards its attack station. *U101* and *U123* were both briefly sighted, exchanging recognition signals by semaphore as the 'wolfpack' gathered to begin its assault, the first torpedoes beginning to explode in the distance as *U46* opened fire. Captain Finn Skage of Norwegian SS *Snefjeld* later reported:

> On Friday 18 October, my noon position was 57.55N, 12.39W, convoy was in 9 columns. First ship was torpedoed (rear of outside port column) at about 1930. Convoy made emergency turn to starboard when a ship in one of the starboard columns was torpedoed. At approximately 1945 hrs an emergency turn to port was made and immediately afterwards a third ship was attacked. After this, formation of convoy became ragged and U-boats appeared on surface using flares and gunfire. I think there were at least four U-boats.

As ships began to burn and men struggled through pools of thick oil from ruptured fuel bunkers, Kretschmer was unable to make his first attack until 2202 hrs. His boat was lying near the convoy's path as it approached and he opted for a long-distance shot targeting the front right column of ships, firing from outside the convoy body as a destroyer raced past. In the darkness, Bargsten fired Tube I, the target a fully laden 6,000-ton freighter some 5,000 metres distant. However, he missed, probably due to the excessive range. *U99* now thundered forward as Kretschmer charged at the front of the convoy and began shooting. Four minutes after his first attempt, a second torpedo shot from the stern tube at the same ship, now only 700 metres away, hitting the 6,055-ton SS *Empire Miniver* below its forward mast. The British cargo ship was carrying 4,500 tons of pig iron and 6,200 tons of steel which accounts for it going down in only twenty seconds. Despite the fast sinking, thirty-five of the thirty-eight crewmen survived to be rescued later by HMS *Bluebell*; Chief Engineering Officer Alexander McGhie Paul, Fourth Engineering Officer Alfred Barlow and Fireman Herbert Edwards were all trapped in the doomed ship's engine room and unable to escape the inrushing water.

A fresh attack was foiled by an error in the calculation of the gyro angle and the bow shot going wide as the *Torpedorichtungsweiseranlage* (TDW – Torpedo Direction Computer) had not been properly calibrated and the settings did not match what Bargsten had on his UZO. Kretschmer opted to use his own judgement for the remainder of his shots. He had more immediate concerns, though, as the U-boat was trimmed high for maximum manoeuvrability and was spotted in the moonlight and glare of an exploding star shell by gunners aboard another merchant ship which immediately opened fire with its own gun while turning to ram. *U99* veered sharply away at full speed and left their assailant behind, the merchant ship rejoining the convoy body while Kretschmer prepared a fresh approach to attack the rearmost ships of the convoy's right wing. Elsewhere, crippled ships within the convoy started to burn as the other U-boats pressed home their attacks.

> I tried to get through the escorts into the convoy, which was my own peculiarity of attacking, and failed the first time. They saw me and shot star shells so that I had to go away again. But the second time I succeeded and got inside the convoy, going up and down the lanes and looking for the most important valuable ships and had the opportunity to expend all my torpedoes, I had twelve in all.[25]

In the space of thirty minutes the 3,854-ton Greek SS *Niritos* and 4,815-ton British SS *Fiscus* were both sunk. The Greek carried 5,426 tons of sulphur and a single man from the twenty-eight-strong crew went down with the ship as it settled bow first into the water. *Fiscus*, on the other hand, left only a solitary survivor, Ordinary Seaman Edward Sidney King, from its crew of thirty-nine. The torpedo tore open the forward hull in a brilliant explosion as the ship began to burn fiercely with a green flame. It carried steel, lumber and a cargo of aircraft in crates upon the deck and finally sank after leaving a towering pillar of smoke 200 metres into the sky. King was found hours later clinging to some debris by a lifeboat from the Norwegian freighter *Snefjeld*. He later recounted what happened in a sworn deposition in Cardiff on 19 November 1940.

> This vessel had reached a point about 350 miles west of Eire. Position in convoy, third ship in column three from port. Other columns having from three to six ships in each. Deponent was lying dozing in his bunk when a violent explosion occurred and ship took a heavy list to starboard. One packing case was lying alongside No. 2 hatch. It was not lashed to the deck. Deponent got on to the packing case, when the sea washed him into No. 2 hold, the hatches of which had been blown off by the explosion. Evidently, the torpedo had struck No. 2 hold, starboard side,

blowing off beams and hatch covers. The hold was full of water. Deponent sank and rose to the surface when he grabbed the rope lashing around the packing case. The case floated away, the fore deck of the ship being by this time under water. The packing case swept clear of the ship and when deponent looked around the ship had disappeared, and the sea was a mass of wreckage. In deponent's opinion vessel sank within a minute of the explosion.

After about two hours on the packing case deponent sighted three Indian firemen clinging to the ice box about twenty yards away. He called to them and helped them on to the packing case. They died from exposure the next morning. Deponent did not see any other members of the crew. He remained on the packing case until picked up on 21 October 1940 by a lifeboat full of survivors from Norwegian ship *Thalia* [incorrect – he may have thought the lifeboat was from the Greek *Thalia*, as there were four survivors from that ship on board]. This vessel had been in deponent's convoy and had been sunk about an hour and a half after the *Fiscus*. The lifeboat was sighted by a flying boat on 24 October 1940 and the occupants picked up on the same day by one of HMS. [This was HMS *Clematis*. Date discrepancies here are probably simply due to different time zones used in reports.] The boats of the *Fiscus* were swung out ready for launching. One raft was in the starboard fore rigging and two others aft in main rigging, one on each side. Master [Ebenezer Williams] had given strict orders on 17 October 1940 that every man was to wear his life-saving waistcoat continuously and deponent knows that all deck personnel wore them accordingly.[26]

Destroyers began to close *U99*'s position and Kretschmer pulled away at full speed to reload and prepare for a fresh attack, noting in his KTB that he would 'now begin to dismantle this convoy from the back'. At 0138 hrs an electric torpedo left Tube II and ran for 63 seconds before hitting 5,154-ton SS *Empire Brigade* carrying a full load that included 750 tons of copper, 129 tons of ferrous alloys and 980 tons of steel. The warhead exploded between the bridge and forward mast and *Empire Brigade* went down by the bow in only fifteen seconds. Almost miraculously, thirty-five of the forty-one men aboard survived and were later rescued by HMS *Fowey*. Just over twenty minutes later 5,875-ton Greek SS *Thalia* was hit in the bow and sank within forty seconds, taking its cargo of steel, zinc and lead to the bottom along with twenty-two of its twenty-six crew.

Two more torpedoes missed because of faulty aiming and gyro failure, before, at 0302 hrs, the Norwegian 1,643-ton steamer SS *Snefjeld*, was hit by a third torpedo shot. The Norwegian had stopped after appeals for help were heard from survivors of the *Thalia* in the water. Three boats were lowered and four men located and dragged from the cold Atlantic water. As two of the boats were about to be raised aboard once more, lookouts actually saw *U99* nearby and minutes later the G7e hit the starboard hull near Hatch 2. The Norwegian second mate, steward and mess boy were all injured in the explosion, which destroyed both the lifeboats being recovered. The ship's first mate, who had been in one of the boats, was flung into the water astern by the blast, fighting his way back to the surface and managing to climb back aboard near the Number 4 hatch. He attempted to open the door to the chart room, but it was completely ablaze, the ship heeling to starboard, which caused the deck cargo of timber to shift and begin toppling overboard. Only the ship's motorboat, which had been lying off to starboard, survived the blast and began to pick up some of the crew while the rest launched a small dinghy. While there were injuries amongst the crew, none of Master Finn Skage's twenty crew were lost.

The ship broke in two after an hour and sank later in flames, the 719 standards of timber that had been carried aboard burning brightly until extinguished in the dark water. The Norwegians and the four Greeks then began an odyssey that lasted for days. They stayed near the site of their ship's sinking until midday before starting to row for land after no rescue ships or aircraft were sighted. The motorboat's engine had seized and in worsening weather the two small boats were separated though they remained in visual contact with light signals. At dawn on 20 October they reunited and found an empty raft from *Thalia* which carried survival supplies. Another empty lifeboat, fully equipped and from the *Empire Brigade*, was also found and some men transferred aboard from the small dinghy. It was then that they found Edward King, standing forlornly on some floating debris. Eventually, on 23 October, they were located by HMS *Clematis*, which rescued them and landed them all three days later.

The sinking of the Norwegian did not mark the last of Kretschmer's successes against SC7. The escorts were firing starshells into the night sky, though they had little effect in the bright moonlight and did not cause any lasting problems for the attacking U-boats. Kretschmer was within the convoy body itself and the escorts appeared to be looking frantically outward in search of the attackers. Nevertheless, Kretschmer was certain that sooner or later he would be located and his exit from the ragged convoy potentially barred and so he made his final attacks. A failed torpedo shot at 0356 hrs passed behind a steamer as *U99* headed towards the rear of the convoy. The target ship had begun to straggle behind the main group and *U99* wheeled about to fire a second torpedo at the straggler; this was the last available shot, a G7a from the stern tube. After forty-six seconds the 'eel' exploded against the hull stern and frantic radio distress calls began flooding from 3,106-ton Briton SS *Clintonia*, carrying 3,850 tons of pulpwood bound for Manchester, as the hull settled into the water.

Kretschmer had now expended all of his torpedoes and, after studying the ship through binoculars, decided to attempt to sink it with shellfire. As he began moving into position, gunfire began to hit the battered ship from its far side and Kretschmer took *U99* carefully around *Clintonia* as many of the shells were passing over the hull, the gunners aiming too high when they should have been concentrating on the waterline. It was Kaptlt. Karl-Heinz Moehle's *U123*, which had briefly taken over the role of shadower after having fired all torpedoes, tailing SC7 as the remains of the convoy shuffled towards Great Britain. His gunfire finally sent the freighter to the bottom. The British ship's cook, Norman Pringle, was killed in the attack, the torpedo explosion hurling him violently head first into the ship's gun platform, but the remaining thirty-five crew successfully abandoned ship in two boats and watched the destruction of their ship before later being rescued by HMS *Bluebell*. Aboard *Bluebell*, Leading Supply Assistant Don Kirton remembered the difficulties of recovering survivors from the battered convoy:

> You could see the red bulbs on their lifejackets showing in the water. We put scrambling nets over the side. Two of the lads would get over to help them up and over the gunwhales, and there were eager hands to take them forward where there was shelter.

Many of them were violently sick from the fuel oil that they'd swallowed. Some were completely naked.[27]

Kretschmer headed for Lorient, his torpedoes spent, arriving in harbour to a rapturous reception on 22 October, after only nine days on patrol in which he claimed the destruction of seven ships totalling 45,000 tons (including *Clintonia*), and was credited with six totalling 38,606 tons. The triumph of the U-boats was broadcast almost immediately by the *Wehrmachtberichte* on Saturday 19 October:

> German U-boats have sunk in the last few days thirty-one enemy merchant ships totalling 173,650 grt. Of these, twenty-six steamers were sunk from strongly defended convoys. Among these successes are those by the U-boat under the command of Kapitänleutnant Frauenheim with ten steamers totalling 51,000 grt, the U-boat of Kapitänleutnant Kretschmer with seven steamers for 45,000 grt, and the U-boat of Kapitänleutnant Moehle with seven steamers for 44,050 grt total.

Even without the inflated tonnage, it was a remarkable achievement by Kretschmer and fully vindicated his method of penetrating a convoy screen and attacking from within while only using one torpedo per ship. In Paris, Dönitz was elated at what he perceived to be demonstrable proof that his 'wolfpack' theory worked:

> Conclusions:
> 1. The operations prove that the principle on which the development of U-boat tactics and training has been based since 1935, namely that of countering concentration in convoys with a concentration of U-boat attacks, is right. This concentration has been made possible by the development of communications since the World War.
> 2. Such operations can only be carried out with commanding officers and crews which are thoroughly trained for them. It follows that there must be extensive and long training in wide sea areas. This training would not be possible if we did not have the Baltic Sea free of enemy interference.
> 3. Such operations can only be carried out if there are enough U-boats in the operations area. In this war this has so far only been the case from time to time.

4. The more U-boats there are in the operations area the more frequently such operations will be possible.

5. Also, if there were more boats, the British supply routes would not be left free of U-boats after such attacks when, as today, nearly all the boats have to return because they have used all their torpedoes.

6. Successes such as in these operations cannot always be expected. Fog, bad weather and other circumstances can sometimes ruin every chance.

The main thing governing results will always be the ability of the Commanding Officer.[28]

Kretschmer's was perhaps the most impressive tally of the U-boats involved and Dönitz radioed to the returning boat that there would be a formal reception awaiting them. In a rare exception to his custom, Kretschmer did not order his men clean shaven for their return, as they had hardly been at sea long enough to begin to grow the familiar U-boat beards. Indeed, once ashore he was photographed with the beginning of his own small beard, an uncharacteristic portrait of the young captain.

U99 eased into port in the wake of the returning Type IX *U37* with a minesweeper escort. Passing Île Saint-Michel, both U-boats were alerted to a sudden British air raid, *U99* firing twenty 20 mm flak rounds at a solitary Bristol Blenheim that dropped out of the clouds and flew low over the harbour, dropping four bombs before disappearing as quickly as it had arrived. It was one of twelve such opportunist attacks launched during October by either single Blenheims or in groups up to six. This foreshadowed the eventual bombing of Lorient that would virtually destroy the town by the time of its liberation in 1945.

Kapitänleutnant Victor Oehrn's *U37* had been active in the North Channel and sunk six ships in combats unconnected with the attack on SC7 and both boats received an ecstatic reception from the assembled people ashore, amongst them Generalleutnant Kurt Renner, commander of the 211th Infantry Division stationed in and around Lorient for coastal defence and training. The bloody convoy battle that Kretschmer had taken part in had been an unmitigated disaster for the Allies, who lost in total twenty merchant ships with a further two damaged. One hundred and forty-one merchant sailors were killed in what the Germans had already begun calling 'The Night of the Long Knives'. Only U-boats running out of torpedoes and the diversion of others to attack convoy HX79 relieved the pressure, twelve ships were also sunk from that Halifax convoy.

During Kretschmer's personal meeting with Dönitz in which the events and decisions recorded by U99's war diary were pored over and analysed in depth, Kretschmer was again admonished for his meagre use of radio transmissions which made BdU coordination of patrol lines more difficult. However, Kretschmer was unapologetic.

> I was told to do so right from the beginning but our tactics in the beginning were what we like to call 'mission tactics' so that submarines at sea do not only obey all orders coming from [BdU] Operations Control. Operations Control only gives directions but no orders and that's how we started the war. But soon the development came so that Operations Control issued specific mission orders; and to be able to do that, Operations Control must know what the battlefield is like and what the submarines in that battlefield are like, how many torpedoes they have, how much fuel they have, what the weather is like and so on.
>
> And so, all these submarines were asked to give information to Operations Control and this was a lot of traffic, radio traffic that was known by British Intelligence; when they took their bearings, they knew where every boat was and so it was quite easy for the enemy to react and circumvent our submarines. I did not like to do all this, which was required from Operations Control, and when I returned from one patrol, I was asked by Dönitz whether or not I was not inclined to obey orders. I said 'not all of them'. I am a fighting instrument and I have got a mission and I know what to do and while there are also regulations which must be followed, it is not necessary for me to be told . . . what to do at sea. I was quite successful at convincing him, but he said that he could not allow this for all the newcomers.
>
> There was a development during the war which I have not experienced myself but everything was later ordered. When the submarines had assembled around the convoy, they had to make a signal 'I am here' with the short signal code, and then [BdU] Operations Control would give the order: 'Attack!' This would

have been very bad for me because I was the only submarine which went *into* the convoy and so when all the others would shoot their spreads and salvoes from outside the convoy, the [enemy] would reach me and sink me right from the beginning, so I could not have followed this tactic . . . Anyway, I would very likely have tried to be there early, fire my torpedoes from inside the convoy and then wait until the others had arrived.[29]

Kretschmer's results in action spoke for themselves and in his own quiet way he was every part the maverick, determined to follow his own instinct and intuition rather than conform to military orthodoxy. His innate ability to digest and analyse a situation immediately, and also examine it later with microscopic detail, had already shaped his boat and crew into one of the most consistently effective parts of the U-boat service and Dönitz in turn exercised his own good judgement of men to allow Kretschmer the latitude to act with a measure of independence in operations.

The BdU comments in the war diary were to the point:

Excellently executed attack on the convoy, which has been rewarded by a corresponding success.

U99 was only in port for eight days, long enough to refit and replenish for the next patrol. Twenty-two men were granted two days' leave in Quiberon before the boat returned to sea at 1700 hrs on the penultimate day of October. Ironically, the U-boats' successes against SC7 and HX79 had successfully denuded the Atlantic of U-boat striking power as boats were forced to return after exhausting ammunition or for repair. Dönitz had desired 300 U-boats with which to begin the war, allowing 100 on station at any one time while another hundred were in transit to and from port and the last hundred in the shipyards. At sea, in the Atlantic focal point of his war against Britain's trade lines, he had but a tiny fraction of that offensive strength. Dönitz was relying on the BETASOM boats to take some of the burden from his paltry forces, but they generally performed below expectations. In Kretschmer, Dönitz knew he had a commander who understood the reality of the struggle and never lingered in port whenever possible.

As *U99* left Lorient, it was escorted by two *Vorpostenboote* of the 4th Flotilla as far as the offshore location designated Punkt 2 where

Kretschmer took his boat down for its regular test dive after leaving harbour, heading south as his escorts returned to Lorient. Within two hours, *U99* was surfaced and headed at cruising speed in the sweeping arc destined for the North Channel. The U-boat ran headlong into a brief storm the following day that forced Kretschmer to submerge for seven hours after visibility was reduced to barely 100 metres. The boat carried another two passengers, a member of the Propaganda Kompanie named Lander who had been assigned to document *U99*'s patrol in both still photographs and film and Oblt.z.S. Hans Harald Ipach – formerly of the Luftwaffe – who was aboard for experience before transfer to *U95*.

By 1530 hrs on 3 November, Kretschmer was 150 miles west of Galway Bay, Ireland, when lookout Matrosenobergefreiter Johan Waltl sighted smoke on the port bow, slowly solidifying into the shape of a coal-fired freighter moving fast and steering a zig-zag course to the north-east. Kretschmer immediately ordered an interception and Petersen plotted a course and speed that would put *U99* ahead of the steamer in an attack position. Two hours later a second smoke trail appeared to port, appearing to be following the same course but still at some distance. Perhaps there were two targets on the menu.

After darkness had fallen, *U99* was finally in position to launch a surfaced attack on the first steamer and at 2140 hrs Bargsten fired a G7e from Tube II at the ship's port side from a range of 1,260 metres. The torpedo ran for eighty-four seconds before exploding between the boat deck and after mast and the ship began to settle by the stern. Kretschmer decided to head towards the second steamer as quickly as possible, his sinking victim now showing lights as the crew abandoned ship while transmitting a plain language distress call that confirmed its identity as the 5,376-ton SS *Casanare*. The steamer had travelled from the Cameroons with a cargo of 1,500 tons of bananas; nine members of Master Johan Allan Moore's crew were killed in the destruction of their vessel, the remaining fifty-four successfully taking to their lifeboats.

At 2202 hrs the second steamer was reacquired in the moon and starlit night, followed by a third even more distant. The unidentified second ship suddenly turned about and reversed course at full speed, obviously alert to the sinking of *Casanare* and unwilling to risk its own safety with a known U-boat presence. However, the third steamer ploughed relentlessly forward and Kretschmer switched his attention to this ship, beginning one of the most drawn-out attacks of his U-boat career.

The oncoming 'third steamer' was the 18,724-ton armed merchant cruiser HMS *Laurentic*. This majestic ship had been built in Belfast's famous Harland & Wolff yards for the White Star Line, plying the trans-Atlantic passenger routes as SS *Laurentic* until White Star was merged with the Cunard Line in 1934 and the ship reduced to shorter-range cruises. Following collision with another ship in the Irish Sea in 1935, the passenger liner was laid up in shipyards and in some state of dilapidation when requisitioned by the Admiralty in August 1939 for conversion to an armed merchant cruiser; equipped with seven 5.5-inch guns, three 4-inch anti-aircraft guns and four .303-inch anti-aircraft machine guns. Captain Eric Paul Vivian, RN (retired), a veteran of the previous war recalled to active duty, was taking his ship from its previous station near Gibraltar to the Clyde, following in the wake of SS *Casanare*. He had a faulty gyrocompass which placed the ship slightly off its intended course and, unfortunately, straight in front of Kretschmer's torpedo tubes. The signals received from the sinking freighter, and accompanying U-boat warning, were tardily passed to Vivian by his signals staff and it was only when Vivian was in full possession of the facts and had begun deciding his best course of action that Kretschmer took the decision out of his hands.

> 2202 hrs: I close the third vessel which continues onwards. As
>   we get closer it becomes evident that she is a passenger
>   liner with two funnels and a foremast. The after mast
>   is stepped. Presumably an auxiliary cruiser. In the
>   bows some of the scuttles have not [sic] been plated
>   over so definitely a warship. She is not proceeding at
>   full speed.[30]

At 2250 hrs a single electric torpedo was fired from Tube IV in a surfaced attack. The range was considerable; *U99* was still 1,537 metres from its target and the torpedo run took nearly two minutes before it hit below the second funnel in the engine room. The great ship slowed and began transmitting in plain language: 'Torpedoed engine room, all fires out.' Unwittingly, the radio operator's message had just informed Kretschmer that his victim would be unable to move and so he could take his time about a finishing shot – the ship was failing to sink despite the large hole torn in its side and clouds of smoke and steam billowing over its deck from the shattered engine room. The deck lights came on and red distress flares were fired while the boats began to be lowered. Kretschmer, who had urged the propaganda cameraman to come to the bridge to film by the light of the star shells, was able to identify the *Laurentic* positively, and prepared to make a finishing shot as what he believed to be the second mysterious steamer reappeared in the distance. In this assumption he was mistaken; the new ship heading his way was a second armed merchant cruiser, HMS *Patroclus*, its presence so near *Laurentic* purely coincidental, but fortuitous for *U99*.

The passenger liner SS *Patroclus* was a veteran of the routes from Liverpool to the Orient, having been built for the Blue Funnel Line and launched in 1923. On the day before Great Britain declared war on Germany it was also requisitioned into the Royal Navy and converted for military use with the installation of six 6-inch guns and two 3-inch anti-aircraft weapons. The 11,314-ton steamer had been on escort duty in the Atlantic before being recalled to Liverpool, en route when SS *Casanare* was torpedoed.

Captain Gerald Charles 'Bill' Wynter, DSO, RN (retired) – another veteran of the last war – had received *Casanare*'s original distress message and ordered his ship diverted to rescue survivors. Heated debate broke out with some of his officers, particularly his executive officer, and personal friend during peacetime, who had served alongside him aboard destroyers in the last war, Commander R. P. Martin, and navigation officer Commander Harrison, RNR, who both strenuously objected. Martin apparently said to his superior: 'If we go over there and stop, we shall be sunk within half an hour, sir!'

To this Wynter replied, 'If I don't stop, I will never be able to show my face in Liverpool again! I'm going to help those poor chaps!'

His officers attempted to remind Wynter that Admiralty standing orders issued in July 1940 forbade armed merchant cruisers from stopping and rendering themselves vulnerable to U-boat attack under any but the most exceptional circumstances, but Wynter remained adamant, rebuking his officers with a final 'The Admiralty is not in command of this ship!'[31]

While the arguments continued aboard *Patroclus*, HMS *Laurentic* had been hit and holed, and at 2328 hrs Kretschmer fired what he hoped would be a finishing shot from his stern tube at the listing ship. However, the electric torpedo vanished without trace, Kretschmer assuming a pistol failure or depth-keeping problems that allowed the contact-fused

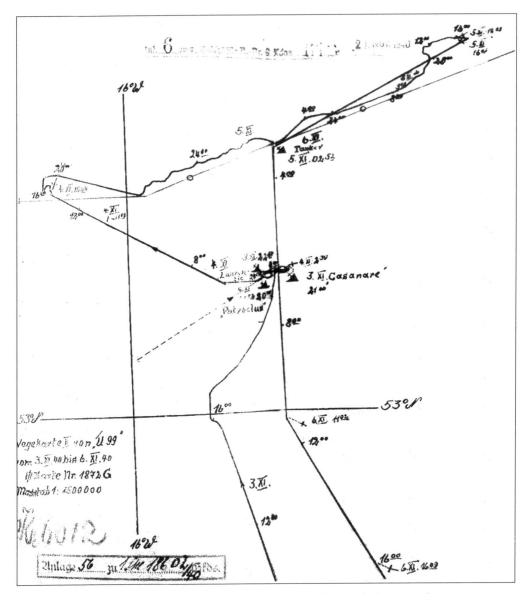

Detail from the track chart of *U99*'s sixth patrol showing the
engagements with *Laurentic*, *Patroclus* and *Casanare*.

torpedo to pass below the hull that lay stationary, broadside on, at only
800 metres range. Within minutes *U99* had turned and closed the
distance yet further and a third torpedo left Tube I, detonating after a
run of only thirty-nine seconds but showing no appreciable effects. The

blast was observed below the bridge but ,alarmingly, a well-aimed star shell burst above the surfaced *U99* and gunners aboard HMS *Laurentic* began to open fire with high explosive shells, forcing Kretschmer to break away rapidly for the cover of darkness and in the direction of the newly arriving HMS *Patroclus*, which demonstrated that it had no idea where the attacking U-boat was by dropping two depth charges in an attempt to frighten away any submerged attacker, before slowing to a halt and preparing to lower boats. The armed merchant cruiser had circled for some time before judging the night dark enough to close and rescue survivors.

At two minutes past midnight, as the first lifeboats with survivors were being recovered, *U99* fired a contact-fused steam torpedo at the stationary *Patroclus* and hit it forward of the bridge. Able Seaman Alfred Miles was aboard at the time.

> We were watching as we picked up survivors of the *Laurentic*. When someone shouted 'Torpedo!' we looked up and sure enough we could see coming towards us a line of white foaming water, at that we all ran to the other side of the ship and then there was an enormous bang which rocked the ship. We were all trained in what to do in the event of a mine or torpedo attack, to go to the appropriate station (the boat deck). Which we did and were then addressed by Lieutenant Commander Martin, who was the captain's second in command.
>
> He told us what had been happening, that other ships had been sunk and that was probably the U-boat's last torpedo. Almost as he said it, another torpedo hit us and another enormous bang; a great big sheet of flame flew up. In the light of the sheet of flame you could see debris flying through the air. Not wishing to be hit by any of the flying debris I ran and crouched by the bottom of the funnel.
>
> Things were getting serious then and we were told to go to our 'Abandon ship' stations This in my case was the portside after well deck. When we got there the petty officer in charge told us to scout round for anything that would float and throw it overboard, hatch covers, wooden fenders, anything that would float. We were fairly close to the after gun position where I knew the gun crew had wooden forms that they used to sit on when

they were on watch. I told Arthur I was going there and he came with me.

It was while we were rooting out these wooden forms and stuff that the third torpedo hit us. At that I thought it was time we got back to our 'Abandon Ship' positions. We did and there was no one there, I looked over the side and saw them disappearing in a boat, I also saw an empty Carley float about to pass by and decided it was time to go. I called to Arthur to tell him I was going and I jumped, I didn't dive because I was wearing an inflatable lifebelt at the time and wasn't sure whether diving would injure my neck.

Having jumped in I then had to reach the Carley Float. Swimming in my uniform, with boots on and wearing a duffle coat was difficult but I managed to haul myself aboard. The Carley float soon filled up, there was about twelve of us altogether; with our combined weight it was partially submerged and we were all sitting on it waist deep in water. Some of the others thought it was a good idea to sing but that didn't last long. We just sat there in the dark.

About 2 o'clock in the morning a destroyer appeared (I knew it was 2 o'clock because I had wristwatch on and I always carried a torch with me). We all shouted and cheered, we felt a great relief, then it disappeared again, I never felt so down in my life. We sat in the water again for another five hours until the destroyer came back and picked us up. I never saw, or heard of Arthur again since that night on the port side after well deck.[32]

It had been a disaster. The first torpedo caused significant damage and also destroyed two of *Laurentic*'s lifeboats as they were being taken aboard, killing their occupants and accounting for the majority of casualties suffered by the *Laurentic*'s crew. Many men aboard *Patroclus* were killed instantly in the blast and Lieutenant Frederick Stuart Piddock had both legs shattered. He would not survive the sinking. However, even at that late stage the ship was not robbed of movement and Martin again suggested that the ship manoeuvre to safety. However, Wynter refused, this time on the grounds that some of his own men were also now struggling in the water after having been blown overboard. Kretschmer's second torpedo followed twenty minutes later and hit Number 4 hold, the German crew surprised to see empty barrels spewing out of the hole torn in the hull; these were carried aboard for extra flotation in the event of damage in the same manner as on Germany's *Sperrbrecher* ships. It was at that point that Wynter ordered the ship abandoned and the magazine flooded to prevent an explosion. Another twenty minutes passed before a third torpedo arced from the reloaded Tube V and also hit beneath the bridge in the cross-bunker. HMS *Patroclus* was now visibly heeling over to starboard and settling deeper into the water, but still refused to go under.

Kretschmer had the identity of his third victim confirmed by further radio transmissions and decided to finish it off with gunfire rather than use yet another torpedo. He edged his boat closer as the gun crew raced on deck and opened up; four shells were fired of which two hit the target, setting fire to ammunition in the after well deck over the after well magazine. Aboard *Patroclus* most men had already left the ship when Commander Martin and a small group of survivors found themselves without a boat to go to. Instead, as the U-boat's shells began landing they manned the 3-inch starboard gun. In his after-action report, Martin recounts that: 'CPO Creasy, the chief gunner's mate, was gunlayer; AB Ellis the trainer; I was loader with Lieutenant Commander Hoggan ammunition supply . . . after our fourth round the shelling ceased and our target disappeared, so ending the action.' Their shells had been fired with great accuracy, spraying the conning tower with water, and though they were incorrect in believing that they had hit *U99* they did cause Kretschmer to cease fire immediately and pull away lest a shell hit render them unable to dive, commenting in his war diary that the ship's 'time-fused shells are well aimed'.[33]

There was no other course of action than to use another torpedo and at 0118 hrs a fourth was fired from the safe distance of 1,880 metres from the stationary ship. This exploded beneath the foremast in Number 3 hold but had no visible effect other than the release of more buoyant barrels and blowing one of the ship's guns overboard.

> It will take the crew a good while to reload torpedoes so I use the enforced break to sail past *Laurentic* – which is still afloat and even more buoyant if anything – to the scene of *Casanare*'s torpedoing.
>
> 0215 hrs: I start questioning the crew of one of the five lifeboats in the position in which *Casanare* sank but am suddenly

interrupted as an illuminated Sunderland appears and starts circling us on a radius of about 500 metres.

0239 hrs: We dive.

Nearly one and a half hours later *U99* resurfaced with freshly loaded torpedoes. The Sunderland was nowhere to be seen, but as Kretschmer returned to finish off the armed merchant cruisers the distant sight of HMS *Achates* was visible steaming at full speed to the scene. Kretschmer had limited time in which to sink both ships and HMS *Laurentic* received its second *coup de grâce* at 0453 hrs which hit its stern and finally sent it under, stored depth charges exploding as it sank to the seabed 2,000 metres below.[34] HMS *Patroclus* proved unendingly defiant, a fifth torpedo exploding in the forward hold but with no discernible effect until the sixth struck amidships in the engine room and finally broke the ship in two abaft the foremast, the stern capsizing and rapidly sinking and the forward section going slowly under. HMS *Achates* was too near for comfort by this stage, searchlights probing the darkness and star shells soon fired above a battleground littered with bobbing heads, wreckage and lifeboats. *U99* made speed away from the scene, heading north-east for three hours before being forced to dive by an approaching aircraft that dropped a bomb but far wide of the boat which spent the next three hours submerged.

Kretschmer's victory was considerable as was the loss of life suffered by the Royal Navy. HMS *Laurentic* had 49 men killed, leaving 368 survivors while HMS *Patroclus* lost 56 men leaving 263 men to be rescued by HMS *Hesperus* and HMS *Beagle*, the former destroyer under the command of Lieutenant-Commander Donald G. F. W. MacIntyre, RN, who would come to feature prominently in Kretschmer's life shortly. A Royal Navy board of enquiry established fault with Captain Vivian for the unacceptable delay in being handed *Casanare*'s distress signal, but withheld its letter of censure as the distraught Vivian was hospitalised with depression and considered a suicide risk, due to be invalided out of the Royal Navy. Captain Wynter was also found to be 'grievously at fault' both for stopping to rescue survivors and not getting under way once more after the first torpedo had struck. However, he was not present to be reprimanded. After he had, mistakenly, believed all men off his ship he had dived into the icy Atlantic waters and drowned despite being known as a strong swimmer. It is possible that he had been weakened by health issues, equally possible that the loss of his ship caused enough shock for this distinguished officer to drown himself intentionally. However, Martin later recorded his opinion that:

> Bill Wynter was an old and dear friend. It just happened that on this occasion he made the wrong decision and paid for it with his own life – an eventuality that is always present when you command a ship at sea in wartime.[35]

In Lorient, there was jubilation at Kretschmer's success and by Dönitz's reckoning Kretschmer had now sunk 217,198 tons of enemy shipping, earning him the Oak Leaves to the Knight's Cross, which was awarded the same day, the second given to a member of the U-boat service, the first having been awarded to Günther Prien on 20 October 1940. Kretschmer's success was picked up by other U-boats at sea. War Correspondent Wolfgang Frank (senior officer of PK men assigned to the U-boat service) was aboard Prien's *U47* at the time:

> Later that day we received a W/T signal. Kretschmer . . . reported sinking three ships: the *Laurentic*, 18,000 tons, the *Patroclus*, 11,000 tons, and another of 5,700 tons. Shortly afterwards another message announced that Kretschmer had been awarded the Oak Leaves as the second U-boat commander to pass the 200,000-ton mark. This award provided a topic of conversation for the next twenty-four hours.[36]

On Monday 4 November, Kretschmer was mentioned in the *Wehrmachtberichte* for the third time. However, his was not the only award as Kretschmer recommended Stabsobersteuermann Heinrich Petersen for the Knight's Cross. His navigation and prosecution of his duties as IIIWO had been outstanding since he had been with Kretschmer in *U23* and this recommendation was approved; Petersen was awarded the Knight's Cross on the following day, 5 November. He was the first non-commissioned officer of the U-boat service to receive the award, forty-sixth member of the Kriegsmarine and third non-captain within the U-boat service (the two previously being the brothers Gerd and Reinhard 'Teddy' Suhren, LI aboard *U37* and IWO aboard *U48* respectively).

At 1403 hrs *U99* surfaced once more to an empty sea. Lookouts climbed atop the conning tower as the boat headed north-east until smoke was sighted on the horizon a little over an hour later. Kretschmer had found convoy HX83, which he estimated to be made up of thirty merchant ships, including several tankers, under escort by six warships. An approaching Sunderland caused an emergency dive and brief loss of contact, but before long *U99* was running surfaced at speed to reach an advantageous position. In total Kretschmer sent three brief contact reports as he awaited nightfall. With darkness came a temporary loss of contact and *U99* dived so that hydrophones could be used to pinpoint the oncoming convoy. With periscope raised he sighted the escort screen and surfaced to keep station with them on the port bow of the convoy, the moon shining strongly and providing a bright unfiltered light that was both blessing and curse.

At 0252 hrs he took his chance at long-distance attack in the bright moonlight. His target lay towards the front of the convoy: three overlapping ships, at least two thought to be tankers. His last torpedo, a G7e, leapt from Tube III and ran true for four minutes before hitting 6,993-ton British tanker MT *Scottish Maiden* in the stern. Master John William Albert Gibson's ship had already experienced difficulties only days into the crossing of the Atlantic, colliding with the tanker MT *Kars* in howling westerly winds and heavy rain as two subsidiary convoys – one from Sydney and one from Bermuda – joined HX38 Both ships suffered damage above the waterline but were considered sound enough to continue towards Great Britain.

Carrying 3,000 tons of diesel oil and 6,500 tons of marine fuel oil, the tanker slowed to a stop and began to burn, sixteen men being killed and the remaining twenty-eight, including Gibson, abandoning ship to be picked up by HMS *Beagle*. As destroyers fired star shells into the night sky, Kretschmer transmitted the convoy details once again, escaping detection by the escorts due to his extreme range. He continued to shadow until late that day before beginning his return, passing the spot in which *Scottish Maiden* was hit and prepared to finish it with gunfire but finding only debris as the ship had finally sunk. It was the sole loss to HX83, *U28* firing three torpedoes after gaining contact but missing with every shot. By late morning on 8 November, after a voyage of 1,900 nautical miles surfaced and 102 submerged, *U99* had once again made fast alongside the hulk *Isère* in Lorient harbour.

The response to returning U-boats was always exuberant ,with soldiers, sailors and airmen lining the dockside along with nurses and female auxiliary personnel and, occasionally, local dignitaries or visitors from Germany and their wives. This time, the atmosphere was even more jubilant as the latest recipient of the vaunted Oak Leaves and a new Knight's Cross winner were both welcomed home from patrol. Awards and decorations were also distributed to other worthy members of the elite crew, including the Iron Cross First Class to Horst Elfe. A small sheaf of telegrams was handed to Kretschmer by the commander of the 7th U-boat Flotilla, Korvkpt. Herbert Sohler. Amongst them were messages from BdU, Grossadmiral Raeder and Adolf Hitler:

> In grateful acknowledgement of your heroic achievement in the battle for the future of our people I bestow upon you, on the occasion of the sinking of 200,000 grt of enemy merchant shipping as the sixth officer of the German Wehrmacht, the Oak Leaves to the Knight's Cross of the Iron Cross.
> Adolf Hitler

> To the commander *U99*,
> My heartiest congratulations, with proud acknowledgment of your achievement, on your being awarded the Oak Leaves to the Knight's Cross.
> Commander in Chief

> To *U99*
> Congratulations. Carry on the same way.
> Your BdU.

The day following his return, Kretschmer made the journey to BdU headquarters in Boulevard Suchet, Paris, to meet Dönitz and examine the events of his war patrol. BdU headquarters was shortly to become officially operational in Kernevel – control passed over from Paris at 0900 hrs on 11 November – but until then the trip to Paris and its pleasant surroundings was at least a welcome break from the coastal town of Lorient, even for Kretschmer who perhaps did not enjoy the fleshpots of the city as avidly as many of his peers.

There he received confirmation that he was to fly the following day to Berlin and be awarded the Oak Leaves in person by Hitler. Five Iron Crosses First Class were allocated for distribution amongst the crew of *U99*, and amongst the recipients was Kassel who consistently freed

Kretschmer of his obligation to talk to the German press between patrols.

Dönitz's written appreciation of Kretschmer's achievements, appended to the typed copy of the boat's war diary, was brief:

> Conclusion of the BdU:
> 1. Very good, successful, and fortunate, operation.
> 2. It was correct that the commander waited and fired at the *Patroclus* steamer over intervals of time, which allowed observation of impact, until it had sunk.

Within the pages of his autobiography published in 1958, he spent longer detailing the efficacy of Kretschmer's tactics in general, and the sinking of the two armed merchant cruisers in particular:

> Kretschmer was an outstanding U-boat captain and a man of rare imperturbability. He was quick in sizing up a situation and in realising how best he could exploit it; and, having made his plan, he delivered his attack with calm determination and great skill. The outcome of the encounter between the small U-boat and the two auxiliary warships which were far its superior in both size and strength was that in the course of a single night, Kretschmer sank them both . . . Kretschmer's narrative showed that the British auxiliary cruisers had not displayed the discipline and efficiency of a warship in action, and they had certainly not expected to be attacked at night by a U-boat on the surface.[37]

However, he continued to point out yet another major flaw in the U-boat's primary weapon and one that the British had already noted: its lack of destructive power upon detonation:

> But the episode also proved that the effectiveness of our torpedoes left very much to be desired. By loading them with empty barrels the British had admittedly made their auxiliary cruisers very hard to sink, but even so the number of torpedoes which *U99* had to fire was disproportionately great. Similar cases were not infrequent, with the result that U-boats often found themselves unable to engage subsequent targets because of lack of torpedoes.[38]

Chapter Six

Oak Leaves

Twenty-five of *U99*'s crew were given home leave in Germany and the remainder headed from Lorient to Quiberon, while Kretschmer himself boarded a Siebel five-seater aircraft bound for Berlin, where he was given a luxurious room in the Kaiserhof Hotel. His initial port of call on 12 November was Shell Haus on the Tirpitzufer, overlooking the Landwehr Canal in the Tiergarten district. Within this unique modernist architectural building the staff of Oberkommando der Kriegsmarine had been controlling every aspect of Germany's naval force since 1934. Raeder received Kretschmer in his office, once again offering his congratulations to one of his service's brightest young officers. He apparently also enquired about the naval situation in Lorient and what might be lacking that would enable a more efficient running of U-boat operations. Kretschmer's reply mirrored one oft-repeated by Dönitz since the war's beginning: cooperation with aerial reconnaissance for convoy location. However, the well-established inter-departmental rivalries that bedevilled nearly every level of the Third Reich's political and military structure had conspired to keep Luftwaffe assets firmly beyond the reach of the Kriegsmarine. What cooperation there already was, was minor, inefficient and largely ineffective.

Göring jealously guarded his political power as the Reich's 'second man' and he considered his military prestige to be one of the cornerstones of that political stature. He and Raeder had clashed repeatedly since before the outbreak of war over creation of a dedicated German naval air arm, Göring furiously proclaiming once that 'everything that flies in Germany belongs to me'. Their dispute was both protracted and intractable, and while Kretschmer may have felt he was saying something new and revolutionary to Raeder, it was nothing of which his commander-in-chief was not already aware and for which he had already lobbied long and hard.

A more profound meeting for Kretschmer followed at noon on 12 November, a car arriving at Shell Haus that morning to transport him the short distance to the Reich Chancellery where he was met at the entrance steps by Karl-Jesko von Puttkamer, Hitler's naval adjutant, and guided towards the ornate reception room where the official presentation took place at precisely midday as Hitler entered the room and met with his latest warrior hero. The small box containing the Oak Leaves was handed by the *Führer* to Kretschmer before they posed for a formal portrait together. Once the ceremony was complete, Kretschmer was invited to sit with Hitler and discuss matters for some time in a relatively informal manner. His leader appeared genuinely interested in the state of the U-boat war and asked Kretschmer's opinion of how best to support and assist the U-boats in their battle. Once again, Kretschmer was commendably honest, repeating the need for aerial reconnaissance as well as increased numbers of U-boats in action, exactly the same principles repeated *ad infinitum* by Dönitz to his superiors in Berlin.

> Hitler nodded, and having listened attentively, rose from his seat and said: 'Thank you Commander. You have been admirably frank, and I shall do what I can for you and your colleagues. You will be lunching here with me.'[1]

As the meeting ended Puttkamer showed Kretschmer into the dining room where lunch would be served; he was given the seat of honour on Hitler's immediate right. That same afternoon Hitler was to meet Soviet Foreign Minister Vyacheslav Molotov to continue what had begun as difficult discussions with Ribbentrop during the morning. The conversation around the table naturally turned to their Soviet allies, Kretschmer maintaining a discreet silence unless engaged on naval matters as he witnessed first-hand the inner circle that surrounded his country's most powerful man. Sadly, there is no record of Kretschmer's impressions of Hitler, as they would have made fascinating reading. Several other U-boat veterans that this author has spoken to at length were also in Hitler's company at various times, sometimes because of their rank and position, but more frequently as part of a similar medal presentation and subsequent lunch. Interestingly they were almost all impressed by the presence of the man they met, despite claiming no particular affinity for National Socialism. Regardless of their political bent, Adolf Hitler was their undisputed leader and during the early years of the Second World War still appeared to exude a certain palpable energy in his relations with front-line officers for whom he harboured respect born from his own time in the trenches of the First World War. That evening, after departing the Reich Chancellery and enjoying a meal at his expensive hotel, Kretschmer was a guest at the State Opera where *Tannhäuser* was being performed; he was the sole occupant of the state box generally reserved for visiting dignitaries.

Although proud of his achievements and somewhat cautiously flattered by his reception, the trappings of fame in Berlin were not his forte and Kretschmer longed to return to sea. Within four days he was back in Lorient, travelling first to Kiel to visit friends and collect some belongings left behind by the flotilla move and then flown directly to Lorient aboard a Focke-Wulf Condor aircraft of Hitler's personal flight, *Die Fliegerstaffel des Führers*, the exact type so desperately needed for service in the Atlantic.

Maintenance on *U99* continued into the third week of November, as the crew returned from leave in Germany and Quiberon. The U-boat was taken from the shipyard and moored by the hulk of the *Audacieuse*, a French minesweeping gunboat captured and used as a pontoon next to the *Isère*. There the U-boat was demagnetised in an effort to nullify any potential influence mines dropped by submarine or aircraft outside the harbour entrance. Finally, at 1600 hrs on 27 November, Kretschmer put to sea once more, escorted by two *Vorpostenboote* to his familiar test-diving station where he submerged for one and a half hours and nearly seven nautical miles, swinging south to begin his journey to the operational area.

The manpower aboard was increased by the presence of Kaptlt. Dietrich Lohmann, attached to *U99* to gather experience as a *Konfirmand* before being due to transfer to the *Baubelehrung* for *U554* in the Blohm & Voss shipyard, Hamburg. Lohmann was already an acquaintance of Kretschmer's, having also been a member of 'Crew 30' but had remained as a watch officer, division officer and adjutant of the sail-training ship *Horst Wessel* before becoming a training company commander. He did not enter the U-boat service until April 1940 and the voyage aboard *U99* would be his first exposure to the war at sea.

Lohmann later went from the training boat *U554*, to *U579* which was damaged within the shipyard by bombs before finally going into combat as commander of *U89* of the 9th U-boat Flotilla. He mounted five war patrols and sank four ships before *U89* was depth-charged and lost with all hands north of the Azores on 12 May 1943.

On the last day of November, Kretschmer was directed to the quadrants AM44 and AM47 by BdU, expecting enemy convoy traffic to pass south of Rockall where Dönitz had begun to gather his available boats. Weather conditions deteriorated as *U99* spent hours scanning a sea devoid of targets. Submerging to use listening gear yielded no result and only a distant burning ship, fast-moving destroyer and aircraft came into view. The attack periscope failed, effectively rendering the boat unable to mount any attacks by day. As Kretschmer was digesting this latest mechanical development, his radio operator reported a fresh message from *U101* to BdU on the evening of 1 December: 'Convoy, AL5883, 50°, 9 knots.' The U-boats had found inbound HX90.

Kretschmer altered course to the track calculated by Petersen and *U99* began the chase. However, though the wind had slightly lessened, the swell running from the west made any forward momentum difficult. Atop the conning tower the men on watch were securely fastened by belts to the inner casing as rolling waves towered above the small U-boat, utterly dwarfed by the full power of the Atlantic. As *U99* climbed each steep incline the diesels struggled to push the boat forward until it breached the crest and tumbled down the far side, propellers briefly thrashing in thin air as the stern lifted from the water.

0315 hrs: We can't make headway against the sea even at three-quarters speed, boat at one point dipping completely below the surface despite the fact that the rear hydroplane was set at an upwards inclination of 5 degrees. The conning tower hatch slammed shut by itself so there was no great deluge of water inside.

0400 hrs: There is a severe drop in air pressure in the boat due to diesel fumes. The bridge watch is safe and sound as they are lashed on. Even with engines at maximum speed against the sea we can only make the equivalent of half speed.[2]

Each time the boat crashed beneath the surface of the water as a result of the huge swell, the engine air intakes shut automatically, causing the high-running engines suddenly to draw air from the interior of the boat itself. With external hatches closed, the resultant sudden decrease in pressure caused considerable pain to the crew's eardrums. (U-boat diesels were supplied by air intake masts and valves fitted within the external skin of the conning tower, running against the outside of the pressure hull. Here their inlet was considered to be the highest point of the boat, the most likely area to remain dry even in heavy seas. The fresh air was sucked through pipes towards the stern where they entered the interior through air inlet control valves. These valves were, of course, closed before the U-boat submerged in order not to allow any ingress of seawater. Exhaust, in turn, was vented through further piping that led to valves on either side of the stern.)

U99 battered its way west towards the reported convoy position until a large shadow loomed out of the surrounding darkness at 0514 hrs less than half a mile distant. Bargsten, who was in command of the watch on duty, called Kretschmer to the tower immediately and they both studied the emerging shape of a large zig-zagging auxiliary cruiser, a converted modern passenger liner with two funnels, a foremast and stepped after mast. Kretschmer immediately moved to attack but the sudden sighting of the destroyer HMS *Viscount* bearing down on the U-boat at high speed from the east thwarted his painfully slow approach manoeuvring. Kretschmer only had time for a single snapped shot before he was forced to dive away from the destroyer's approach; any idea of escaping surfaced was impossible in such heavy seas. At 0546 hrs a steam torpedo was fired from Tube IV at long range, estimated to be 3,600 metres. Then the conning tower watch and their commander were tumbling through the hatch into the control room as *U99* immediately dived, the screws of the hurrying destroyer passing almost directly above. While Kretschmer had at first feared it to be an escort for the merchant cruiser, *Viscount* was actually making full speed to rendezvous with incoming HX90 after having escorted OB251 before being detached.

After three minutes, the dull crack of an explosion echoed through the salt water, the torpedo having struck HMS *Forfar* on the starboard side by the engine room, bringing the ship's main aerial crashing down and rendering it unable to make steam. All engines were knocked out of action and the engine room, aft shaft tunnels and diesel room all began to flood. The 16,402-ton ship had been built for the Canadian Pacific Line and entered service as SS *Montrose* on the Liverpool–Montreal–Quebec run during 1922. On 6 September 1939, it had been requisitioned by the Admiralty, renamed HMS *Forfar* (to avoid confusion with the destroyer HMS *Montrose*) and equipped with eight 6-inch guns and two 3-inch anti-aircraft guns. The ship, commanded by Captain Norman Arthur Cyril Hardy, RN, was assigned to the Royal Navy's Northern Patrol during December 1939 and was en route to join the Western Patrol and escort convoy HX90 when Kretschmer's torpedo struck. The Second Officer, Lieutenant Robert Antrobus, RNR, had sighted *U99*, reporting a 'suspicious object, possibly a submarine', but unfortunately for *Forfar* no action was taken as the sighting could not be verified and Antrobus was considered to be 'of an imaginative nature and rather apt to get excited'.[3] Apparently, he had previously reported sightings of submarines which transpired to be unfounded. This time, however, he had been correct and Kretschmer's torpedo brought the ship to a sudden standstill. Midshipman Allan Kerr had just come off watch when *U99* attacked.

It was a black night, with no moon, and the fitful starlight occasionally obscured by cloud. I undressed, said my prayers and turned in quite happily. My sound sleep was soon broken by a terrific crash! Immediately I was awake. 'Torpedoed' flashed through my mind and just as quickly I prayed and switched on my light. Never will I forget the eerie silence that prevailed. The engines had stopped and the lights were dimming rapidly. 'Action Stations' was sounded on the klaxons, but this seemed to drain the last few dregs from the dynamo for it petered out and all went black. I pulled on my uniform and an old jersey on top of my pyjamas, a scarf, cap and raincoat as well as the all-important lifebelt. I can still distinctly remember being annoyed when one of my shoe-laces broke as I pulled on my shoes.[4]

Aboard *U99* the sound of HMS *Viscount*'s screws had receded and there was no trace of HMS *Forfar* to be heard. Kretschmer ordered the boat surfaced and at 0612 hrs, *U99* emerged, its bridge watch seeing HMS *Forfar* lying motionless in a spreading pool of oil. The hit was confirmed, but *Forfar* was a long way from sinking. Mindful of the number of torpedoes it had taken to sink HMS *Laurentic* and *Patroclus*, Kretschmer ordered another fired, though he was eager to join the attack

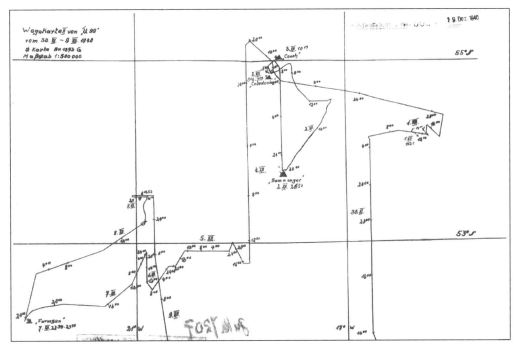

The seventh war patrol, including the sinking of HMS *Forfar*.

on the sighted convoy. The distant sound of a U-boat's cannon could be heard as *U47* shelled SS *Dunsley*, which had straggled from HX90. The second torpedo left Tube I at 0639 hrs, after the U-boat had crept to within 930 metres of the cruiser. It exploded amidships but showed no discernible effect to the watching men on *U99*. The blast had actually destroyed one of the boats being swung out in readiness by the crew and caused a significant number of casualties. As star shells were fired into the sky along with red Very lights signalling the ship in distress, *Forfar*'s boat deck collapsed onto the promenade deck below, killing many at their boat stations and destroying lifeboats in the process. Four minutes later torpedo three struck, drenching sheltering British crewmen on deck as water came jetting out of the engine room vents. The sound of grinding, breaking metal was audible throughout the ship, though externally it appeared only to have developed a slight list to port. Captain Hardy gave the order to abandon ship and men began to lower boats into the water as HMS *Forfar* started to settle slowly.

Midshipman Kerr had already taken control of the lowering of boat number P2:

Men now came down the rope ladders and as she settled some even jumped from the Promenade deck right into the boat. There would be nearly 20 men in the boat now and I was trying to slip the painter when someone in the water screamed my name. I was dripping with oil fuel even now, as the painter was thickly covered in it, however I got good grip of the young fellow who I think was Radio Cadet Fraser. Another chap and myself were endeavouring to haul him inboard when with a shattering roar we went sailing into the air. The fourth torpedo had struck directly below my boat blowing us right out of the water. I thought this was finish. I can remember being down under and striking out mechanically for the surface. Just previously I had seen a Carley float for'ard of the boat. I swam to this to find the Postie, PO Lazenby and L/S Frank Mayo already 'on board'. There were many others inside and all round so I just hung on for a while. Even in these circumstances the lads had to laugh at my appearance. Now capless, with hair and face coated thickly in that treacle-like oil I am sure I was an odd sight.[5]

The fourth torpedo had come from *U99*'s stern tube and the explosion helped start the disintegration of the ship, already beginning to break in two before the fifth and final torpedo hit it in the stern at 0657 hrs and detonated the aft magazine. Finally, the great ship broke apart, the stern collapsing upon itself, splintering decking, before heeling over to starboard and going below the waves, sinking slightly faster than the bow section, stored depth charges exploding on the way to the bottom a thousand metres below. The loss of life was severe: 172 men were killed leaving only twenty-one survivors. Captain Hardy went down with his ship, last seen still on the bridge as HMS *Forfar* broke in two and Lieutenant Antrobus, whose warning had remained unheeded, also died. HMS *Viscount*, HMCS *St Laurent* and SS *Dunsley* – which had survived Prien's attack – rescued the scattered survivors hours later, by which time *U99* had retreated, diving to reload all five tubes. Kretschmer recorded the successful destruction of the ship, though incorrectly identified it as SS *Caledonia*, an armed merchant cruiser renamed HMS *Scotstoun* and already sunk in June 1940 by *U25*. The error was rectified shortly thereafter by B-Dienst intelligence sources and appended to *U99*'s war diary after return from patrol.

HMS *Forfar* was the fifth armed merchant cruiser to be sunk on the Northern and Western Patrols since August 1940 and the Admiralty withdrew them from the area, redirecting their use further into the Atlantic where they could serve their original purpose of defending against potential attack by German surface raiders.

By midday, Kretschmer had caught up with the convoy, but was forced to shadow in preparation for a night attack due to the inoperative attack periscope. As *U99* moved towards a position suitable for attempting to break into the convoy body, a solitary detached steamer appeared from the south and Kretschmer switched his attention to the newcomer, the 4,276-ton Norwegian freighter SS *Samnanger*. Master Andreas Hansen's ship was travelling from Hartlepool to Pepel in Sierra Leone in ballast and had already straggled from convoy OB251 when Kretschmer's lookouts sighted it. After signalling BdU the position of the convoy, he began trailing the single Norwegian until attacking under the cover of darkness. At 2050 hrs a single G7e hit *Samnanger* amidships with an impressive explosion, the ship slewing to a halt and beginning to list. Unwilling to use more torpedoes, Kretschmer edged closer and his gun crew began firing mixed high explosive and phosphorous shells into the ship's hull, fifty rounds setting the steamer ablaze before it heeled over and sank. Kretschmer recorded no sighting of survivors or boats, and whether any escaped the blazing hulk or not, none of the thirty crew survived the loss of their ship.

By this stage the convoy was too far east to be caught by *U99* before it reached the safety of the defensive mine barriers across the North Channel. Instead, Kretschmer turned almost due north and slowly searched for stragglers and soon a distant tanker was sighted that appeared to be stopped and lying motionless apart from the rise and fall of the heavy Atlantic swell. Cautiously approaching what could be a deliberate trap, Kretschmer and his watch officer scanned the ship for any trace of activity, content to lie nearby until dawn. With the spreading light it became obvious that the ship had been abandoned: there was some battle damage showing and all the lifeboats were missing. The ship's name was visible, confirmed soon thereafter when a life-ring was recovered from the sea with the title 'MV *Conch*' written upon it in bold letters.

Master Charles George Graham's 8,376-ton motor tanker was carrying 11,214 tons of Admiralty fuel oil from Trinidad to the Clyde as part of convoy HX90 which came under sustained attack after being sighted by *U101* on 1 December. In total six U-boats – *U43, U47, U52, U94, U95* and *U101* – as well as the Italian boats *Argo, Giuliani* and *Tarantini* made contact with HX90 and between them sank nine merchant ships and damaged three others before the convoy reached the safety of the North Channel minefields. Among those ships damaged was MV *Conch*, hit by a single torpedo from *U47* and beginning to straggle behind the main body. Kapitänleutnant Gerd Schreiber's *U95* then hit *Conch* with two torpedoes out of four fired, destroying the engine room and forcing the crew to abandon ship before Schreiber was driven away by HMCS *St Laurent*, which subsequently rescued all fifty-three crewmen.

Kretschmer found the deserted ship still riding high on the swell and at 1019 hrs the stern tube was fired from 920 metres and hit the engine room causing a sympathetic gas explosion, that sent a column of water and debris a hundred metres into the air as the tanker began sinking by the stern. Within a minute, MV *Conch* was gone.

As operations against HX90 were officially ended, *U47, U95* and *U101* began their return to France, low on ammunition and fuel. The remaining boats were moved south to lie in deep formation along the next expected convoy's route reported by the B-Dienst intelligence source. In Lorient, Dönitz was reliant on weather reports to plan his operations and had attempted to use Italian boats for this purpose, but his effort proved to have been in vain.

> As no weather reports have been received from the Italian boats, I find myself forced to detail one of our boats for this. It will have to be one of the five in the attacking positions ready for the convoy, announced by radio intelligence. This is very undesirable, but I have no alternative. I do not think any danger need be feared from the probably very inaccurate bearings of the undivided short weather reports, but when there are many regular reports made from approximately the same area, the enemy is likely in the end to discover this boat's ops. area. This, new very modest attempt to cooperate with the Italians has failed. Two of them were ordered to make the weather reports. Neither of them produced messages which were any use.
>
> This is unfortunately not the only disappointment. I did not expect that the Italians would at once sink a lot of shipping. They

are still too unaccustomed to this theatre of operations. They
have never yet operated in similar waters under similar weather
conditions. They are not adequately equipped for it. But I did at
least hope that they would contribute to a better reconnaissance
of the operations area. In actual fact during the whole time I have
not received one single enemy report from them on which I could
take action. All they have produced are several very delayed,
mainly incomplete or inaccurate sighting reports. They have
never managed to maintain contact even for a very short time.
During the period in which the German boats sank 26,000 grt
in the same operations area, the Italian successes amounted to
12,800 tons at the best (8,000 of these doubtful) and one destroyer.
I am not at all sure that their presence in the operations area of
the German boats, the way they let themselves be sighted, their
radio traffic, their clumsy attacks do not do us more harm than
good.[6]

On 4 December *U99* was told to report weather conditions at 0300 hrs,
1300 hrs and 1700 hrs and Dönitz may have been shocked to discover
that the storm had worsened considerably; Kretschmer reporting Gale
Force 10 and 11 winds. Attempts to locate the enemy were virtually
impossible and, if they had been found, the successful use of weapons
was unlikely. Frequent dives were required both to rest *U99*'s crew and
provide an opportunity to listen for the sound of distant propellers. Not
until 2221 hrs on 5 December was a large freighter sighted by lookouts
clinging to their precarious position atop the wildly swaying conning
tower. The wind was holding at a cyclonic Force 11 and yet Kretschmer
dared to attack at a range of only 300 metres. A single torpedo was fired
from Tube I, which predictably missed in the hideous conditions. All
the two antagonists could do was look at each other until contact was
lost once more.

The Atlantic storm showed no signs of abating and with monotonous
regularity, Kretschmer recorded in his war diary: 'Surfaced. Use of
weapons impossible.' Once again, a steamer was sighted at 1135 hrs on
7 December and Kretschmer ambitiously dived to attack. The Force 10
wind blew from the north-west and the ocean undulated in a towering
swell. The attack was almost instantly foiled by the non-functioning
attack periscope and an absolute inability to use the larger navigation

periscope in such a heavily rolling ocean. Kretschmer contented himself with surfacing and shadowing the ship to attempt a surface attack under cover of darkness. The ship, 5,237-ton Dutch SS *Farmsum*, was headed for Buenos Aires with a load of coal. Master Bartele Jansma had taken his ship originally from Blyth before joining the westward convoy OB252 that departed Liverpool under escort by corvette HMS *Arbutus* and destroyers HMS *Chelsea*, *Cottesmore*, *Verity*, *Veteran* and *Wolverine*. The thirty-two merchant ships immediately ran headlong into the Atlantic storm and were dispersed, *Farmsum* straggling from the first day of joining the convoy, until Kretschmer sighted it.

While *U99* tailed the Dutch ship and the wind gradually began to drop, a distress message was received during the early afternoon, transmitted by a Greek freighter which had been disabled by what was sometimes the common enemy to all mariners, the weather: '*Aghia Eirini*, position 52° 38′ N – 22° 52′ W at 10.51 GMT wants immediate assistance. 29 on board. All holds full of water.' For Kretschmer there was no question of going to its assistance. 'I plan first to sink the enemy steamer that I have in sight, and then operate against *Aghia Eirini*. This ship, a Greek of 4,330 grt, I can probably sink with artillery fire.'[7]

The Greek ship had arrived in Great Britain during September as part of convoy SC5 carrying iron ore and now on its outward voyage, from Cardiff for Buenos Aires, its steering gear had failed. The large freighter crashed broadside-on to the sea, taking on considerable amounts of water as it drifted towards the rocky Irish coastline. Meanwhile, *U99* ploughed onward, shadowing the slowly moving *Farmsum* for hours until darkness allowed Kretschmer to position himself for a surfaced attack. Despite the wind dropping to a Force 5 south-southwester, the position was still difficult as both vessels were buffeted by the dramatic swell that continued to run strongly. At 2239 hrs a close-range shot was fired from Tube III. After only a thirty-seven-second run, the torpedo impacted and exploded against the stern. However, due to the sea conditions and the fact that BdU had ordered depth settings for torpedoes adjusted to only two metres in such conditions, it had broken surface more than once while speeding towards the target, the final peak of the swell throwing the contact-fused torpedo out of the water so that it hit above the waterline and the explosion resembled a 'dry' artillery strike. The blast lifted the stern gun and its platform high into the air and over the side, but apart from water entering from waves breaking against the hull, *Farmsum* showed no sign of sinking. The ship had, however, stopped and radio transmissions began frantically to pour from its radio shack as it reported the attack, providing Kretschmer with the identification of his target that he needed. Before long the crew could be seen taking to their boats.

Eleven minutes later a second torpedo sped towards the target, again breaking the surface during its run, but this time hitting the stern below the waterline and detonating with a column of dark water blown seventy-five metres into the air. Though this was clearly an effective hit, the stationary merchant ship still showed no signs of going down and so a third torpedo was fired, set to run at a depth of three metres and hitting the Dutch ship amidships, this *coup de grâce* sending the ship heeling over to port and sinking within one minute of the torpedo's detonation. Of the thirty-one crewmen aboard (all of them Dutch apart from a British cook), nineteen were later rescued by HMS *Ambuscade*, a destroyer based in Iceland for trans-Atlantic escort duty. All of the survivors had severe frostbite and were hospitalised after being landed at Greenock, four of them subsequently dying despite medical care.

Without waiting to assist survivors, Kretschmer immediately ordered course set for the last reported position of SS *Aghia Eirini*, reaching the scene at 0230 hrs the following morning but finding only the bare Atlantic swell. He considered it unlikely that the ship had gone down, expecting to have heard a final distress call made on the international 600 m frequency. More likely, it was either drifting or sailing in the direction of the North Channel, and *U99* began to trail this predicted course. At 0923 hrs, another message was received:

> *Aghia Eirini*. Lost every try to come near the shore in spite of the ship's holds being full of water. The helm is out of action now again. Position at 0725 GMT 53° 07' N – 18° 12' W.

Kretschmer urged his crew on as he altered course to attack what would probably be the last ship of his patrol with weather conditions so foul and ammunition so low. One last transmission was received aboard *U99* not long after, the exasperation and barely concealed anger of the ship's master flowing through the words his radio room sent:

> To the Admiralty. No hope to come near the shore. We are asking for your immediate help. Helm out of use. Ship is full of water

three days ago. No ships to our rescue three days ago. Position 54°
06' N – 18° 18' W approx. Master.

However, Kretschmer was never to find the Greek freighter, which
eventually ran aground and was wrecked at Achill Head, Clewbay, on
10 December. Instead he was forced to alter course after his lookouts
sighted a large passenger liner during the afternoon, the ship clearly
having been converted to an auxiliary cruiser. The sudden appearance
of an approaching destroyer then forced *U99* to make an emergency
dive, the enemy propellers being tracked as they swept past too near
for comfort. At that most inopportune moment, the port electric motor
failed as a result of the strain caused by the weather conditions. Schröder
requested the boat surfaced to give time to carry out repairs and after
careful listening through the hydrophones Kretschmer was content to
bring his boat up once more. No 'all round look' was possible through
the conning tower periscope which remained inoperative, but there was
no sound of propellers detected and Kretschmer chanced his hand and
surfaced. As he led his men of the watch onto the conning tower, they
were shocked to see the auxiliary cruiser lying stopped only a matter
of two to three nautical miles distant. Immediately he called for an
emergency dive, but *U99* took an inordinately long time to submerge on
only the starboard electric motor, no forward momentum having been
gathered as the diesels had not even been started. The auxiliary cruiser
was heard to begin moving and almost immediately the high-pitched
propellers and probing ASDIC of two destroyers were detected, rapidly
approaching nearer.

The boat slowly clawed its way downwards as a single destroyer passed
almost directly overhead, dropping ten depth charges that exploded
close enough temporarily to disable hydroplanes and an instrument
panel within the control room, though these were swiftly returned
to service. As quickly as it had begun, the attack was over and the
destroyers could be heard slowly receding into the distance. Kretschmer
once again gradually brought *U99* to the surface at 2031 hrs after
darkness had fallen. A distant destroyer could be seen lying stopped
near the position that had been occupied by the auxiliary cruiser but
Kretschmer had had enough and ordered course set to the south and
away from the enemy while Schröder attempted to repair the damaged
electric motor. However, with the tools available, the motor refused to

restart and at 0422 hrs on 9 December Kretschmer signalled BdU that he was returning with engine trouble. Three days later *U99* entered Lorient in the wake of Sperrbrecher I *Saar* and made fast against the hulk of the *Audacieuse*.

Although his patrol had undoubtedly not ended as Kretschmer had hoped, it had still been a success, four pennants decorated with the boat's horseshoe insignia fluttering from the raised periscope – one edged in red to denote a military ship sunk – as the boat docked to an enthusiastic reception. As usual, Kassel fielded the myriad questions and interview requests received from the German press, freeing Kretschmer of the obligation as much as possible. Amongst the accounts of the U-boat's actions at sea, the *Kieler Neueste Nachrichten* – the most important daily newspaper in Kiel since the end of the nineteenth century – published on 17 December a somewhat lurid account of the sinking of Kretschmer's third auxiliary merchant cruiser.

How the Auxiliary Cruiser *Forfar* Sank in Three Minutes
By War Correspondent Hans Kreis

Kretschmer has returned to port; four pennants fly above the periscope. The tonnage he has sunk is 35,000 grt, and included in this is a large British auxiliary cruiser, the *Forfar* of more than 16,000 tons, as well as a big tanker and two merchant ships. There is considerable joy out here at the U-boat base on the Atlantic coast. This was the sixth war cruise which Kapitänleutnant Kretschmer had carried out with such magnificent success. He has only recently been decorated by the *Führer* with the Oak Leaves to the Knight's Cross of the Iron Cross. This makes him the first German U-boat commander to have sunk more than a quarter of a million tons of shipping. Notwithstanding all the measures of defence adopted by the British, he has sent to the bottom thirty-six of their vessels or ships sailing for them, making up approximately 250,000 grt; three British auxiliary cruisers totalling 57,000 tons as well as a number of tankers figure in this.

During his cruise in the Atlantic before this last one he sank the two auxiliary cruisers, *Patroclus* (11,300 tons) and *Laurentic* (18,700 tons), in a heavy sea and in face of a strong counter-attack. In this last patrol he encountered the *Forfar* in mid-Atlantic during a night in which our U-boats operating there scattered a large convoy and sank a tonnage of nearly 130,000 grt.

The *Forfar* swiftly met its fate; those on board could not determine from what bearing or range the attack was being made – whether the submarine was operating on the surface or submerged; the auxiliary cruiser's firing was indiscriminate, while red star shells and distress signals [probably the wrong way around as the red flares were distress signals fired by hand-held Very pistols, as opposed to white star shells] were discharged into the darkness; and still Kapitänleutnant Kretschmer closed to attack the vessel.

Suddenly a terrific detonation crashes through the night, bringing to the submarine the signal of success, while on board the cruiser everything is shaken and it starts to heel badly; the torpedo has struck in the engine-room, destroying life, machinery, bulkheads and decks, the hull being damaged to the very keel. The back of the *Forfar* is broken, its stern rises from the water and the huge ship of 16,000 tons disappears, making a wonderful impression even in the darkness.

The dull thuds of depth charges detonating below the surface are heard – depth charges which had been intended for German U-boats. They were in the fore part of the ship, and have been exploded by the pressure caused by the increasing depth as the ship sinks. Scarcely three minutes after the discharge of the torpedo, nothing of the British auxiliary cruiser but wreckage is visible.

As ever, Kretschmer reported directly to Dönitz to discuss the events of his latest patrol. The weather had played a major part in preventing greater success for all of the U-boats in the Atlantic at that time, but once again, *U99* had achieved more than most and Dönitz offered no criticism of the way that Kretschmer had conducted his mission.

BdU comment: 'Very successful, well-executed operation.'

Following this latest exposure to the worst weather experienced by *U99* thus far, the boat needed a complete refit, which would keep it in the shipyard for months. The opportunity was also taken to give the crew a proper break as the strain of patrolling was beginning to show. While Kretschmer's unyielding quest for efficiency remained undiminished, the traces of natural combat fatigue could be found amongst all of the men from *U99*. Three weeks' leave was granted to all men and Kretschmer invited all who wanted to to join him at the mountain resort in Krummhübel (now Karpocz), Silesia, the majority of their tab to be paid by the Kriegsmarine.

Coupled with the rest and relaxation were major changes that would be taking place amongst the tightly knit crew of *U99*. Both Bargsten and Elfe were to leave and begin training to take over their own commands, relieved of their duties aboard *U99* before Christmas but not actually departing Lorient until January 1941. After completing his commander's course in Flensburg, Oblt.z.S. Klaus Bargsten was posted to take charge of *U563* while it was being built in the Blohm and Voss yard in Hamburg. The boat was commissioned in March 1941 and Bargsten made four patrols in *U563* before transferring to command *U521* during June 1942. On 2 June 1943, *U521* was depth charged and sunk in the western Atlantic north-east of Norfolk, Virginia. Bargsten was the sole survivor; he lived out the war and passed away on 13 August 2000 in Bremen.

Oblt.z.S. Horst Elfe officially left *U99*'s complement on 12 December 1940 and was appointed commander of the Type IID *U139* nine days later. Later he mounted two Baltic war patrols during 'Operation Barbarossa' before transferring to take over command of Kaptlt. Claus Korth's veteran Type VIIB *U93* on 6 October 1941. His tenure was brief, the boat being sunk on its second patrol with Elfe in command, depth-charged north-east of Madeira and going down with six men killed. Elfe survived the sinking and later Allied interrogators noted that his 'crew did not seem to have a very high regard for his skill as a commanding officer and some of them held him responsible for the loss of his ship'. However, the boat crew's morale appeared 'to have been of a high standard and the Captain was, on the whole, popular with his crew, despite their contention that he was responsible for the loss of his boat. This may have been due to some extent to the fact that he kept them well supplied with beer and brought them each a small present at Christmas time.'[8]

With the departure of the two officers, Kretschmer required replacements and reputedly was offered a shortlist of men from which to choose his new IWO. He singled out Oblt.z.S. Hans-Joachim von Knebel-Döberitz with whom he had sailed in *U23*. Knebel-Döberitz had joined the Kriegsmarine in 1936 at the age of eighteen, transferring to the U-boat service two years later and making his first cruise with Kretschmer aboard *U23* during January 1940. Following his tenure aboard *U23*, Knebel-Döberitz had transferred to *U58*, then spent six months ashore on Dönitz's staff before engineering a return to front-line service in which he was fortunate enough to receive a transfer to *U99*. His tenure within BdU had reached the logical end for the young officer. Of Germany's nobility, Knebel-Döberitz's family were no friends of the Nazi Party and were under surveillance for their pronounced views, and he had inherited their thorough distaste for Germany's political elite. In the informal surroundings fostered by Dönitz at his headquarters, Knebel-Döberitz was able to speak without self-censorship, though he correctly foresaw a time when his personal politics could cause conflict and perhaps even reflect badly on his commander. Hence, he judged that it was time to return to combat duties.

However, there was to be no replacement for Elfe. Instead, the reliable veteran Stabsobersteuerman Heinrich Petersen would assume the duties of IIWO, his place as IIIWO and the boat's quartermaster taken by 29-year-old Obersteuermann Rudolf Ellrich. Additionally, the U-boat service was about to start sending *Fähnrich* (midshipmen) aboard combat boats in order to accelerate their U-boat officer training by gaining experience in a fighting boat. A small number of *U99*'s other veterans were also transferred to different U-boats where the benefit of their experience was considered essential to new crews 'learning the ropes' in the Atlantic. Kretschmer later lamented the change in his crew:

> At the end of 1940, I sent two of my officers off to commanding officer school, because I figured that these two fine officers would make good commanders and this way could better contribute to winning the war, while hoping that at the same time I would get similarly good replacements. Unfortunately, however, that was not the case, which partly contributed to my last patrol in the beginning of 1941 turning out a disaster that cost the boat and the lives of three crew members.

Kretschmer, too, was under some pressure to transfer from *U99*. The war had entered its seventeenth month and already some of the original U-boat commanders, such as Otto Schuhart (*U29*) and Werner

Hartmann (*U37*) had come ashore to take either a post within the BdU Staff or command of a training facility. This transfer served a twofold purpose in that it not only allowed a period of rest and tranquillity for men already mentally and emotionally stretched by the difficult nature of U-boat warfare, but also allowed them to pass on their experience to the second and third generation of U-boat commanders coming into active service. Production of U-boats was still far below the desired level, but there remained new boats being committed to action, and generally their captains had begun the war either as watch officers – such as Erich Topp, Wolfgang Lüth and 'Adi' Schnee, who was bringing *U201* into the Atlantic for the first time during January 1941 – or had still been in training. The potential benefit of being instructed by a man such as Kretschmer could have been incalculable and Dönitz attempted to persuade him to come ashore during January 1941, at least for a matter of months.

However, Kretschmer had no desire to become a 'desk warrior'. He possessed neither the patience nor the predisposition for office politics that was frequently required of staff officers and knew that he would quickly become bored and frustrated at trying to train prospective commanders to act as he felt was required in combat. After all, he had already preached the benefit of convoy penetration to his peers and could not even persuade them to make the tactic a standard method of attacking. What chance would he have had with raw officers?

There is a mistaken belief that Kretschmer was the lone hold-out amongst the war's earliest commanders as regards taking an offered post ashore. This is, in fact, far from the truth. As well as his close associates Prien and Schepke, many of the notable veterans were still at sea, including Fritz-Julius Lemp (*U110*), Heinrich Liebe (*U38*) and Jürgen Oesten (*U106*). Nonetheless, it was a matter that Dönitz pursued with all of them at one point or another and Kretschmer was no exception. Dönitz took the opportunity to attempt to pressure Kretschmer into a training assignment during December 1940 when Kretschmer shared the back seat of Dönitz's staff car with Wolfgang Lüth of *U43* as they were driven from Lorient via Paris to Köln from where they would head onwards to their respective homes for Christmas. Dönitz repeatedly requested that Kretschmer come ashore as a training officer, and was repeatedly turned down. Regarding Lüth, who would rise to be one of the two most highly decorated officers of the Kriegsmarine, Kretschmer later wrote: 'We were alike in several ways. Neither of us was a gossip or a braggart, we both had strong nerves and we both kept our heads before the enemy . . . basically Lüth was a Prussian like me.'[9]

Despite repeated badgering from Dönitz during the long car journey, Kretschmer refused to budge and would remain in command of his Golden Horseshoe boat.

The period of relaxation in the Silesian mountains almost certainly recharged not only Kretschmer's spirits, but also those of his crew who joined him. Despite clashing with a publisher despatched by the Propaganda Ministry to pressure Kretschmer into writing a book to help recruitment of fresh U-boat personnel – or at least allow his name to be attached to the book as author – the war barely intruded at all.

After three weeks' home leave, the crew returned to Lorient. Back in the familiar environs of France's Atlantic ports, Kretschmer dined with Prien and Schepke at a restaurant in a small village near Lorient. Robertson recalls in his book that this evening occurred following Kretschmer's return from his Oak Leaves presentation in Berlin, but both Schepke and Prien were at sea during that period, and after Kretschmer's return on 12 December Schepke had already sailed again, staying at sea until January. In the retelling of the event, Schepke had also already won the Oak Leaves which places any such celebratory meal after 1 December 1940. The event must have taken place in either January or February 1941 when all three were ashore, although this too appears unlikely as Schepke had returned to Germany with *U100* at the end of his December patrol and remained there during the period in which he was awarded the Oak Leaves, he and his crew being fêted, photographed, filmed, interviewed, given a winter sports holiday and taking part in speeches and broadcasts during their stay in Germany while Goebbels's propaganda machine used every angle possible of the commander and crew almost without pause over the duration of their ten-week stay. Regardless, according to Robertson, at the time of this meeting between the three aces, Schepke apparently appeared slightly frayed, perhaps actually beginning to show the strain of months of successful Atlantic patrols. His tonnage claims had become steadily more inaccurate, probably reflecting the difficulty of verified identification from intense convoy action. Nonetheless, he was still one of the leading U-boat men of the time, as Kretschmer analytically explained in a letter written on 12 July 1989:

Take the tonnage sunk and divide it by [months in service] and you get the efficiency per month. Or divide it by the number of days in service (292 for *U100*) you get the efficiency per day of service. Better, of course, would be to find the efficiency per day of operational service, i.e. from the first day of the first patrol (leaving port). All this could be shown by means of a diagram. The x-axis would show the time in operational service, the y-axis the tonnage sunk. The resulting mathematical curve would give the overall figure of tonnage sunk. The angle between this curve and the x-axis would indicate the efficiency of the submarine. If the crew at all times kept the boat's equipment, armament and engines in a good state, then the periods in port could be comparatively short, which again would count favourably for the efficiency curve. I hope you were able to show and prove that Schepke's efficiency in *U100* was much better than those of the slow tonnage collectors like Topp in *U552* etc. By the way, Dönitz had his staff book-keeping the tonnage sunk by submarines in order to get the figure per day and per month. The latter was published.[10]

The written accounts of the evening meal between the three aces also includes Schepke suggesting that they make a wager amongst themselves as to who would first exceed the amount of 250,000 tons of enemy shipping sunk. Of course, this too is problematic for the dating, as Kretschmer was mistakenly believed to have surpassed that number during December. If any such bet had ever been made, then Otto Kretschmer had won.

Chapter Seven

The Final Patrol

Back in Lorient, one of the Wehrmacht regiments stationed near the port city had unofficially adopted *U99*, the regimental band leader, Hans Thissen, going as far as to compose a stirring piece named the 'Kretschmer March', with a ceremony laid on in which to debut the piece publicly and present Kretschmer with a copy of the sheet music. In exchange, Kretschmer intended to present a life-ring that had been retrieved from the sinking tanker *Conch* on 3 December. The event became a full military parade and the German Rundfunk requested the opportunity to record the ceremony for later broadcast. According to most accounts of this event, Kretschmer flatly declined to be recorded, though correspondents were admitted to cover the ceremony in written words only. Kassel most definitely conspired with the broadcasting unit to equip a sailor with a wrist-mounted microphone and, as Kretschmer presented the life-ring to his Army benefactors and made a short speech of appreciation for the musical composition, the sailor stood immediately behind and to Kretschmer's right, his arm and microphone extended and the words successfully captured for later transmission. However, despite assertions that Kretschmer forbade a press presence, the event *was definitely* captured for cinema broadcast; footage survives of the entire ceremony and the cinema camera itself was caught in some stills from the event that have also survived.

As the U-boat was finally prepared for sea once more during February, two *Fähnrich* arrived to take their place amongst Kretschmer's crew. They were Günther Rubahn and Volkmar König. König remembers his happiness to be attached to such an impressive command:

I was amongst the first *Fähnrich* that they assigned to duty aboard a combat U-boat. I came to U-boats by accident. Once you had completed your officer's training you took a position somewhere in the fleet to 'learn by doing'. I was very proud to be posted to the U-boats. After having served with a naval artillery unit in France, my orders were to report to the 7th U-boat Flotilla in Lorient, the port of the aces and I was very excited. My friend from naval school in Kiel and I decided to visit our respective parents on the way to France and we boarded separate trains. The idea was we would meet up afterwards and continue onward together. However, engine trouble on my train stopped it near Cologne and he arrived before me. But it was actually good luck for me and terrible for him as he was immediately assigned to Günther Prien's *U47* which was sunk with all hands on the next patrol. That could have been me if we had met as planned and journeyed together.

When I arrived in Lorient I was sent to *U99*, Kretschmer's boat. This was really quite something for me as he had already become a famous ace. I was only twenty years old and he was eight years my senior, the 'Old Man'. He was not what you would call 'friendly' with the men aboard his boat but he obviously cared about them deeply. He was also courageous, intelligent and inventive in his approach to U-boat methods. His authority over every one of his crew was absolute and unquestioned and they each had total respect for the 'Old Man'

As soon as I reported to my captain he turned to me and asked, 'What do you know?' And I, of course, couldn't really give him an answer so he just shook his head and said, 'My goodness, what do I have aboard my boat.'[1]

The first of the three aces to leave Lorient was Prien on 20 February, bound for the North Channel approaches once more, and Kretschmer was amongst the crowd there to see him off as the U-boat with the 'snorting bull of Scapa Flow' on its conning tower left for its tenth war patrol. Prien was the most famous submariner in Germany, probably the most famous member of any submarine service worldwide, and had already been immortalised in German film, radio and writing. He had taken war correspondent Wolfgang Frank on patrol to record *U47* in action, which later formed the basis of a wartime book that was arguably more accurate than most of its contemporaries, and was subsequently updated and reissued after the end of hostilities. Unlike Kretschmer, Prien had initially revelled in the attention, the accolades of the nation his reward after a life that had been beset by prewar hardship at every turn before the Kriegsmarine had accepted him following the *Niobe* sinking. However, by 1941 the sheen had worn off his fame and he appeared weary of the adulation when so many of his original crew had moved on from *U47*, some already claimed in combat aboard other boats.

> 'Little Prien,' said Kretschmer, calling him by his nickname, 'I shall be following you in a couple of days. Have a convoy ready.'
>
> 'I shall do that thing,' replied Prien with a laugh. 'Just leave it to Papa's nose to smell something out.'
>
> 'Good luck and good hunting,' said Kretschmer, and shook his hand.
>
> 'Thank you Otto. I have a feeling about this trip. I feel it is going to be a big one for us all. Goodbye.'[2]

Two days later, on Saturday 22 February, *U99* put to sea heading for the same area as Prien. The boat slipped from harbour alongside the larger Type IX *U105* that was headed for the hunting grounds of the South Atlantic, which these 'cruiser U-boats' better suited. *U99* carried fourteen torpedoes this time, hoping for more moderate seas that would allow the transfer of external torpedoes to the boat's interior. This departure was rather more spectacular than those that had preceded: an Army band played the 'Kretschmer March' from the deck of a *Vorpostenboot* which accompanied *U99* as far as the harbour entrance.

Ahead of him, Prien had picked up the trail of westbound convoy OB290 and began to follow, though beaten away repeatedly by British aircraft that forced *U47* to dive to safety. Crashing through huge breakers into the turbulent Atlantic, Kretschmer was ordered to make all speed to Prien's convoy. *U73* and *U97* – the latter having already expended all torpedoes – were ordered by Dönitz to join Prien in the difficult job of shadowing while *U99* was brought up as quickly as possible to the scene. During the early morning on 26 February Prien began his attacks and by the day's end had sunk three ships and damaged a fourth, though he was eventually forced away with accurate depth charges from the escort. Kretschmer had arrived in the general area that Prien had reported, but found nothing in the atrocious visibility. He dived to allow Kassel to sweep a wide arc with his hydrophones, being rewarded by the low rhythmic thump of merchant ship screws to port, unfortunately accompanied by the higher-pitched sound of destroyers. Kretschmer altered course and, using rough estimation of distance to the ships, he brought *U99* to the surface and found the sleek dark grey conning tower of *U47* lying virtually stationary dead ahead, lookouts more alert this time and spotting the emerging U-boat immediately while others gazed in the opposite direction where, beyond them, the squat shapes of merchantmen were visible. The two boats exchanged signals before attracting the attention of a pair of destroyers that immediately changed tack to run down the Germans. Kretschmer and Prien were immediately forced to dive as there was no darkness to hide them, *U99* towards the convoy and *U47* breaking north and attracting a brief flurry of depth charges.

Prien's position reports enabled a single Focke-Wulf Fw 200 of I./KG40 to find and attack the merchant ships during the afternoon and five more Fw 200s that evening as OB290 began to disperse, sinking eight ships and damaging several more. It was an inkling of what was possible with greater Kriegsmarine–Luftwaffe cooperation, though only made possible by Prien's accurate contact reports rather than by aerial reconnaissance.

Contact was then lost with OB290 and both Prien and Kretschmer were ordered to search the same area in case of stragglers, the weather degenerating into drifting fog banks over a still undulating long, high and heavy Atlantic swell as they scoured the area for ships. *U99* passed several wrecks burning after the Luftwaffe attack, but sighted nothing worth attacking. Finally, late on the night of 27 February, Kretschmer sighted the 4,223-ton British steamer SS *Holmlea*, which had straggled behind inbound convoy HX109, but missed with a single torpedo shot before losing the merchant ship in the thick mist. During the dark hours of the following morning *Holmlea* was found by Prien who damaged the ship with gunfire before a torpedo finished it off.

Prien and Kretschmer appeared to cross each other's paths regularly during this patrol, flashing Morse recognition signals and occasionally sailing close enough together to converse via megaphone as they carried on the hunt for enemy shipping. Luftwaffe aircraft from Norway reported sighting an outbound convoy east of Rockall Bank, but their position was reported as 'inexact' to BdU. Nonetheless, in response Dönitz ordered a patrol line established by an increasing number of converging U-boats:

> *U70, U108, U552, U95, U99, U47* are to take up reconnaissance lines from AL 3794 to 6259, at 1000 hrs. Two Italian boats are to extend the flanks. In this way, assuming a convoy speed of 9 knots, and if the course lies between 250° and 290°, the boats will be *ahead* of the convoy.[3]

It was an imprecise science, but logical as the assembled U-boats moved their line slowly east into the face of what was assumed to be outgoing traffic. The U-boats ordered to take part in this patrol line were each given an individual area, stationed at roughly equal distances of about seven nautical miles from each other, though this of course depended on the navigation officer's accuracy at determining the boat's position in what was frequently bad visibility. Dönitz intended to occupy as wide a strip of ocean as possible and *U99* remained in its allocated position for an entire day, keeping in contact with other U-boats and forced to dive eight times by destroyers and Sunderland flying boats.

However, either the Luftwaffe had been wildly in error regarding the location of the ships, or they had changed course, because the U-boats found only an empty horizon. Dönitz moved them slightly to the north, but it was not until the evening of 6 March that Prien once again transmitted a contact report, just south of Lousy Bank at the entrance to the North Channel: 'Enemy in sight. AM1452 north-westerly course. Speed eight knots.' Prien had found outbound OB293: thirty-seven ships, either in ballast or carrying trade goods, bound from Liverpool to North America.

Kretschmer was ordered by BdU to proceed at full speed to Prien's sighting, charging on the surface in intermittent visibility to the general area before submerging to use the greater detection range of the hydrophones. Prien was maintaining contact by proceeding in a series of spurts, before withdrawing once more, to ensure that he followed the course of the convoy. *U99* sighted *U47* at about 1800 hrs on 6 March, but was again forced to dive by British destroyers emerging from the mist at a distance of about 1,000 metres and heading straight for them. As the U-boat descended the screws were heard passing overhead more than once, with a scattering of depth charges nearby but none of any danger to *U99*. *U47* later resurfaced to report the boat attacked with depth charges, before heading back into action against OB293.

At 0424 hrs on 7 March, Prien signalled once more the speed, position and course of the convoy before attacking. Forty minutes later two torpedoes hit the 20,638-ton British whaling factory ship *Terje Viken*, credited to Prien in *U47*, although according to the exhaustive research completed by German historian Axel Niestle, possibly fired by Kaptlt. Joachim Matz in *U70*, who believed that he had missed with a fan shot of three torpedoes. The huge ship was the largest vessel of its kind in the world, and was being used as a tanker, but travelling in ballast on this voyage. The first torpedo hit on the starboard side approximately thirty metres from the bow, passing through the ship and holing it also on the port side. Immediately afterwards the second torpedo struck the ship slightly forward of the first, exploded and completely wrecked the forward hold. Meanwhile, of Prien there was no more sign.

What exactly happened to Günther Prien and the crew of *U47* remains unknown to this day. Originally, he was claimed as sunk by HMS *Wolverine* on 8 March, but we now know for certain that in fact the boat depth-charged severely was the oddity *UA*, commanded by Fregattenkapitän Hans Eckermann. This large U-boat had originally been built for Turkey but entered Kriegsmarine service at the outbreak of war. Though *UA* was damaged, Eckermann successfully returned to Lorient after briefly acting as weather boat further to the west. *U47* disappeared, lost somewhere near OB293, possibly to depth charges, floating mines that had broken lose from defensive minefields and not been rendered safe, a diving accident as a result of the new and inexperienced crew aboard, or, the most popular theory and one to which Otto Kretschmer also subscribed, a victim of its own torpedo. If the gyroscope failed within an active torpedo it would likely begin to circle and become a danger to the U-boat that fired it. Somewhere, thousands of metres below the surface in this area, the wreck of *U47* lies undisturbed on the seabed and is unlikely ever to give up the secret of what caused its destruction.

Meanwhile, Kretschmer had caught up with OB293 – helped by the Very lights being fired by ships already attacked and on fire – and he tried immediately to break through the visible destroyer screen and get amongst the merchant columns to use his favourite tactic.

When I approached a convoy which had been shadowed, then it was quite simple. During the night, find out where the escorts were. That was very easy and I went on to penetrate the screen on the surface, and I got in. And, of course I knew, or expected really, all of them had come across the ocean already, that they were tired and also the merchant ships in the convoy, they were tired, and they would not be on the alert all the time and so, the point was to try to think what the enemy was thinking and then make decisions.

So I went into the convoy and was able to pick out the best targets, the largest ships, the tankers for instance, and shoot from short distance only one torpedo. A well-aimed torpedo at point-blank range. And so it saves torpedoes and if the ships did not sink, and normally they don't because it takes them at least one hour until all the holds are full of water and they then sink, so I could wait for an hour and leave the convoy and find my targets that were not sinking astern of the rest of the convoy. Some had been hit and sunk immediately and [the others] I was able to sink by gunfire, so I spared torpedoes and so was able to sink more ships in one patrol than other submarines.

Kretschmer closed the convoy's starboard column, approaching two ships that had already been damaged by torpedoes: the *Terje Viken* and the 6,568-ton British cargo ship MV *Athelbeach* hit by torpedoes from Matz in *U70*. Both were proceeding slowly but showed no sign of going under and so *U99* fired torpedoes at close range around 0640 hrs, hitting *Terje Viken* on the port side and *Athelbeach* in the stern, which brought it to a halt. Despite the heaving seas, Kretschmer ordered his gun manned and proceeded to pump shells towards the damaged *Athelbeach*, though most missed in the long troughs and peaks of the swell. Apparently Kretschmer was angered at what he considered bad gunnery, no doubt bemoaning the loss of Horst Elfe to another boat, and before long some wild shots began to be returned from the drifting freighter. Kretschmer opted to end the encounter and fired a third torpedo, which hit the ship's stern and capsized it and sent it to the bottom. *Athelbeach*'s master, Malcolm McIntyre, and six crew members were lost, while thirty-seven survivors were later rescued by the corvette HMS *Camellia* and landed at Greenock.

The drifting whale factory ship had also been disabled though Kretschmer had moved some distance away while attempting to finish the cargo ship with gunfire. Once *Athelbeach* turned over, *U99* returned to where he had left *Terje Viken*, which had been abandoned. A part of the crew rejoined their vessel to determine whether there was any hope of saving the huge ship, but it was too far gone and they once again took to their boats. Half an hour later, the great vessel slowly capsized, remaining a drifting wreck for a week before it was shelled by a British salvage tug and sunk on 14 March. Two of the crew had been killed in the attack, but the remaining 105 survivors were recovered by the destroyer HMS *Hurricane* and returned to Greenock. The *Terje Viken* was the largest ship attributed to Kretschmer and the fourth largest vessel listed as sunk by U-boat during the Second World War.

But Kretschmer had no time to rest on his laurels. Enemy destroyers were hard on his heels and both he and Matz were coming under extreme pressure. *U99* had fallen behind the convoy while finishing the two ships, no longer hidden amongst the merchantmen and distinctly vulnerable to counter attacks from 'sweepers' trailing the formation. It had begun to grow unpleasantly light and Matz's *U70* was briefly sighted passing across *U99*'s bows as he attempted to regain contact with OB293. Matz had already reported a damaged conning tower from being rammed by the Dutch tanker *Mijdrecht* after *U70* had hit it with a torpedo, but he was determined to continue his attack and expend all torpedoes. The boat's tower was badly dented aft, the direction finder had been ripped away, both periscopes put out of action and everything on the bridge smashed. Though the lights barely flickered within the U-boat interior, the crew later described the U-boat as having rolled over on one side, as though struck by a huge wave. Nevertheless, no internal damage or pressure hull breach had been caused except a single stream of water, over two inches in diameter, entering the boat through the broken shaft leading to where the direction finder had been.

Aboard *U99* a petty officer on watch reported a mast ahead on the starboard bow, Knebel-Döberitz ordering a sharp watch maintained on this mast when, unexpectedly, what they thought was an 'old-type destroyer' broke from out of a rain squall making directly for *U99*. A pair of corvettes were approaching rapidly and both *U99* and *U70* made rapid alarm dives to escape, Matz continuing his course while Kretschmer moved under the drifting wreckage of *Terje Viken*. For Matz it was too late to evade as corvettes HMS *Arbutus* and *Camellia* hounded *U70* with depth charges. A chaotic uncontrolled descent that exceeded 200 metres was only checked by both electric motors set at full speed ahead, hydroplanes on maximum rise and all tanks blown. *U47* would not be the only boat lost that day: Matz's *U70* broke the surface and came under immediate fire before sinking; twenty-five of the crew, including Matz, were rescued by their attackers. However, neither the loss of *U47* nor *U70* was able to be confirmed immediately by the Germans as Kretschmer, though nearby when *U70* was sunk, did not witness or hear the boat being destroyed. Dönitz hoped that the reason for their sudden absence of signals was a disabled wireless transmitter, a problem that *U47* had reported while outbound. Eventually the fate of *U70* was confirmed but Prien's boat was not officially declared lost until 26 April when there was no chance of the boat still being at sea. Feldpost number 18837 was no longer accepting correspondence. However, so great was the likely blow to German national morale that his loss was not publicly acknowledged until 23 May 1941.

Kretschmer escaped severe retaliation, though his crew counted at least fifty-one depth charges dropped on them over a period of nine hours in numerous attacks at twenty or thirty-minute intervals. The first and second attacks sent the U-boat reeling, though they became gradually less focussed as Kretschmer hid under the drifting hulk and amidst the turbulence created by the depth charges themselves. The ensuing charges appear to have exploded either some distance from or above the U-boat, which suffered no damage and managed to evade a firm ASDIC lock. As the attackers faded away, Kretschmer ordered all tubes reloaded and eventually resurfaced to an empty sea.

By 12 March, Dönitz was lamenting the thinning of his North Atlantic attack force by cumulative damage or reassignment to the wearisome weather reporting demanded by SKL on behalf of the greater Wehrmacht war machine.

> *UA* was forced to begin the return passage owing to depth charge damage; *U37* has taken over as weather boat. The fantastic position therefore arises whereby of four boats stationed in the northern operational area (*U74*, *U99*, *U37*, *U95*) two are detailed for weather service and therefore at a great disadvantage while one of these is even at sea without torpedoes exclusively for

meteorological work. *U70* and *U47* are not taken into consideration here.

For days *U99* patrolled an empty ocean while more U-boats put to sea to join the North Atlantic patrol lines, amongst them Schepke's *U100* which had departed Kiel on Sunday 9 March to return to action, though delayed by medical issues and mechanical breakdown in Brunsbüttel for three days. Finally, on 15 March, Kaptlt. Lemp in his new boat *U110* reported an eastbound convoy south of Iceland in quadrant AE7983. The sighting re-energised an exhausting period of boredom aboard *U99* of the sort which could dangerously dull the senses. Kretschmer requested a beacon signal the following day from *U110* and Dönitz vectored as many U-boats as he judged to be within the immediate vicinity towards an interception point for Halifax convoy HX112. Commanded by Rear Admiral Burges Watson, HX112 was an eastbound North Atlantic slow convoy of forty-one merchant ships whose ocean escort was heavy cruiser HMS *Norfolk* and auxiliary merchant cruiser HMS *Ranpura*, handing over to the local escort of 5th Escort Group – HMS *Walker, Vanoc, Volunteer, Bluebell* and *Hydrangea* – and augmented by reinforcements HMS *Sardonyx and Scimitar*. Lemp immediately attacked and at 2320 hrs destroyer HMS *Volunteer*, steaming in the port wing position of the escort screen, detected on its hydrophones the fast propeller of an inbound torpedo, which duly struck the motor tanker *Erodona* and set its cargo of fuel ablaze, killing thirty-six of the fifty-seven crew. The G7a torpedo track was visible from the destroyer, which traced it back to the presumed firing position accompanied by HMS *Vanoc* but failed to find *U110*. However, though *Vanoc* subsequently returned to HX112, *Volunteer* was unable to find the convoy in the prevailing thick weather as it possessed no radar. Though the attention of the destroyers forced Lemp away and he temporarily lost contact, he had also robbed HX112 of one escort vessel. At 1220 hrs *U37* also sighted the enemy in Quadrant AE8793 and sent beacon signals for the remaining U-boats and at 1920 hrs *U99* reported that it too had made contact, but only after a position request from BdU.

Kretschmer had arrived at the convoy's reported position but initially found nothing, a dive to sweep the area with hydrophones pinpointing the merchant-ship propellers to the south. *U99* surfaced again and raced through drifting fog banks towards the expected convoy.

On the 16th I was trailing the convoy HX112 after Lemp (*U110*)
had discovered the convoy the night before, had attacked and
given exact position signals, so that I could come down from the
vicinity of Iceland. The weather was misty with bad visibility
during the night. Therefore, I had to dive [while] still on my
southerly course from Iceland in order to find the convoy with my
passive sonar. Lemp's navigation had been so correct that I soon
found myself in the midst of the convoy – ships all around me. So
I surfaced, only to discover that I popped up between a port escort
and the first line of the convoy proper. Diving immediately, I let
the convoy pass over me and surfaced a safe distance at the rear,
then trailed during the daylight of the 16th when the visibility
improved very much so that we could detect Sunderlands before
they saw us. This meant diving and surfacing all the time.
On the starboard side of the convoy I could see two destroyers
attacking a submarine underwater with depth charges [original
emphasis]. This made me change from the rear to the port side
of the convoy to a station (surfaced) behind the horizon (as seen
from the convoy).[4]

Kretschmer manoeuvred carefully to achieve a position from which
to launch his night attack, keeping the mastheads of the convoy in
sight until darkness fell, the distant sound of depth charges still echoing
through the water. Finally, after hours of preparation, Kretschmer
brought *U99* racing towards the convoy and slipped between two escorts
on the port wing before he began a string of attacks, targeting the largest
ships that he could find.

Knowing nothing so far of Schepke's position I guessed that
the attacked submarine was *U110* (Lemp). At dusk, the convoy
changed course to starboard, now heading for the North Minch.
At nightfall I attacked, penetrating the escort screen and shooting
from inside the convoy – as usual. Travelling with the convoy
in one of its lanes, I managed to sink six [*sic*] merchant ships
(starting with the tanker *Ferm* which went ablaze, and ending
just after midnight with the Swedish motor vessel *Korshamn*.[5]

Norwegian MV *Ferm* was indeed struck in the bow shortly before
midnight, the explosion causing huge fires to break out as it began to

list to port and sink by the bow. The explosion was so impressive that Knebel-Döberitz later told interrogators that 'a sheet of flame shot out of the tanker turning the night into daylight'. Almost miraculously, all thirty-five men aboard survived the blast and abandoned ship in three boats, to be picked up shortly afterwards by corvette HMS *Bluebell*. The corvette's captain, Lieutenant-Commander Robert Evan Sherwood, RNR, asked the 61-year-old Norwegian master, Bernt Anton Thorbjørnsen, whether there was any chance of reboarding the damaged ship and attempting to save it, but Thorbjørnsen and his entire crew considered the risks too great: the holds were filled with fuel oil and flames still raged unabated aboard the ship. Instead, the Norwegians recommended an Admiralty tug be despatched to examine the drifting wreck; the drifting MV *Ferm* was subsequently taken in tow but sank on 21 March. Meanwhile, some of the Norwegian crew had volunteered to go aboard the damaged tanker *Franche-Comté* and assisted its safe passage to port.

The 5,728-ton SS *Venetia* carrying 7,052 tons of maize from Baltimore to London was hit by a torpedo fired at an oblique angle and sunk. Master Alexander Mitchell and his crew of thirty-seven plus two gunners were all rescued by HMS *Bluebell*, while 9,314-ton Admiralty motor tanker MT *Franche-Comté* was also hit and damaged by a single torpedo, although Kretschmer believed the ship left in a sinking condition. Aboard Canadian steamer SS *J. B. White*, Master J. W. R. Woodward clearly saw a U-boat on his starboard beam inside the body of the convoy and turned the 7,375-ton freighter to ram as a torpedo streaked ahead of the ship's bow. However, seconds later a second and a third torpedo slammed into the hull and the ship, carrying 2,500 tons of steel and 4,500 tons of newsprint, was doomed. Able Seaman Charles Goodwin and Boatswain Jack Henry Visser were both killed, but Woodward and the remaining thirty-seven crew abandoned ship and were picked up shortly afterwards by HMS *Walker*.

A second Norwegian ship was also hit by Kretschmer: 8,136-ton motor tanker MV *Beduin*, was struck astern of the pump room, the explosion so powerful that the deck plates were blown upwards and left standing vertically twenty feet in the air, while the fore and aft gangway disappeared. All lights throughout the ship went out and the engines immediately stopped, though there was fortunately no outbreak of fire. With the convoy already under attack, the ship's master, Hans Hansen, had ordered most of the crew to remain near lifeboat stations while he, Third Mate Hans Johan Hansen and three crew manned the bridge. The order was rapidly given to abandon ship, four men being killed in the attack, at least two of them overcome with strong leaking gas fumes from the 11,000 tons of petroleum cargo. Even those in the lifeboats began to feel the effect of the gas and rowed to windward as rapidly as possible to escape the fumes.

As the survivors drew away, they saw the hull of their ship begin to break in two, the lifeboats still within a spreading pool of petrol and at great danger in the event of fire beginning aboard the stricken tanker. By morning the survivors could see the *Beduin*'s bow standing vertically in the air, drifting almost a mile away from the stern. On 19 March, the bow was finally sunk after being shelled by a British trawler; the stern had been taken in tow by the tug HMS *St Olaves* on 18 March, but also sank within two days. The lifeboats and their occupants were finally recovered by trawlers on 18 March, many treated in hospital after having sustained burns from being sprayed with highly corrosive petroleum.

The final victim of Kretschmer's near perfect convoy attack was 6,673-ton Swedish MV *Korshamn*, hit and sunk by torpedo. Twenty-five of Master S. Lantz's crew were killed in the destruction of their ship, which was carrying a full load of 7,979 tons of general cargo to Liverpool from New York. The large merchant ship sagged in the middle and snapped in two, seeming to alter course towards the attacking *U99* in a final defiant attempt to ram.

Of his shots fired, Kretschmer missed with only a single torpedo and had fired one other that turned out to be a dud. Though he had raced at high speed on the surface along the merchant columns, often fully exposed in the light of burning ships and exploding torpedoes, he had rarely been glimpsed as escort ships fired star shells outwards from the convoy body, oblivious to the presence of a U-boat within.

Within *U99* there was jubilation at their successful attack, the single most successful convoy attack of their career thus far. As radio messages from some of the stricken ships confirmed their identities and their tonnage was collated for the war diary, the claimed tally by about 0300 hrs on Monday, 17 March, amounted to 59,000 tons for this single night's action. The total claimed for the entire patrol was a record-breaking 86,000 tons. The reality was short of these expectations but was still impressive. In total, *U99* had sunk five ships totalling 34,505 tons from HX112 and damaged another of 9,314 tons. The entire patrol's successes added up to a staggering 61,711 tons of enemy shipping sunk in twenty-four days at sea. The crew considered their achievement to be unique within the U-boat service. With no torpedoes remaining, Kretschmer decided to return to Lorient and ordered course laid for home, while fighting still raged around HX112.

> Having spent all my torpedoes, I left the convoy on a northerly course, because in the west I suspected a minefield on the Lousy Bank, having seen some floating mines. This course to the north and then safe of the bank to the west brought me into the attack group consisting of the destroyers *Walker* and *Vanoc* under the command of Commander Donald Macintyre in HMS *Walker still chasing a submarine which turned out to be U100 (Schepke)* [original emphasis].[6]

Schepke's *U100* was in deep trouble. The boat had reached the convoy on the evening of Sunday 16 March, and sighted escort HMS *Scimitar* astern while attempting to close the merchant formation. Diving, *U100* remained submerged for about one hour before surfacing into darkness. Shortly afterward while closing the convoy once more, another destroyer was sighted, and Schepke crash-dived and was briefly depth-charged, though the destroyers lost all contact and *U100* later surfaced unscathed astern of the convoy. However, to the German lookouts' dismay, the merchant ships had managed to distance themselves from *U100* by making an emergency turn to starboard and back to port an hour later, the long-legged zig-zag having left the submerged boat behind. As Schepke raced to pull ahead of the convoy once more HMS *Walker* sighted the small fluorescent wash created by the U-boat at 0048 hrs, immediately turning to ram and forcing Schepke to crash-dive once more.

A second pattern of ten depth charges was dropped on medium settings, at least half of them exploding near the U-boat's hull, damaging the depth gauge and smashing lightbulbs. Contact was briefly lost before *Walker* relocated *U100*, summoning Commander J. G. W. Deneys's HMS *Vanoc* to join the hunt. With Macintyre directing from *Walker*'s bridge, *Vanoc* dropped six depth charges set at 350, 250 and 150 feet. This time the damage was considerable: all pumps were put out of action, instruments smashed, floor plates wrenched loose and water began entering the bilges while the hydroplanes no longer appeared functional. The boat's supply of compressed air ruptured, causing an unpleasant increase in internal pressure within the boat and soon nearly exhausting the storage tanks. Schepke was convinced that the British above would hear the noise of the escaping air and indeed, aboard *Vanoc*, a hydrophone operator reported a distinct 'noise of a bubbling nature' while men on deck smelt the distinct odour of diesel oil from the U-boat's ruptured fuel cells.[7]

While HMS *Vanoc* continued the hunt, Commander Macintyre took HMS *Walker* towards distress signals coming from drifting lifeboats, finding the thirty-eight survivors from *J. B. White*. After getting the lifeboats alongside, they had to be hurriedly slipped once again when the destroyer's ASDIC operator reported a contact, though this was soon found to be 'non-sub' and *Walker* continued to embark the remaining Canadian survivors. Once they were secured, HMS *Walker* returned to the scene of *Vanoc*'s continuing hunt.

In the meantime, the disabled *U100* had sunk deeper into the depths reaching 230 metres before Schepke ordered what little remained of their compressed air to blow tanks and bring the boat to the surface. Though the torpedo tubes were not yet ready for action, he had little choice and crew men remembering him voicing the hope that he could at least attempt to torpedo one of his attackers.

As *U100* broke the surface, lookouts scrambled on to the conning tower and sighted HMS *Vanoc* at no more than 500 metres. Aboard the destroyer Deneys had brought his ship to 15 knots in order to join *Walker* for a coordinated hunt for their wounded quarry. The radar operator immediately reported a contact to starboard at 1,000 yards, steering slowly from right to left. Schepke became flustered when his diesels refused to fire, then found trouble with the electric motors which finally came to life, the young captain ordering astern on the starboard motor, when he should have ordered ahead. He quickly realised his mistake, but there was no time to correct it and bring the U-boat into a firing position. HMS *Vanoc* was moving at sufficient speed for ramming and the wheel had been thrown hard over, to close fast on the virtually stationary boat. For a moment Schepke saw a glimmer of hope, shouting 'It's all right, the destroyer is going to pass under our stern' through the conning tower hatch before he suddenly recognised his error and that the boat's position was hopeless and ordered his men to prepare to abandon ship. Moments before impact the destroyer's engines were stopped and seconds later the destroyer's bow hit *U100* almost at right angles to the conning tower, running up and over *U100* which passed beneath 'B' gun. The hull flank of *U100* and its conning tower were stove in by the impact; Schepke was caught and crushed between the smashed side of his bridge and the periscope housing. Flister, the officer under instruction, was standing immediately behind his captain and later told British interrogators that Schepke was wedged in place and dragged under by the sinking U-boat. Flister was also caught up in the twisted guard rail of the after part of the bridge and pulled underwater as *U100* sank but managed to free himself and got to the surface. Kretschmer later praised Schepke's actions in remaining on the bridge during the action which killed him.

> Schepke himself did not leave the bridge of *U100* for two reasons:
> 1. He had to con his boat up to the last moment trying to avoid the ram.
> 2. By tradition the captain must stay at his post until his ship sinks under his feet (as I did on the bridge of *U99*).
>
> Half a year or so later Lemp, the captain of *U110*, acted against this rule and left his command before the boat sank with the terrible result that the enemy entered *U110* and seized all the secret documents including the coding machine, which meant the beginning of the end of the successful U-boat operations.[8]

On the other side of the hill, Petty Officer Telegraphist Walter Edney was aboard *Vanoc* during the brief battle.

> After a little more than a mile, the silhouette of a U-boat could be seen on the surface, so without hesitation our Captain gave the order to 'Stand by to Ram'. This we did, in no uncertain manner, at full speed, hitting the U-boat amidships and toppling her over. It brought *Vanoc* to a sudden standstill, embedded in the U-boat which was only cleared by both engines, full astern. The U-boat rose high in the air and sank, the Captain still on the bridge wearing his white cap but badly injured went down with her. There were few survivors, just five from a crew of fifty who had probably jumped overboard before the collision . . . We

next swept the surface of the waters with our searchlight in order to pick up survivors. I well remember and will do so always, the cries of those men in the icy waters: '*Kamerad*'. In my youth, my bitterness towards them was extreme. They had sunk our ships and many of our seamen drowned at sea. Their air force (the Luftwaffe) had bombed our cities relentlessly killing thousands of innocent civilians. I just had to shout, 'Leave them there.' Fortunately, perhaps, the older members of our crew had more compassion and pulled up the side as many as they could, before the next alarm. It had amounted to just five, one officer and four men.[9]

Aboard HMS *Vanoc* there was jubilation. Despite the ship's ASDIC dome being wrecked by the impact leaving a leak in the ASDIC compartment through the training unit, there was relatively little damage. The keel had been cut away from the stem to Number 11 bulkhead and Number 2 store was holed, but *Vanoc* was in no danger and the destroyer immediately began to rescue German survivors, who, according to Flister, were in good spirits despite the loss of their boat through knowing their enemy was preparing to pull them from the water. Six had been hauled from the water when the situation became 'somewhat awkward and confused'.[10] A second U-boat had appeared out of nowhere only 1,000 yards away and HMS *Walker* had opened fire.

> Whilst recovering these survivors, the *Walker* ASDIC operator reported a U-boat echo, which, on investigation, placed it directly under our stern (where we were stopped, recovering survivors). There was only one answer, to get away quickly and depth charge, which we did, followed by a run over the spot by HMS *Walker* who also dropped a bank of depth charges. Any further swimmers that may have been in the water (and there were some) could not possibly have survived this fierce attack. After a short while, a U-boat surfaced just astern of us, so close that it was necessary to move out of the way fairly quickly for fear of being torpedoed or fired upon.[11]

Following the expenditure of all of his torpedoes, Kretschmer had ordered course set for the north of Lousy Bank and went below to discuss the events of the patrol with Kassel and Hesselbarth in order to complete the boat's war diary. Accounts of the sinking say that Petersen had taken command of the watch and at 0300 hrs was ordering coffee and sandwiches brought to the men in their oilskins as they scanned the horizon. It is difficult to verify exactly who was in charge of the watch when HMS *Walker* was sighted. It is entirely possible that Petersen was there as IIWO but his experience and coolness under pressure – plus the fact that he was extremely familiar with Kretschmer's methods at sea – seem at odds with a hurried crash dive. Some accounts state that 'the *Obersteuermann*' was on watch, and perhaps by this they mean Obersteuermann Rudolf Ellrich, an inexperienced IIIWO more likely to be rattled by the sudden appearance of an enemy destroyer and whose orthodox U-boat training would be more likely to recommend diving. Unfortunately, none of the protagonists are with us any more to provide a definitive answer. But perhaps it is enough to know that Kretschmer blamed the inexperience of some of his crew for the decision to submerge rather than follow his standing orders as suddenly alarm bells rang throughout the boat and the bow immediately began to tilt downward. The watch officer had ordered an emergency dive.

> Through the fault of my starboard forward lookout, a petty officer, who had not seen anything of the approaching HMS *Walker*, we had almost run into the destroyer. Only the vigilance of the officer on watch, who from time to time took a look around covering also the quarter of the petty officer, saved the boat from that fate, but unfortunately, he sounded [the] diving alarm in contrast to my standing order not to dive in such a situation, but to show the stern with high speed and call me onto the bridge, whereupon I would take command of the situation. So, the boat became stationary in the midst of the hunting destroyers. *U99* got a full load of depth charges from HMS *Walker* which brought an inrush of water and sent the boat dropping like a stone.[12]

HMS *Walker* had been circling HMS *Vanoc* in order to provide anti-submarine protection while the latter picked up survivors from *U100*. At 0337 hrs *Walker* obtained an ASDIC contact, though Macintyre was sceptical at first.

> I was electrified to hear the ASDIC operator, AB Backhouse, excitedly reporting 'Contact! Contact!' But I could hardly credit

it, for not only was it unbelievable that in all the wide wastes of the Atlantic a second U-boat should turn up just where another had gone to the bottom, but I knew that there were sure to be areas of disturbed water persisting in the vicinity from our own and *Vanoc*'s wakes. The echo was not very clear and I expressed my doubts to John Langton, but Backhouse was not to be disheartened. 'Contact definitely submarine,' he reported, and as I listened to the ping the echo sharpened and there could be no further doubt. With a warning to the men aft to get any charges ready that they had managed to hoist into the throwers and rails, we ran into the attack. It was a great test for John Langton for, with the maddening habit of the beautiful instruments of precision provided for us, they all elected to break down at the crucial moment. But much patient drill against just such an emergency now brought its reward. Timing his attack by the most primitive of methods, Langton gave the order to fire. A pattern of six depth charges – all that could be got ready in time – went down. As they exploded, *Walker* ran on to get sea-room to turn for further attacks, but as we turned, came the thrilling signal from *Vanoc* – 'U-boat surfaced astern of me.'[13]

The crew of *U99* heard the distinctive sound of the destroyer's propellers passing directly overhead, before the dreaded explosions came; six of them, thought by the Germans to have exploded beneath the keel of their boat, which had sunk to a depth of 120 metres. Gauges were smashed, the boat rocked violently, buffeted by what Kretschmer knew were the closest depth charges he had ever experienced. Deeper and deeper *U99* plunged, the gauge measuring 140 metres and still sinking, hull plates groaning as they passed well below the official crush depth of a Type VIIB hull. Kretschmer registered the boat as having reached at least 185 metres, before it was confirmed by Schröder that the electric motors were disabled, the propellers no longer turning and *U99* incapable of maintaining its place in the water column. The boat had a pronounced list and water had begun to enter through the aft torpedo room hull and fractured pipes. Fuel had also begun to leak into the boat and the hull groaned ominously as it threatened to collapse finally. There was no longer any alternative; *U99* would either sink into oblivion or attempt one last blow with compressed air – while the tanks remained undamaged by the depth charges – to reach the surface whereupon it would be at the mercy of the warships above.

Kretschmer ordered the main ballast tanks blown with compressed air and Obermaschinist Artur Popp tugged at the levers that controlled the venting of air into the tanks. For several heart-stopping seconds the lever remained stuck fast until Popp, with assistance from another man in the control room, gradually managed to crack the valve open. Compressed air whistled through pipes into the ballast tanks and Petersen's robotic reciting of the boat's depth finally showed *U99* slowing before beginning an ascent. An almost half-hearted attempt to stop their ascent before surfacing failed to have any impact as *U99* rocketed through the water and rose nose first into fresh Atlantic air before crashing down to lie motionless on the surface. As was the custom for such events, Kretschmer led the way out of the conning tower hatch. His intention was to attempt to run for it, but Petersen immediately reported the steering gear out of action as well as electric motors. While Knebel-Döberitz swung the manual steering gear into its ready position, news reached the conning tower that virtually everything, including the fuel tanks, had been disabled.

> Before the final crush (the electrical motors were out of action) I got to the surface with compressed air where the boat lay with a list to starboard in a pool of diesel oil. I could not get away because also the diesel engine would not do it (shaft or propeller trouble). *Forward I saw a destroyer (later known to be HMS* Vanoc) *stopped, picking up survivors (as I found out later) of U100* [original emphasis] until they discovered me and after a gun shot came round to some distance off my port side together with HMS *Walker* who had been at my starboard quarter some distance away – both firing at me with all they had, 4-inch guns and 40 mm pompoms. *Both still thought they were firing at U100 as Donald Macintyre later told me. HMS* Vanoc *had rammed U100 and sunk it thereby killing Schepke. The greater part of the crew was in the water swimming to the stopped HMS* Vanoc, *some of them making jokes when U99* popped up and was discovered by HMS *Vanoc* who *stopped picking up survivors (five had already been saved)* and moved away to fight *U99*, which they thought was *U100*, having come to the surface again. This was told to

me by Korvettenkapitän Siegfried Flister, the only officer who survived and stayed together with me at Cockfosters Camp and No. 1 Camp at Grizedale Hall in the Lake District . . . He was on board *U100* as . . . *Konfirmand*.[14]

Aboard *Vanoc* there was momentary confusion. Survivors from *U100* were still in the water swimming around the destroyer's propellers when *U99* was sighted, Deneys immediately guessing that Kretschmer was about to fire torpedoes. With HMS *Walker* beyond the U-boat, but still in the line of fire, they could not bring guns to bear and he had no alternative but to bring his ship ahead and to port with the intention of providing *Walker* with a clear field of fire. No more survivors from *U100* were ever found. Unfortunately, Macintyre aboard *Walker* also turned to port, and both ships were forced to stop in order to avoid collision. Deneys then ordered full ahead and both destroyers at last opened fire on *U99* at 0354 hrs, but ceased two minutes later.

At this point, reliable witnesses aboard *Walker* reported sighting a third U-boat astern:

> When *U99* was brought to the surface by *Walker*, I saw a destroyer (*Vanoc*) with its broad silhouette lying stopped at a distance of half a mile directly ahead of me. My engines were out of order, all my torpedoes were spent earlier during the night, *U99* lay with a list to starboard in a pond of oil. But if I had only a single torpedo left I certainly could have sunk HMS *Vanoc*, the other destroyer being farther away on my starboard quarter so that he could not have interfered. Of course, I had some shells for the gun left, but with the list it was virtually impossible to man it. The immediate firing by the destroyers made it also impossible to man the gun which was enveloped by tracer shells from the pompoms. Of course, at the time I had no idea that *Vanoc* was about to pick up survivors from *U100*. Fate could have taken another turn. Flister told me in the interrogation camp at Cockfosters that the greater part of the crew of *U100* were in a comparatively good mood when they realised that *Vanoc* was picking up survivors. Some of them suggested having a race towards the side of the destroyer which, however, stopped the operation when *U99* was discovered on the surface.[15]

Kretschmer's boat was doomed. There was absolutely no chance to escape or fire back and the crew were ordered to put on lifebelts and make their way above decks. Kretschmer shouted confirmation to his men that the boat was going down and both Knebel-Döberitz and Schröder agreed that it would remain afloat for perhaps another ten or fifteen minutes, beginning to open valves and hatches to make certain that it would go down. As Knebel-Döberitz made his way forward, he suddenly heard splashing in the control room, and saw a thick stream of water entering through the conning tower hatch. Spurred onward, he climbed the ladder into fresh air and found that the whole crew had gathered together on the bridge and deck.

> As Donald Macintyre has told me, they stopped firing because there was the acute danger of hitting each other in the heat of battle. They had not hit my boat with their guns. Of course, there were many water spouts around my boat and many far over. Their 40 mm pompom shells with their sensitive anti-aircraft fuses did damage only to the paint. They fired from my port side and my boat had a considerable list to starboard so that no shell could explode on the bridge. My order STAND BY TO ABANDON SHIP [original emphasis] could be followed without danger as the men could hide on the bridge and on the sheltered side (starboard side) of the conning tower. Well after the firing had stopped, my aftermost (No. 1) ballast tank which had apparently been damaged by the depth charges, slowly flooded again so that the stern submerged until the water got into the boat through the conning tower hatch. But in the meantime, the engineering officer who together with the first lieutenant was down in the boat, had blown the ballast tanks with the rest of the compressed air. The result: the stern came up again after I had got the two officers through the inrushing water back onto the bridge. But about half of the ship's company, i.e. those who had been standing on the upper deck, were washed overboard. I saw their heads sticking out above the waves, keeping together in accordance with my order in case of sinking and drifting in the direction of one of the destroyers. [Drifting is incorrect insofar as the men were stationary but the ships drifted before the wind.] As the captain is responsible for the life and well-being of his

ship's company in peace and war, I decided to make a signal for their rescue to the captain of the destroyer. As I was the only one on board who was confident in the English language, I spelled the words to the Morse lamp operator: 'From captain to captain: Please save my men drifting in your direction. I am sinking.' (Meaning that I cannot save them myself because I am sinking.) Donald Macintyre in his book states that my operator made a mistake ('sunking' instead of 'sinking'), but HMS *Walker* acknowledged every word, lit his starboard signal searchlight and took them aboard over the scrambling nets.[16]

A final radio message had been despatched in plain language, while the Enigma machine and its code books were thrown overboard. It was not received by any land-based listening stations, but instead was picked up by both *U46* and *U37* and relayed onwards to Lorient. There remains some discrepancy in various accounts of *U99*'s last battle about what exactly was received, so we shall defer to what was recorded by BdU in the last sheet of Kretschmer's typed war diaries. It is believed that both Knebel-Döberitz and Kassel added words to the message actually transmitted by Funkmaat Otto Stohrer, which is recorded as saying: 'Bombed, boat sunk, Heil Hitler. Kretschmer 2 destroyers, 53 tons.' ('*Bomben, Boot versenkt, Heil Hitler. Kretschmer 2 Zerstörer, 53 Tonnen.*')

Once the British ceased fire they withdrew slightly, laying end-on lest the U-boat still prove to be dangerous. Merchant seamen who had been rescued from the SS *J. B. White* had assisted the Royal Navy gunners and in their enthusiasm excess piles of ammunition lay near the destroyer's guns in case firing resumed. Macintyre briefly considered sending a boat possibly to effect a capture, or at least search of the disabled U-boat, but before long the option was removed as *U99* went down.

Aboard the listing U-boat, Kretschmer – now seen to be smoking one of his ever-present cigars – had ordered scuttling charges set, though crewmen reported that access to the compartment in which the explosives were stored was impossible. The U-boat lay noticeably stern-down once again as water continued entering the boat but was refusing to sink and so Schröder offered to go below and flood the ballast tanks and ensure *U99* sank. It is believed that he also opened the galley hatch but as the rest of the crew bobbed in the water, the stern suddenly sank, *U99*'s bow rising out of the water as Kretschmer shouted for

Schröder to join him on the conning tower. Kretschmer heard no reply as water rapidly flooded through open hatches, though some crewmen recall hearing Schröder shout something inaudible as the boat sank. Kretschmer suddenly found his feet no longer on the solid deck plates of his conning tower but in mid water when *U99* rapidly disappeared from beneath him. Schröder was never seen again and went to the bottom with his boat, to be posthumously awarded the German Cross in Gold on 19 March 1942.

HMS *Walker* moved to windward of the swimming Germans, allowing the ship to drift on to them as scrambling nets were lowered. Gradually the U-boat men clambered aboard, some in the last stages of exhaustion as the cold Atlantic took its toll on their stamina. Willing British hands pulled them aboard, Leading Seaman Albert Edward Prout jumping in to the water fully clothed to assist those who could not manage to pull themselves from the sea. Kassel was thought to be dead when he was dragged aboard, but the slightest trace of life was detected and he was thawed in the warmth of the ship's galley, making a full recovery and later acting as an interpreter for the enlisted prisoners from *U99*. Two men of Schröder's engine room crew were not found: Maschinengefreiters Heinz Schneider and Herbert Löffler. One of the unfortunate men lost his lifebelt and could not swim while the other had apparently suffered concussion during the attack and fell from the scrambling net, never to resurface.

Kretschmer was the last to leave the water and when it was finally his turn to climb the nets he found his seaboots so full of water and his limbs so tired that he could not move. Unaware on the bridge that he was still hanging below, HMS *Walker* had begun to get under way and Kretschmer was increasingly buffeted by the wake before being spotted and dragged aboard by Stabsbootsmann Gerhard Thoenes (*Seemännische Nr. 1*, equivalent to a Royal Navy coxswain) with help from a British sailor, flopped on the deck still wearing his cap and with his prized Zeiss binoculars around his neck. His mind rapidly clearing despite the nervous exhaustion and effects of a chilling sea, Kretschmer moved to throw his binoculars overboard but was stopped by Sub-Lieutenant Peter Sturdee, who immediately relieved him of this valuable prize which was passed up to Macintyre on the bridge.

Kretschmer was escorted to Macintyre's day cabin with his officers where they stripped off their wet clothes and were provided with dry clothing and tots of rum to recover their dulled circulation. It was not only for the prisoners' health that their wet things were taken away, but for the opportunity to remove every scrap of personal material that could be found stuffed carelessly into pockets before the owners had had a chance to gather their wits. Though their uniforms would be dried and returned to them, they were searched minutely for anything deemed of any intelligence value at all. Many in the Royal Navy – including Macintyre – harboured a suspicion that at least some U-boats had developed the technique of attacking from within the convoy itself and a sketch was found in one of the *U99's* crewmen's pockets of a U-boat doing exactly that, flanked by merchant ships on either side and firing torpedoes in angled shots to left and right. Such innocuous-seeming items could become a bonanza to intelligence officers capable of investigating the smallest information scraps. In fact the Royal Navy had already captured the man responsible for this type of attack. While his officers were taken to the wardroom, Kretschmer sank into an armchair and was soon fast asleep as exhaustion took over. He awoke hours later to find MacIntyre silently observing him. Kretschmer thanked him for the rescue of his crew, the two men shaking hands before Macintyre returned to the bridge.

HMS *Walker* was now overcrowded with an extremely unusual group of people. All bar three of *U99's* crew were accommodated alongside the thirty-eight survivors of SS *J. B. White*. While the majority of the captured Germans were orderly and polite, it appears that only Knebel-Döberitz caused any small problem.

> While the Germans were thawing out, John Langton, anxious not to have pneumonia cases on his hands, ordered whiskey for the Germans. Von Knebel-Döberitz haughtily refused to drink with us, pompously ordered the remainder not to drink with us, and ended with a Nazi salute and a 'Heil Hitler!' Mr. Chaplin, the gunner, was on to him like a terrier and warned him that if he valued his life that was the last time that he would try on anything of that sort. The others were told to drink up and after a slight hesitation they did so and tension relaxed. The merchant navy officers could not resist some minor digs at the Germans. While their uniforms were being dried off, not only the medals and insignia were taken as souvenirs but even the fly buttons. Great were the complaints

when the Germans discovered their losses. The rules of treatment of PoWs forbade the confiscation of medals and insignia and Peter Sturdee had quite a job extracting them from their purloiners to return them. The flies were never recovered and I never did hear how the Germans managed without.[17]

During the day that followed, HMS *Walker* and *Vanoc* both managed to rejoin the convoy; the identity of *Vanoc*'s U-boat was now confirmed and elation spread through the naval escort as they realised that they had destroyed two of Germany's greatest aces. Macintyre allowed the Germans on deck under guard as they sailed alongside the massed merchant ships that showed little trace of the depredations caused by *U99*. Indeed, there was some grim satisfaction for the British crew as they observed faint traces of bewilderment amongst their captives who vainly searched for any trace of the chaos and destruction they had wrought. There were still mustered a considerable number of merchant ships, which had dressed their columns for the final approach to Great Britain and provided a sight of great material power. Kretschmer was also seen transfixed by an unofficial insignia sported by HMS *Walker*, that of a horseshoe. According to Macintyre's recollections Kretschmer remarked to Lieutenant (E) G. F. 'Chiefy' Osborne (Chief Engineering Officer aboard HMS *Walker*) on the odd coincidence that the destroyer should also sport a horseshoe as an emblem, though the British horseshoe was inverted so that the ends pointed upward. Osborne's reply was to inform Kretschmer that the British belief was that if the shoe pointed downward, the luck would run out of the open ends. Kretschmer could only regretfully smile in return.

Life aboard the crowded destroyer assumed a somewhat bizarre semblance of normality, though there were occasional bouts of under-standable aggression from some of the Canadian merchant's crew who had lost friends to *U99*'s attack. However, *Walker*'s crew managed the situation with an admirable combination of firmness and restraint. Kretschmer himself was found to be an urbane 'guest' who fully fitted the description 'officer and a gentleman'. At one point he even became the fourth bridge player in a game organised by 'Chiefy' Osborne with the master and chief engineer from *J. B. White*.

As the convoy reached the relative safety of the Minches, both HMS *Vanoc* and *Walker* were detached from the escort to head for

Liverpool, where they had been ordered to land the prisoners. Aboard HMS *Walker*, Kassel made a sincere speech to many of the destroyer's crew within the crowded mess deck and thanked them on behalf of the crew for their excellent treatment and hospitality to men who were, after all, the enemy. HMS *Walker* docked at the Prince's Landing Stage where a welcoming reception party awaited them, including Sir Percy Noble, Commander-in-Chief Western Approaches, and many members of his staff. The feeling that the Royal Navy had drawn the teeth of Dönitz's U-boats was tangibly in the air, though nobody doubted that the struggle was far from over. However, the three leading aces had been taken from the battle, Kretschmer the prize. The sole exponent of the tactical approach of penetrating the lanes of the enemy convoys and shooting from within was a threat no more to the vital merchant supply lines keeping Great Britain alive.

For many aboard *Walker*, the sinking of *U99* and its leading U-boat ace brought decorations. On 6 May, the Distinguished Service Order for 'skill, enterprise, and resource in successful actions against enemy submarines' was awarded to Commander Donald George Frederick Wyville Macintyre, RN. The Distinguished Service Cross was granted to Lieutenant John Christopher Langton, RN; Distinguished Service Medals to Temporary Acting Petty Officer Albert Edward Prout, Able Seaman Alec Backhouse and Able Seaman Leonard Jack Stickley, RNVR. Sub-Lieutenant Peter Doveton Sturdee was Mentioned in Despatches.

Within the Wehrmacht there was a stunned disbelief that the U-boat service had lost its three pre-eminent heroes. Fähnrich zur See Herbert Werner was serving aboard *U557* when news of the disaster arrived, a moment memorialised within his autobiographical account of the war:

> I was in the petty officers' wardroom when [Günter] Gerloff came rushing down the aisle asking, 'Have you heard the bad news?'
>
> 'Haven't heard anything', I said. 'What are you talking about?'
>
> 'Kretschmer and Schepke are supposed to be sunk. I can't believe it.'
>
> But the news was confirmed by Leutnant Siebold. *U99*, with Kretschmer in command, and *U100* under Captain Schepke, had indeed been destroyed while attacking a convoy in the North Atlantic. Both great captains had been considered indestructible, and their loss – the first to be admitted publicly in eighteen

months of U-boat action – reminded us that the sea war was increasing in intensity as the British built up their defences . . . The double tragedy, which had occurred on March 17, stunned and baffled the country.[18]

Chapter Eight

Captivity

The landing of Kretschmer and his crew in Liverpool attracted a crowd of vengeful spectators, Kretschmer leading his men ashore clad in his dried uniform tunic and leather U-boat trousers. There were many within the port city with strong connections to the Atlantic convoy war and while Kretschmer was taken separately by car under armed guard from the dock, the remainder of his crew marched through Liverpool streets lined with angry British civilians. Policemen and British troops shepherded the German crew towards Lime Street Station; spectators were kept at bay, though many threw stones or whatever they could find to hand at the hated U-boat foe as they were marched towards their transport. It was undeniably ugly, but completely understandable after both the reality and the unrelenting propaganda of the struggle against Dönitz's men. During the 1940 Blitz Liverpool was also the second most heavily bombed city after London; a raid that had taken place on 28 November resulted in what Winston Churchill described as the 'single worst incident of the war' when bombs hit an air-raid shelter in the city's Durning Road, killing 166 people.

The disturbances along their route to Lime Street delayed the Germans' arrival at the station and correspondingly they missed their planned London-bound train and were escorted back to Walton Prison, which had also suffered during the Luftwaffe bombing. Officers, NCOs and enlisted men were segregated; Kretschmer was incarcerated in his own small cell. The following day the entire crew minus their commander were transported by train to the 'London Cage', an establishment organised by Military Intelligence Section 19 (MI19) and run by Major Alexander Scotland, head of the Prisoner of War Interrogation Section

(PWIS) of the Intelligence Corps (Field Security Police). Nine 'cages' had been established within England and Scotland in total, London's located within a stately home at Number 8 Kensington Palace Gardens, also being used as a transit point for prisoners of war.

Kretschmer's capture was announced by Winston Churchill in the House of Commons on 21 March and so German radio was obliged to answer the question surrounding what had happened to one of their favourite fighters and admitted the death of Schepke and capture of Kretschmer, though news regarding the mysterious fate of Prien was still withheld as it was felt the triple hammer-blow to German morale could be too traumatic. Kretschmer's capture was, of course, widely reported in the British press, generally with some degree of accuracy, although *The People* later published a fanciful account on 13 July 1941 that included its interesting version of Kretschmer's arrival on HMS *Walker*:

> Then Commander Otto Kretschmer came aboard the destroyer. He gave a stiff Nazi salute, and said 'Heil Hitler.' The destroyer skipper said, 'None of that stuff here.' Kretschmer smirked and Heiled Hitler again.[1]

Once the Germans were safely behind walls, skilled interrogators immediately began sifting through their prisoners from *U99*, their evaluation summed up in an Admiralty report '"U 99" Interrogation of Survivors'. It makes fascinating reading, not least of all regarding the interrogators' impressions of the men they had captured at a stage of the war when U-boat prisoners were not yet abundant.

> The crew gave the impression of having attained a higher degree of cooperation and having worked better together than in the case of U-boat crews interrogated in recent months. The senior Petty Officers were more experienced and had been with the U-boat a considerable time. Among the ratings, also, there were fewer new hands. The crew of *U99* had an exaggerated idea of their importance and dignity; these inflated opinions were no doubt due to the extraordinary degree of public adulation to which they had become accustomed. Special aeroplanes and bouquets at railway stations had since become part of their daily lives when ashore.

For the first time in this war, no criticism of their officers was noted; on the contrary a marked degree of loyalty and admiration for their Captain was expressed by the men . . .

[Kretschmer] gave the impression of being a quiet, deliberate man, and looked more like a student than a U-boat Captain. He prided himself on being able to take advantage of whatever the passing moment offered and made no elaborate plans for attacking convoys. He admitted that he had become weary of the war some time ago, and latterly had gotten no satisfaction from sinking ship after ship . . . His political views were less extremely Nazi than had been assumed. On seeing the craters of a stick of bombs near Buckingham Palace he was genuinely shocked that an attempt had so obviously been made by his countrymen to bomb the Palace. He spoke English quite well, though he lacked practice. His whole demeanour was calm and quiet, and he seemed anxious to be friendly; he was also less suspicious of British Officers than was his First Lieutenant.

The First Lieutenant of *U99* was Oberleutnant zur See Hans-Jochen von Knebel-Döberitz, aged twenty-three years. His family were of the Junker class, i.e., of the landed aristocracy, living in eastern Pomerania; he was the first member of his family to enter the navy, which he joined in 1936. In the autumn of 1938 he transferred to U-boats, and during the earlier part of the war served in a 250-ton U-boat, in which he made two cruises. His former captain had since been lost. He also served in another U-boat and in *U23* under Kretschmer. He was, for some months, Adjutant to Vice-Admiral Dönitz, the Admiral Commanding U-boats.

Knebel-Döberitz only joined *U99* before her last cruise and expected to have been appointed to the command of a U-boat had he returned in *U99*. On the surface, he seemed a very thorough Nazi, but actually he was rather ashamed of many of the Nazi methods, and most of their leading personalities. He maintained a facade of loyalty towards the regime, whereas in reality he was only loyal to his class and to his country. He showed every promise, however, of becoming later more arrogant and even ruthless. He spoke a little English, but suffered from an inadequate general education much influenced by half-understood propaganda. He was a bachelor, and had few interests apart from the navy.

The Engineer Officer, Oberleutnant (Ing.) Gottfried Schröder, did not survive the sinking of *U99*, and was drowned while trying to ensure and to hasten the sinking of the U-boat; this was subsequently admitted to have been unnecessary.

The Lieutenant-Commander under instruction, Kapitän-leutnant Horst Hesselbarth, aged 28, was a Westphalian, and formerly served as Torpedo Officer in the cruiser *Leipzig*. After a brief technical U-boat course he joined *U99* shortly before she sailed, and was thus captured on his first cruise. He gave the impression of being a rather dull and not very intelligent man without personality, but possessed some sense of humour and was interested in sport.

The two midshipmen had joined the navy in 1939, and were on their first cruise, to test their suitability for U-boats. They had not yet had any preliminary U-boat instruction, and had only been through a short infantry course on joining, followed by some naval training. They were both typical Nazis, unmovingly certain of a supreme German victory in 1941, and repeated the usual propaganda when discussing any subject.

The Chief Quartermaster (*Stabsobersteuermann*) Heinrich Petersen, who was fulfilling the duties of junior Officer in *U99*, was an able and experienced man who had served in the navy for many years. He had been under Kretschmer for a long time, and was the only man in the German Navy below commissioned rank to be awarded the Knight Insignia of the Iron Cross. This dignity had gone to his head somewhat, so that at first, he behaved rather arrogantly.[2]

From the Kensington Cage, the entire crew were transferred to Trent Park, Cockfosters, North London. There, British intelligence had established another transit and interrogation centre amidst the lush surroundings of a stately home. Before the outbreak of war, it had been agreed by all branches of the British services that a Combined Services Detailed Interrogation Centre (CSDIC) should be formed, under the responsibility and control of the War Office. Their task was to deal with selected enemy prisoners of war of the Wehrmacht and Waffen-SS. Within twenty-four hours of war being declared, the nucleus of the CSDIC had opened in the Tower of London where selected prisoners of war or internees were held for comprehensive interrogation by specially qualified officers. On 12 December 1939, the Centre moved to Trent Park where the War Office had requisitioned the stately home. The splendid rooms were comprehensively equipped with electronic surveillance: bugging devices were placed in light fittings, plant pots, fireplaces, a billiard table and even the trees in the grounds to gain vital intelligence which could assist the Allied war effort.[3]

The converted manor house in which the crew were confined was set in its own grounds, ringed by barbed wire. Kretschmer was given his own room on the first floor, which also held other captured Wehrmacht officers. The crew were accommodated in converted stables where they received harsher treatment designed to instil fear of reprisals against them if they did not cooperate with their interrogators and provide more than the barest information required of captured personnel. Though they maintained their discipline throughout, even the slightest mention of seeming trivialities of their time in port and at sea was collected and added to the picture obtained by skilled British intelligence officers. It is fair to say that their accumulated knowledge of the inner workings of the U-boat service already far exceeded the Kriegsmarine's grasp of Royal Navy operations and personalities.

As well as his value to the German war effort, Kretschmer was considered by Captain George Creasy as the greatest prize that the Royal Navy could have taken. For the Director of Anti-Submarine Warfare, Kretschmer could provide an invaluable insight into the workings of the U-boats in action. Allied counter-measures and defensive tactics were already improving and would, before long, completely overtake German technological and tactical abilities. But in early 1941 the battle was still being fought with bloody knuckles on both sides. Creasy had already ascertained that the most effective U-boats attacked while surfaced, using the agility and low silhouette of the boat to full advantage during the hours of darkness and had also come to believe that at least one U-boat had attacked more than one convoy from inside the convoy formation itself. After-action reports and eyewitness accounts had showed torpedoes coming from within the ranks of merchant ships, though he judged this such a dangerous manoeuvre that it had likely come about more by accident than design.

Creasy was keen to meet Kretschmer face to face, more to establish the calibre of the man before him than in the expectation of receiving valuable intelligence. In captivity, and surrounded by microphones, Kretschmer and his crew had remained reluctant to discuss matters that could be of any benefit to the Allies, no doubt suspicious that they were indeed being monitored.

Transcripts of many of the tapes have recently been distilled by German historian Sönke Neitzel, Professor of Military History at the University of Potsdam, who has published two books on the subject. Within the pages of his first volume, co-authored with German social psychologist Harald Welzer, he mentions *U99* twice from tapes made of their time in Trent Park. His first could arguably have painted Kretschmer as a more vainglorious man than his reputation would suggest. The Wehrmacht placed great store in rewarding troops with campaign badges and service awards as well as medals for valour or injury. Many such decorations were worn in combat, though generally not within the U-boat service where duty clothes were relatively plain and unadorned.

> In the navy, too, where the tonnage of ships sunk was the dominant criterion, soldiers' attention revolved around decorations. Revealingly, Lieutenant [*sic*] Otto Kretschmer fretted intensely as a PoW over whether his last radio message had reached Dönitz. Along with the regrettable fact that he had had to abandon ship, Kretschmer wanted his superior to know about his successes on his final mission, which had made him Germany's top submarine commander.[4]

While there is no dispute with the factual basis of this passage, the rationale for Kretschmer's fixation on the final message despatched may well have been less orientated towards the acclaim suggested by the words above. Kretschmer was 'correct' in virtually every aspect of his service life, and reporting the success achieved by his boat would have helped Dönitz judge the efficacy of his U-boats for that week, in that action, against that convoy. Additionally, the same message reported the boat lost, of which it was vitally important that Dönitz was made aware. He was already the premier ace in the pantheon of Second World War U-boat heroes, so needed little more by way of accolade. However, it is also true that both Kretschmer and his crew believed they had mounted perhaps the most effective single patrol undertaken by a U-boat since 1939, so there was perhaps at least an element of recognition that they desired.

More troubling was a second passage that was recorded on 22 March 1941 that showed a disturbing insight into excesses committed in fighting on land:

> A navy radio operator offered a moral assessment: 'In Poland it was all right for them to kill captured Poles, because the Poles had killed and burnt captured German airmen, but I think it's wrong that the SS [written incorrectly as 'SA' in the original] troops should have killed innocent French prisoners.' The moral standard here was clear. There was nothing wrong with shooting captured soldiers in reprisal, but it was unjust to kill innocent civilians. It is unclear where this radio operator, who fell into British hands after *U99* sank on March 7 [*sic*], 1941, got his information. It could well have been second hand, which would be an indication how early the Waffen-SS accrued its ambiguous reputation.[5]

While limited information was accumulated by MI19 from Cockfosters' microphones, Kretschmer was taken by car into London to meet personally with Creasy at the latter's request.

> One day a British officer arrived and asked me to accompany him to the director of anti-submarine warfare. There was some difficulty in procuring me a suit of civilian clothes in which to visit Captain Creasy (as he was then). But eventually everything necessary was obtained from the officers' clothing store except a pair of shoes to fit me. But this problem too was solved by one of the interrogating officers, a naval Lieutenant. He jumped up, stood beside me and measured his foot against mine. Seeing that they were the same size, he whipped off his own shoes and presented them to me. They fitted beautifully.[6]

Originally Creasy had desired to meet Kretschmer officially at the Admiralty; however he changed the meeting to one of a more 'private and personal' nature at his quarters at Buckingham Gate instead lest the presence of a U-boat commander in the Admiralty building prove politically embarrassing. On 3 April, with his wife nervously pacing the adjoining room fearing that the young U-boat captain might attempt to overpower her husband and escape, Creasy met alone with Kretschmer in the lounge of his flat. For an hour, the two men talked over glasses of port and cigars, Creasy adroitly steered the conversation between seemingly trivial matters, all the time probing for glimpses of Kretschmer's nature, rather than seeking an intelligence bonanza. Kretschmer equally skilfully avoided subjects that he felt were leading him into areas of U-boat operations that he would not discuss, particularly matters pertaining to Dönitz himself and his manner of handling those under his command. However, internally, Kretschmer was surprised and dismayed at the knowledge that Creasy already had about himself and his comrades.

> Then from his lips I heard a precise account of all my enterprises to date in the Atlantic. Everything he said was accurate. I felt a shiver run through me, and I was hard put to it to preserve my calm and to reply with a polite smile: 'Really very interesting!'[7]

Kretschmer was dumbfounded at the amount of personal information that Creasy could recite, including matters related to Prien, Schepke and Dönitz that were both detailed and exact. Nonetheless, ever the professional, Kretschmer successfully disguised his inner turmoil beneath increasingly noncommittal replies, particularly when Creasy returned to probing for glimpses of information about Dönitz. Nonetheless, Creasy had already achieved his aim. He had wanted to form a judgement about the kind of man that Kretschmer was and therefore an indication of the likely nature of other U-boat commanders. In a preface to Robertson's biography he summarised his impression:

> I saw a young and obviously self-confident Naval Commander who bore himself, in the difficult conditions of recent captivity, with self-respect, modesty and courtesy. His record stamped him as brave and quick-witted; his appearance and manners were those of an officer and a gentleman. When he left me I sincerely hoped that there were not too many like him.[8]

Within an hour, the extraordinary meeting was at an end and Kretschmer was returned through London's streets by car to Trent Park. Along the way, his escorting officer remembered Kretschmer being visibly shocked when he saw bomb damage inflicted on Buckingham Palace, apparently disturbed that the Luftwaffe had hit such a non-military target. In many ways, if accurate, it is a surprising display of naivety on Kretschmer's behalf as the indiscriminate bombing of cities – or at least inaccuracy due to relatively primitive bomb sights and targeting information particularly at night – had been a hallmark of most offensive operations to date since the outbreak of war.

After weeks in captivity, Kretschmer was informed by his captors that he had been promoted to *Korvettenkapitän*, dated retrospectively to 1 March. Prien, too, had been similarly promoted, posthumously of course, though the German public were not yet aware of his loss. The news of Kretschmer's promotion had come through the propaganda *Wehrmachtberichte* programme broadcast on 25 April, which simultaneously announced his capture and the loss of Schepke:

> The U-boats under the command of Korvettenkapitän Kretschmer and Kapitänleutnant Schepke have not returned from patrol. Both boats were recently instrumental in destroying enemy convoys under the toughest conditions and have increased their overall successes considerably.
>
> Korvettenkapitän Kretschmer now has in addition to the destruction of three enemy destroyers – including two on his last mission – sunk a total of 313,611 grt, including the auxiliary cruisers *Laurentic*, *Patroclus* and *Forfar*. Kapitänleutnant Schepke sank 233,971 grt of enemy shipping.
>
> The two commanders, awarded with the Oak Leaves to the Knight's Cross of the Iron Cross in recognition of their outstanding services in the freedom struggle of the German people, have won imperishable laurels with their brave crews. Korvettenkapitän Kretschmer was taken prisoner along with part of his crew.

Once interrogators had finished with Kretschmer and his crew, they were moved onwards to more permanent prisoner of war accommodation. The enlisted personnel were shipped to Warth Mill PoW camp, Bury, which had previously held German and Italian internees, while Kretschmer and his officers were transferred to the Lake District where they were to be incarcerated in the prison compound of Grizedale Hall, a large country house. The War Office had commandeered Grizedale Hall in 1939 from the Forestry Commission and it was officially titled 'No. 1 PoW Camp (Officers)'. This early during the war, the vast majority of inmates were either Luftwaffe or U-boat men – so much so that it became known as the 'U-boat Hotel' – and they were held initially inside the main building before the camp was extended to include thirty huts in the grounds, the entire area encircled with a double perimeter fence with small wooden watchtowers evenly spaced to provide an overview of the prisoners' compound.

Raymond Alexander 'Sacha' Carnegie was a second lieutenant with the Scots Guards in March 1941 and tasked with escorting Kretschmer and part of his crew from London to their new camp near Lake Windermere. Carnegie, an author in later life, recounted the story of his brief encounter with Kretschmer in an article entitled 'Otto the Silent' published in the March 1999 issue of *Saga Magazine*. Based at the Tower of London, Carnegie took five men and escorted Kretschmer and his men on a bus from Cockfosters to Euston station where they boarded a north-bound train:

> He wore the piratical cap of the U-boat captain, but without the well-known white cover; he wore his faded leather trousers tucked into short seaboots. At his throat hung the coveted Knight's Cross.
>
> . . . On the way, the young officers and petty officers of *U99* were excited, cocky and arrogant as they pointed out the damage of the night before, wrought by their comrades of the Luftwaffe. They chatted, they laughed, and they did not in any way seem like prisoners, nor indeed like men who had been through the hideous ordeal of depth-charging . . .
>
> [Kretschmer] did not speak except once when his men grew too boisterous at the sight of some badly broken building or extra-large crater. Then he said something quietly and raised a restraining hand and they all fell silent. He certainly had their total obedience and respect. Looking at him I felt rather useless and amateurish in my nicely creased battledress and blancoed equipment and highly polished boots.[9]

Carnegie and his contingent of Guardsmen watched the German prisoners under the wash of dull blue lights as they travelled from London, all of the Germans gradually falling asleep save for their commander. Kretschmer, he noted, did not sleep, but sat upright and motionless, eyes open but rarely directed anywhere but in the empty space before him. During the hours that followed into the next day, the remainder of the crew awoke and became somewhat boisterous once more, even playing the popular tune 'We March Against England'. Tea from a refreshment trolley was distributed at Crewe and Kretschmer uttered his first word with a brief 'Danke' after returning his paper cup. It was not until the train had reached its destination and the prisoners disembarked to be loaded onto trucks for transfer to their new home that Kretschmer turned to Carnegie and spoke for the first time in nearly twelve hours.

> 'On behalf of myself and my men of the *U99*, I thank you for the kindness shown by you and your men . . .' He paused. 'And for the tea. We found it . . .' a small smile, '. . . very good.' He then raised his hand in a sort of half salute before boarding the truck.[10]

Though the Grizedale Hall compound was commanded by Colonel James Reynolds Veitch, the senior German officers remained responsible for the prisoners' conduct and discipline and were directly answerable to Veitch. This small group of Wehrmacht officers formed the Ältestenrat (council of elders) which acted as a governing body for the incarcerated Germans. While they took responsibility for maintaining discipline and representing the prisoners in all dealings with British authorities regarding their welfare, there was no lawful power held by the council; all disciplinary matters were ultimately handled by the British. It was Veitch's officers who determined any punishment that would be required for breaches of military discipline.

However, as for the men of all nations held in PoW camps, the council actually wielded great authority over the prisoners. It acted as the camp's escape committee, reviewed and, if necessary, censored outgoing mail and could also establish secret tribunals to try men accused of anything from defeatism to treason. This latter activity was in direct contravention of Article 59 of the Geneva Convention protecting the rights of Prisoners of War which stated: 'Excepting the competence of courts and higher military authorities, disciplinary punishment may be ordered only by an officer provided with disciplinary powers in his capacity as commander of a camp or detachment, or by the responsible officer replacing him.'

At Grizedale Hall before Kretschmer's arrival, the Ältestenrat had comprised two Luftwaffe staff officers, Major Willibald Fanelsa and Hauptmann Helmut Pohle, and the captured commander of Kretschmer's old boat *U35*, Kaptlt. Werner Lott, taken prisoner when *U35* was sunk in November 1939. Lott had made the first failed escape attempt from the camp, and also played a major role in the escape of Luftwaffe pilot Franz von Werra in October 1940, though Werra was subsequently recaptured on that occasion.[11] When he arrived Kretschmer became the camp's senior officer and head of the Ältestenrat. Further character assessment via interrogation was undertaken at Grizedale Hall and prisoners were divided into three separate classifications: 'white' indicated the person in question had demonstrated or professed no loyalty to the Nazi regime and appeared indifferent to National Socialism; 'grey' applied to those men who could not be called ardent Nazis but who were not opposed to the tenets of fascism and Germany's National Socialist government in particular; 'black' signified what the Allies considered an ardent and dedicated Nazi. Interestingly, most U-boat officers were graded 'black' as a matter of course, despite many displaying characteristics that would be better described as 'nationalist' than 'national socialist'. While it seems a fine distinction, it remains an important one that is oft repeated in Kretschmer's story.

Hitler himself is alleged to have once complained that he had been forced to wage war with 'a reactionary army, a National Socialist air force and a Christian navy'. Indeed, Raeder was at great pains to keep his service apolitical, devoted not to political affiliation, but to patriotism. While Göring instilled a certain degree of his own political beliefs into his branch of service, the Kriegsmarine remained relatively free of political influence until later in the war than the years in which Kretschmer was at sea. Though there were occasional well-documented adherents to National Socialism within the U-boat service, such as Wolfgang Lüth, in general it was pure patriotic fervour and a single-minded sense of duty that coloured the view of men like Otto Kretschmer. For the Allies, however, U-boat men appeared some of the most menacing characters of the opposing forces, arguably second only to the Waffen-SS. Indeed, Allied interrogation reports equate an unwillingness by captured U-boat men to divulge more than the required information, or any sense of arrogance or surliness among the captives, as pointing to their clearly being 'hard-core Nazis'. This is demonstrably untrue; Kretschmer was a specific case in point.

Kretschmer himself came to be classified as 'black' and yet still displayed no particular affinity for, nor aversion to, Germany's political leadership. Instead, he was what became a later addendum to the 'black' classification, an 'ardent militarist'. Kretschmer may have expressed discontent and even boredom with the destruction wrought by his U-boat patrols while under interrogation, but he was every inch an officer of the Wehrmacht, for whom honour and loyalty were amongst the paramount virtues.

In 1946, after the end of hostilities but while still in custody, veteran U-boat officer Jürgen Oesten who had begun the war in command of *U61* and ended it in *U861*, met Kretschmer in Lodge Moor camp, near Sheffield. He talked with Kretschmer and several other officers and found them all suffering from what he called 'barbed-wire disease'. His experience told him that some men developed an emotional state that remained suspended in the position it was when they were first captured. This mental state remained unchanged no matter how external conditions and the military situation generally developed, and Kretschmer had been captured when the German military star was still ascendant, the Wehrmacht appearing virtually invincible, particularly on land. He was not on hand to witness the rapid decline of the U-boat service's fortunes once the 'old guard' were whittled down, though he no doubt saw the increasing number of prisoners passing through British and later Canadian captivity, many a shadow of the skilled and disciplined mariners who had populated every level of a U-boat such as *U99*. Kretschmer's point of view remained steadfastly loyal to a dominant Germany. Indeed, MacIntyre remembered a conversation aboard HMS *Walker* in which Kretschmer professed bitterness that politicians had made it necessary for 'the only two decent nations of Europe to fight each other'. It was a revealing insight and his captor ruefully wondered whether the 'revelations of the horrors perpetrated by his countrymen at Belsen and such-like places have modified this rather naïve summing-up of the situation'.[12]

However, these musings were some years in the future. For the moment Kretschmer was Senior German Officer at Grizedale Hall when officers of *U570* arrived in the camp during September 1941. Their transfer to the camp had already galvanised the inmates who were determined to investigate what they perceived as a gross dereliction of duty, informed by copious reports in the British press of what had happened aboard *U570* in the North Atlantic.

On 27 August 1941 *U570* surrendered to a Coastal Command Hudson aircraft of 269 Squadron. The inexperienced captain, Kaptlt. Hans-Joachim Rahmlow, had served in surface craft and artillery before transferring to the U-boat service. After a period in training aboard *U58* he assumed command of the new Type VIIC *U570* and took it for its maiden patrol from Trondheim on 23 August 1941. The majority of the boat's complement were similarly inexperienced.

Six days later, *U570* was running submerged in order to provide some respite from the heavy seas, which had caused widespread seasickness amongst the inexperienced crew, when Rahmlow surfaced from a depth of thirty metres after neglecting to check the sky periscope for potential threats. Hudson 'S' was almost directly overhead when the unexpected shape of *U570* broke surface and dropped four 250-pound depth charges that landed nearby. Once more, the crew's inexperience showed as the damage inflicted was relatively negligible and would not have prevented an experienced crew from diving once more. For Rahmlow and his officers, the appearance of gas (thought incorrectly to be deadly chlorine gas from cracked battery cells), smashed instruments and the ingress of a small amount of water proved too much and Rahmlow ordered the crew to prepare to abandon ship, surrendering to the aircraft circling above. Subsequently, although the boat's Enigma machine and cipher material were thrown overboard, *U570* was captured intact and provided an absolute bonanza of information regarding the Type VIIC. Somewhat ironically – considering the impact that Otto Kretschmer would have on part of *U570*'s crew – the boat's chosen *Wappen* was a single horseshoe welded to the front of the conning tower. A photograph included in this book is frequently cited as showing men from *U99* attaching the horseshoe to their conning tower. It isn't. It is actually from *U570*. Kretschmer's boat had two horseshoes, painted gold, one welded to either side of the tower. Rahmlow's boat had a single shoe mounted at the front of the tower.

Amongst the items recovered were the lid of the Enigma machine, providing evidence of the impending introduction of the new four-rotor variant of the machine, plain text messages, and some Enigma key setting information as well as a large array of personal papers, photos and diaries carelessly kept by the crew. The boat itself was later tested thoroughly as HMS *Graph* and showed the Admiralty that – amongst other things – U-boats were capable of diving to far greater depths than previously thought; depth charge settings were adjusted accordingly. A subsequent Royal Navy interrogation report provides an interesting snapshot of the crew that highlights the rapid degradation of parts of the U-boat service since the early days of war, brought about by losses in action and rotation ashore of veteran men:

> The inexperience of this crew was most striking, the Engineer Officer, one or two petty officers and one rating being the only men to have taken part in a war cruise prior to *U570*'s first and last cruise. The chief petty officers were men who had been in the Navy for a number of years, the Chief Quartermaster [Obersteuermann Otto Grotum, who had served aboard Schepke's *U19*] having joined in about 1926; the average length of service of the petty officers was three and a half years while only one rating had more than 18 months' service; about half of the ratings, all very young, joined the Navy in April 1940, and the other half more recently than that date. Most of the technical ratings had done three to six months' U-boat training, the seamen even less.
>
> The chief petty officers, and to a lesser extent, some of the petty officers, expressed great concern at the inadequacy of the training and the lack of U-boat experience, not only of the men, but also of the officers and petty officers; no attempt was made to disguise the incompetence of the crew and the officers were severely criticised by all the men.
>
> The captain, Kapitänleutnant Hans Rahmlow . . . appeared to have been somewhat of a disciplinarian, but was at first quite popular with his crew of young recruits; later many of the ratings joined in a chorus of criticism.
>
> The First Lieutenant, Oblt.z.S. Bernhard Berndt, aged 25 years, entered the Navy in 1935, and served in destroyers until transferring to U-boats some months ago. He was an uninteresting, arrogant young man and professed some contempt for the 'slackness and credulity' of the British. According to the ratings of *U570*, Berndt was a difficult and nagging superior, but neither efficient nor knowledgeable. His views on obligation, promises, or keeping faith were exactly what would have been expected of a rather typical product of the Nazi system.
>
> The junior officer, Leutnant zur See Walter Christiansen . . . was very junior, having been granted his commission in the spring of this year, and hopelessly inexperienced. He behaved

rather like a schoolboy and was simple, cheerful and not very intelligent, but a much more pleasant personality than any of the other officers of his U-boat.

The Engineer Officer, Leutnant (Ing.) Erich Menzel . . . was a man of considerable experience and had served in peacetime and on active service in other U-boats. Personally, he was a vulgar little Saxon with an appalling accent, but an enviable flow of invective.[13]

Following their capture, the crew of *U570* were held in London and interrogated by the British before being separated and sent to various PoW camps. The officers, excluding Rahmlow, were sent to Grizedale Hall, where news of their impending arrival had already generated much unrest amongst the prisoners. The capture of a virtually undamaged U-boat had been widely reported in the British press and Kretschmer and his fellow officers were incensed by what they considered to be potential dereliction of duty or, worse, cowardice in the face of the enemy.

U570's IWO, Oblt.z.S. Bernhard Berndt, IIWO, L.z.S. Walter Christiansen and Chief Engineer, Leutnant (Ing.) Erich Menzel arrived at Grizedale Hall in September 1941 and were greeted with a tangible sense of hostility from the inmates. Kretschmer had already been invited to lecture Luftwaffe officers on the course of action he would have taken in Rahmlow's place, and had expressed no doubt whatsoever that, even if the U-boat had been completely disabled, he would at the very least have made it his priority to scuttle in order to prevent capture. His fellow officers being unwilling to welcome the new arrivals into their ranks until the circumstances surrounding their capture were investigated, Kretschmer formed a 'Council of Honour'. Though this contravened the Geneva Convention, the assembled German officers deemed it acceptable as it did not pass under the official titles of either a court martial or board of inquiry. Alongside Kretschmer was Hesselbarth and two other Kriegsmarine officers and they proceeded to try the three new arrivals and also Rahmlow *in absentia*.

If Robertson's account is accurate, the 'defendants' were provided every opportunity to defend their actions and in due course both Christiansen and Menzel were found not guilty. Berndt, on the other hand, accepted full responsibility for his part in the capture of *U570* and, to his credit, at no point did he alter his opinion that the lives of himself and his crew were of more importance than the destruction of his U-boat. He offered the inexperience of the crew and the circumstances of the attack as defence but it fell on deaf ears. Kretschmer and his officers found Berndt guilty of cowardice in the face of the enemy, as they deemed him to have been capable of assuming command, if necessary by arresting Rahmlow, and then sinking his ship. Rahmlow, too, was condemned as guilty in his absence. Convinced of the imminence of a successful German invasion of Great Britain, Kretschmer ordered Berndt ostracised by all prisoners and later handed over to German authorities after the occupation of Great Britain, tried by court martial and likely executed.

Using the code that Dönitz had established with his men in the event of capture (named the 'Ireland code'), Kretschmer was able to communicate his decision to BdU, hidden amongst seemingly innocuous messages to his family in letters delivered by the International Red Cross. Berndt offered to make amends by committing suicide, which apparently simply attracted more scorn from Kretschmer. However, British newspapers that were freely available to the prisoners soon reported *U570* held in Barrow-in-Furness. There, within the graving dock, it was undergoing minute examination by the Royal Navy before being put through extensive trials. There are two diverging views on whether Berndt proposed an ambitious escape plan by which to regain his honour or was coerced into doing so by his fellow prisoners who deemed his mere presence intolerable. Regardless of the motivation, with full assistance from Kretschmer's escape committee he would break out of the camp and travel to Barrow-in-Furness in order to scuttle the boat with its installed explosive charges. His plan was approved and the German prisoners' escape committee furnished him with civilian clothes, money, forged papers as a Dutch merchant seaman and a map of three potential routes to the port as well as likely locations in which to find *U570*.

On the evening of 18 October, prisoners held an open-air singing session near the wire and directly beneath one of the guard towers, two men cutting a small hole unseen by the sentry above. Later, Berndt was lowered out of a first-floor window of the hall and quickly passed through the wire and into the surrounding countryside. However, his attempt was doomed to failure. Despite no one having witnessed his successful escape from the compound, his absence was soon discovered and local Home Guardsmen mobilised to track him down.

Alex Weir, a thirty-year-old Forestry Commission worker, was amongst those in the local Home Guard who had been alerted by the Hawkshead Police with news of Berndt's escape. During the morning of 19 October, on the fells near Satterthwaite, a man was found sheltering beneath a tarpaulin stretched across a sheep pen. Giving his identity as Dutch, he claimed to be attempting to hitchhike to the Clyde in order to join his ship. However, though his accent appeared convincing, Weir decided to escort the man to Grizedale Hall from where, if his identity as a merchant sailor was confirmed, he could be transported to his ship. As Berndt trudged along the road under armed guard he made a sudden break for freedom as they neared a convenient wood, Weir shouting three times for him to stop before firing at Berndt's legs. At that moment, Berndt stumbled and the bullet hit him squarely in the back. In agony, Berndt was rushed to a nearby farmhouse and his ugly wound bathed while a doctor was summoned, but he died before help arrived.[14]

Following Berndt's death, Kretschmer was quizzed about the entire event, Berndt's hand-drawn maps and skilfully created documents and clothing being obviously the work of more than one officer. He refused to divulge any information and claimed ignorance of the entire affair. His request that Berndt be buried with full military honours was granted, and Kretschmer announced to his fellow prisoners that Berndt's honour had been fully restored. The luckless young officer's body was interred locally in the village of Ambleside with Kretschmer and eleven officers in attendance in full uniform. Due to an unfortunate but genuine error, the last part of Berndt's rank of *Oberleutnant zur See* was misread as his first name and so he was originally buried as 'Lee Bernhard Berndt'. Later, his body was exhumed and reinterred at the German military cemetery at Cannock Chase.

Only a matter of hours after Kretschmer had been returned to Grizedale Hall, Hans-Joachim Rahmlow arrived. His transfer into the camp took the inmates by surprise and he was greeted with outright hostility and informed that, though he had already been found guilty, he too would sit before a Council of Honour to answer the charge of cowardice. Aware now of the likelihood of an illegal tribunal being held within his camp, Veitch ordered Rahmlow detained first in solitary confinement and then moved on to a different camp near Carlisle that primarily held Luftwaffe prisoners.

Alongside Rahmlow, thirty-six-year-old Korvkpt. Hugo Förster was also a new arrival at Grizedale Hall and would be subjected to trial by Kretschmer's Council of Honour. The charge levelled at Förster was that he had deserted his command, *U501*, while under attack by Canadian corvettes. On 10 September 1941, the Type IXC *U501* was attacked by HMCS *Chambly* and *Moosejaw*, both on a training cruise before being ordered to join the escort of convoy SC42. *Chambly* found *U501* by ASDIC and depth charges brought the U-boat to the surface whereupon *Moosejaw* opened fire, the gun jamming after one round and the corvette preparing instead to ram. As the Canadian ship ran alongside the moving U-boat, Förster promptly jumped aboard the corvette.

A naval veteran, Förster had joined the Reichsmarine in 1923 and served aboard the surface fleet until transferred to U-boats in late 1940, *U501*'s first war patrol was also Förster's first and last. Allied interrogators later summarised his actions in combat:

> His lack of experience, his cowardice and other defects were bitterly criticised by his officers and men, some of whom went so far as to threaten to take vengeance into their own hands should Förster not be adequately punished by Court Martial after the war. According to his crew, Förster not only surrendered without a fight, but subsequently thought solely of his own skin, and not of the fate of his ship, nor of the lives of his men, eleven of whom were drowned. He was the first to desert his U-boat and the only man to jump from her to the British [sic] corvette without even getting wet, let alone having to swim for some time before being rescued. Later, when visiting his men, he offered his hand to his Chief Quartermaster [Stabsobersteuermann Robert Lemke], a man of fourteen years' service in the German Navy, who refused to shake hands with him. Förster's own behaviour did not coincide with the attitude towards duty and death, which he had frequently and dramatically enjoined on his crew during the earlier, calm period of their cruise. Some of his men felt that he had not personally proved his favourite dictum to the effect that 'the Germans know how to die'.

The captain of *U501* explained his precipitate leap from his U-boat by stating that he felt compelled to get aboard *Moosejaw* at once in order to insist on the British rescuing his men; otherwise, he added, the German crew might have been left to drown. His explanation, while failing to convince the British, succeeded in infuriating his own men into a state of high blood pressure.[15]

Förster apparently accepted his likely fate when confronted with his trial by the Council of Honour, but by now certain of what was afoot within his camp, Veitch intervened once more and Förster was transferred that very afternoon to a different camp where his military record was not known. Later, in January 1945, he was repatriated to Germany in a prisoner of war exchange and committed suicide on 27 February 1945, unable to live with his public disgrace.

The remainder of Kretschmer's stay in Grizedale Hall passed unremarkably. He was awarded the Swords to his Knight's Cross with Oak Leaves on Boxing Day of 1941, the official declaration read out at a formal parade of camp inmates by Colonel Veitch, Kretschmer the first of only five U-boat commanders to be so decorated during the Second World War.

Chapter Nine

Canada

During March 1942, the population of Grizedale Hall was transported to Canada for incarceration in Bowmanville Camp near Lake Ontario in the grounds of what had once been a 'School For Unadjusted Boys Who Are Not Inherently Delinquent' (Bowmanville Boys Training School). During the summer of 1940 when the possibility of German invasion had loomed large in Great Britain, German prisoners began to be transported to Canada, the majority initially either captured merchant seamen or Luftwaffe personnel. The number increased with each passing year as the number of prisoners taken steadily grew. Following the outbreak of war between the United States and the Axis powers, Canada was seen as an increasingly desirable location for prisoners, no longer bordering on a neutral nation.

Kretschmer remembered his surprise on arrival at the impression that Germany's new foe appeared to have of the Wehrmacht's capabilities.

> Then we were taken to Canada in March of 42, it was just a few months after Pearl Harbor. And there in Canada we got all the Canadian newspapers and the United States papers and the astonishing thing was to read the United States papers. The United States had been attacked by Japan at Pearl Harbor, and of course afterwards Germany had declared war on the United States. But it was very difficult for President Roosevelt to switch the will of his population from the Pacific to the Atlantic, from Japan to Europe, and try to convince them that it was high time to stop the Germans from conquering the whole world. It was astonishing to read this because we asked ourselves: 'With what?!

With what could we conquer the world?' We had nothing, which everybody knew.[1]

Kretschmer and his fellow officers found the camp relatively undeveloped on their arrival despite it already housing approximately 170 Army and Luftwaffe personnel. Unlike Grizedale, Bowmanville was not an officers' camp. Generals were allocated their own rooms; more junior officers were accommodated in rooms housing two to eight men; other ranks were housed in groups of sixty men to a single barrack. The senior camp officer was Generalmajor Georg Friemel who had been captured on 10 May 1940 as an *Oberst* at Ypenburg, The Netherlands, while commanding 65th Infantry Regiment. Beneath Friemel was the senior army officer, Generalmajor Johann von Ravenstein (commander of the Afrika Korps' 21st Panzer Division, captured by New Zealand troops on 28 November 1941), senior Luftwaffe officer Oberstleutnant Hans Hefele (commander of II./KG26, shot down in a Heinkel He 111 bomber during April 1940). Kretschmer's arrival made him the senior Kriegsmarine officer.

It is a mistaken belief that the previous inhabitants had been uninterested in developing those aspects of the camp within their control, but Kretschmer's arrival and a fresh influx of manpower helped energise the development of sports fields, gardens, a theatre company and orchestra as well as various other activities to maintain military discipline among the inmates while keeping then mentally and physically fit. The prolific improvements made by the prisoners surprised even the Canadian guards and by mid-1942 the Canadian War Office judged that the standard of comfort in which Bowmanville prisoners were kept was 'unique'. Relations with the Canadian authorities were cordial and even friendly at times, though escape attempts were frequent and inventive, but unsuccessful.

However, the peaceful coexistence of captors and captured ended in October 1942. During the abortive Allied raid on Dieppe (Operation *Jubilee*) on 19 August 1942, Wehrmacht troops captured operational plans that included instructions for any enemy prisoners taken to be bound in order to prevent them from destroying intelligence material. During the night of 3 October, a British commando raid on the island of Sark (Operation *Basalt*) left two German soldiers dead with their hands tied behind their backs. The pair had been amongst five captured while asleep, their hands secured until they could be taken aboard *MTB 344* that had landed the raiders. This alone violated Article 3 of the Geneva Convention, and when three made a break for freedom, one was stabbed and another shot. Hitler immediately ordered that 107 officers and 1,268 men, mainly Canadian, captured at Dieppe were to be shackled in retaliation. This in turn prompted Churchill to announce in October that Britain would match the German act, both sides then subsequently upping the ante by inflating the number of men to be so restrained.

While Hitler's Axis partners refused to take part in the reprisals, Churchill pressured Canadian authorities into shackling 2,000 prisoners held within their camps; despite protests from the Canadian press, the number was raised to 3,888 prisoners on 10 October as Germany increased the number of men shackled to 4,000. Four Canadian camps were ordered to implement the restraint of prisoners: No. 20 Camp, Gravenhurst; No. 21 Camp, Espanola; No. 23 Camp, Monteith; and No. 30 Camp, Bowmanville. The opposition faced by the Canadians ranged from passive resistance at Monteith and Espanola, to defiance at Gravenhurst where the prisoners threw their 'shackles into the stoves, rendering them useless' and finally to what has become known as the Battle of Bowmanville.

All of the camp's senior officers refused to comply with requests to provide men for shackling, and the Germans began to arm themselves with broom handles and hockey sticks. The 1500 hrs roll call was boycotted and Canadian troops moved in to enforce their order. Fähnrich zur See Volkmar König recalled the events that followed:

> The Canadian camp commandant, Colonel Taylor, had received orders to shackle a certain, by name, number of German army officers and army ranks in retaliation against the shackling of Canadian PoWs in Germany. This order was announced to the German camp inmates. For us it was self-evident that no one would voluntarily submit to this action. Unanimous attitude of all: 'We shall barricade ourselves in the buildings and hoard food supplies. And then let them come!'

Veterans of WW1 (Veterans Guard) were used to guard the PoW camps in Canada. An assault on the camp buildings was not feasible with these, so young regular troops were brought in.

On 10 October 1942, these troops stormed and took the mess hall where officers and other ranks, housed in the wooden barracks, had barricaded themselves. They had come without weapons and had suffered serious injuries since the Germans had used dinner/china ware, jam jars, table legs and even pepper in their defence. Further, the basement of House V [an officers' barracks], where its 'tenants' had taken refuge, was flooded using fire hoses until they were forced to 'surrender'. With raised hands, they left the building and had to 'run the gauntlet' through the lines of Canadian soldiers. Among these was also the engineering officer of the Canadian camp guards, Captain [in fact Lieutenant G. E.] Brent, who used his swagger stick to hit the German officers. We considered his behaviour as defamatory and the Canadian camp commandant was asked to see that this officer should not enter the camp in the future: his security, and well-being, could not be guaranteed after this incident.[2]

Kretschmer himself was the officer who informed the Canadian authorities that it would be unwise for Brent to return to the camp compound but, during the following morning of what was to be a long hot Sunday, Brent entered the compound with a corporal of the Veterans Guard. Kretschmer, accompanied by Luftwaffe pilots Oberleutnant Erwin Moll (Dornier Do 17 bomber pilot of III./KG76) and Oberst Artur von Casimir (commanding officer of KG100), confronted him in front of House IV, out of sight of the perimeter guard towers. Brent greeted Kretschmer with a simple 'Good morning, commander' but received a fist in the face, while Moll hit the accompanying man with the back of his hand to his neck and the elderly Canadian NCO folded to the ground, Moll later remarking, 'I expected that he would fight back, but instead he rolled his eyes and hit the ground which really frightened me as I really did not want to do any harm to him.' Brent was bleeding from his nose and mouth as the Germans dragged him into House IV. König continues:

I was standing beside Captain Brent and was ordered: 'Quick, shackle this man! We will parade him through the camp!' I tied his hands behind his back and pushed him ahead of me towards one of the exits at the rear of our house along which the perimeter fence stretched. I was accompanied by a 'patrol' of House IV inmates. As we exited into the open, Captain Brent and I first, we were challenged from the opposite guard tower: 'Back into the building!' Simultaneously rifles were pointed at us from the tower. Captain Brent threw himself immediately on the ground. We jumped back into the building, I was the last one. As I was in the doorway, a number of shots rang out. One went into the left door frame at a height of about 180 centimetres, another at about 80 centimetres hit the masonry wall left of the door. This bullet disintegrated and I was wounded in my left side by a number of bullet fragments and masonry pieces. As I was diving head first through the doorway, another shot rang out. I received a gunshot that penetrated clean through my left thigh. I was transported to the camp hospital where a number of bullet and stone fragments were removed. One bullet stuck, luckily, in the skin right over my left hip bone while another one is embedded, until this day, in my back.[3]

Meanwhile, with König hospitalised for three days, the battle continued after a compromise offered by the Canadian commander, to exchange those 'captured' but not listed for shackling, for those not yet captured but on the list, was rejected.

On 12 October, an additional contingent of active duty troops [undergoing commando training nearby] was employed and equipped with baseball bats and later – as these proved to be too unwieldy – with rifles and fixed bayonets. A careful inspection of officers made sure that no live ammunition was on hand. After all the buildings had been stormed, all the [126] named members of the army were under their control. These were moved to a farm house, located outside of the fenced camp, and there they were more or less shackled, pro forma, to fulfil the shackling order. Shortly before Christmas 1942, the whole action was ended and as a 'Christmas present' they were allowed to return to the actual camp.[4]

The Canadians had suffered few serious casualties, though there were multiple cuts and bruises and one man had his skull fractured by a flying jam jar. A Canadian guard interviewed after the first day's fighting and sporting a black eye was quoted in the 26 October *Time* magazine as saying that: 'The Nazis are pretty good fellows generally, but they're cross as bears today.'[5]

By the end of 1942, Bowmanville had again calmed down to the familiar routine of life behind barbed wire, though the inmates managed to a large degree to avoid the general sense of apathy that could sometimes overtake men in long periods of incarceration during wartime. Part of their inherent drive was the fact that they had refused to acknowledge that their part in the war had finished. Kretschmer had formed the so-called 'Lorient Espionage Unit' that concentrated on developing the means to escape and while there were numerous attempts by other men, none was more daring than that hatched by Kretschmer and a small group of U-boat officers that culminated in Operation *Kiebitz*.

> I had an atlas that I obtained in England; it was a nice school atlas that we could use to study the Canadian Atlantic shoreline. At the point where the St Lawrence empties into the sea, along the shores of its wide mouth, we located a number of bays. One of them, called the Chaleur Bay, attracted our attention because of a cape that protruded into it and which would favour an escape. The cape was called Pointe Maisonnette.
>
> We could easily reach Pointe Maisonnette in three or four days if walking conditions were the least bit favourable. Once we had reached that place, it would be highly possible to board a U-boat sent by Admiral Dönitz. The critical part was convincing . . . Admiral Dönitz, to send us a U-boat.[6]

Using the 'Ireland Code' Kretschmer had proposed an ambitious escape from Bowmanville during 1943 for himself and four other officers: his previous IIWO Horst Elfe who had been captured on 15 January 1942 after the loss of *U93*; Hans Ey (captain of *U433* sunk on 16 November 1941 in the Mediterranean); Wolfgang Heyda (captain of *U434* sunk on 18 December 1941) and his IWO from *U99*, Hans-Joachim von Knebel-Döberitz. After tunnelling out of the camp they would trek to the predetermined location at Pointe Maisonnette where they would rendezvous with a U-boat for return to France. The plan was successfully communicated to Dönitz, who gave his permission for the attempt to be made, fully aware of the stunning propaganda and military coup that could be achieved by the rescue of Germany's premier

U-boat ace. In Bowmanville, preparations began in earnest and after appeals to use a tunnel already under construction for his escape were denied, Kretschmer and Kriegsmarine volunteers began construction of a second impressive tunnel, both beginning under the floor of House IV.

Unbeknownst to the Germans, Canadian authorities had already broken their 'Ireland code', but rather than prohibit the exchange of mail, they simply monitored it to gather information. The planned Bowmanville breakout was soon revealed, similar to a previously attempted and unsuccessful escape planned from Camp 70 on Prince Edward Island. Escape documents were found skilfully concealed within the binding of a novel posted from Germany, including a map of the eastern Canadian coastline revealing the rendezvous point, a forged National Registration card and Canadian and United States currency. The tunnel, which had reached a hundred metres in length and was later revealed to be 'a masterpiece of engineering' had already been located when a RCMP team had probed the compound at night after being alerted to digging sounds by patrolling sentries. The decision was taken to allow the breakout to happen, apprehend the escapees as they emerged from the tunnel and then replace them with German-speaking volunteers who would impersonate Kretschmer and his men and make the rendezvous. Once aboard the U-boat they were to prevent it diving by throwing a heavy chain suspended from the periscope mount down through the hatches into the control room, while attacking the crew with small arms. The Canadian plan was equally as bold and ambitious as the escape itself, but soon cancelled after British Admiralty officers demanded the U-boat be sunk at its rendezvous point.

However, earth that had been removed from the tunnel and stored in the barrack roof space was revealed when heavy rainfall one night seeped through the tar paper exterior into the compacted soil and caused the ceiling to give way and deluge the sleeping men below in thick mud. Confronted with this evidence of tunnelling, the Canadian authorities could no longer feign ignorance, though they deliberately avoided 'finding' the main tunnel, uncovering a pair of decoy tunnels instead. Finally, the entire game was given away when part of the roof of the remaining tunnel collapsed and the escape was revealed.

Kretschmer and his officers remained ignorant of just how much the Canadians knew, and believed their code still safe. Dönitz had indeed despatched two U-boats to meet the escaped men. The first,

U669, had been sunk on 30 August 1943 while outbound, and therefore the 'back-up' boat, *U536*, was instructed to make the rendezvous. Kapitänleutnant Rolf Schauenburg had been informed by BdU of the details of Operation *Kiebitz*, though ordered not to reveal the plan to his officers and crew until at sea and only if definitely assigned the task. The Type IXC/40 *U536* sailed from Lorient on 29 August and before it had cleared Biscay was ordered by BdU to take over from *U669* and mount Operation *Kiebitz*. Schauenburg gave only a brief outline of their mission to his crew, informing them that they had been tasked with picking up 'escaped U-boat prisoners from Canada, one of whom was a well-known ace'.

U536 set course for the St Lawrence and arrived by 16 September, ordered to remain vigilant for the escapees after 23 September and for a two-week period thereafter. The U-boat was instructed to surface for two hours near Pointe Maisonnette every night and await the prearranged signals from shore. Once contacted, the IIWO, L.z.S. Gunther Freudenberg, and an engine room rating were to take a dinghy ashore and recover the men.

In the meantime, following the failure of their tunnel, Elfe and Knebel-Döberitz conceived a second daring plan for the escape of a single man. Wolfgang Heyda was selected and on 24 September, dressed in a badly fitting Canadian Army sergeant's uniform, he cleared the perimeter wire by use of a jury-rigged bosun's chair that ran along telegraph wires over the barbed wire fence. Heyda hit the ground running. Though his disappearance was revealed during the following day and a description sent to all police stations, Heyda travelled by by train and foot from southern Ontario to Pointe de Maisonnette. Amongst his forged documents were papers authorising him to conduct a geological survey on the Point on behalf of the Royal Canadian Navy. He also spoke excellent English, having studied English Literature at the University of Exeter in England prior to joining the Reichsmarine. He was not apprehended until stopped by sentries while camped near the rendezvous point and finally unmasked during subsequent questioning in the Pointe de Maisonnette lighthouse by Lieutenant-Commander Desmond Piers, who was coordinating the attempt to trap and sink *U536*. Heyda unwittingly revealed a handmade compass and chocolate stamped with the German Red Cross. Three days later he was back in Bowmanville where he received twenty-eight days' solitary confinement.

Nearby, Schauenburg successfully detected the Canadian trap. Throughout daylight he remained submerged, surfacing only for a few hours at night to recharge batteries. At one point a torchlight signal repeating the word 'Komm' was detected but this clumsy deception was ignored. Schauenburg examined the coastline from as close as 200 metres offshore and detected more buildings than expected from the out-of-date chart he was using, and also sighted enemy warships when moving submerged from Chaleur Bay to charge batteries. Schauenburg observed six warships further out to sea, and a corvette replace a departing destroyer directly off the rendezvous point. This confirmed his suspicions and *U536* lay submerged on the shallow bottom throughout 27 September before easing out to sea at slow speed in only twenty metres of water. Despite successfully retreating, *U536* was later sunk by the Canadian ships HMCS *Snowberry*, and *Calgary*, and the frigate HMS *Nene* on 20 November 1943, Schauenburg and sixteen of his men surviving the sinking.

The abortive escape attempt marked the last real military act in which Kretschmer was involved. Though at no point did he become lax in his attitude to military procedure and he still behaved always as a commissioned officer of the Kriegsmarine, his active part in the Second World War was over. On 1 September 1944, he was promoted to *Fregattenkapitän* at which rank he ended the war, still the undisputed 'tonnage king' of the U-boat service.

Kretschmer's status as far as the Allies were concerned was still 'black', an unreconstructed militarist. It was a broad brush with which most U-boat commanders were painted until evidentially proved otherwise. For Kretschmer there also remained the spectre of his illegal Council of Honour that had resulted in the death of Bernhard Berndt. Allied authorities were unwilling to let the matter rest and nor, so it appears, was Rahmlow, whose point of view remained unmodified. Kretschmer's Council of Honour was far from the most heinous of such illegal courts called behind barbed wire during the Second World War. A small number of prisoners were murdered for acting as Allied spies within PoW camps in Great Britain and the United States, occasionally merely for the suspicion of treason, as occurred to Feldwebel Wolfgang Rosterg on 23 December 1944 when he was tried, found guilty, beaten and then murdered for allegedly betraying an audacious – and fanciful – plot hatched by Waffen-SS, Fallschirmjäger and U-boat PoWs in Wiltshire, to break out, steal weapons and march on neighbouring camps in order to liberate prisoners.

Nonetheless, Kretschmer had a reputation amongst his captors as an unrepentant nationalist. His involvement in the *U570* affair, the Bowmanville fracas, Operation *Kiebitz* and the 'Lorient Espionage Unit' loomed large over the reality that he had had virtually no bearing on the conduct of the war since his capture and the end of his meteoric rise to the top of the U-boat service. His attitudes had not softened since 1941, evidenced by his conversation with Jürgen Oesten after the end of the war when he refused to countenance the idea promoted to him by Oesten that Germany's defeat was necessary to ensure the fall of the Nazi Party and, ultimately, Germany's liberation.

This conversation took place in Lodge Moor Camp, near Sheffield, for Kretschmer had been part of the movement of prisoners from Canada back to the United Kingdom during 1946. Shipped aboard the liner SS *Aquitania*, many of the crew from *U99* were reunited with their officers for the first time since 1941. At Lodge Moor, the interviews to determine a prisoner's state of mind and degree of 'Nazification' continued, the most troublesome moved onward to other facilities while some were repatriated to a defeated Germany. Kretschmer was amongst the former and was moved to Camp 165 at Watten, Caithness, in the Scottish Highlands. There, on a desolate Scottish moor, Camp 165 had been a Polish Army barracks before conversion to PoW camp in 1945. By 1947 2,800 men were held in huts whose corrugated iron roofs and concrete floors made them stuffy in summer and freezing in winter. They were not ill-treated, however, and what few escapees there were, were soon defeated by hunger and weather in the bleak surrounding countryside. The compound itself was divided into two areas: Area A and Compound O. The former held what were considered low-risk prisoners who enjoyed considerable freedom and worked unpaid in local industries and farms, while the latter was ringed with barbed wire and guard towers and housed men classified as 'hardcore Nazis or unrelenting Prussian militarists'. Kretschmer was held in Compound O alongside forty other U-boat commanders. Nicknamed 'Little Belsen' by its British guards, its other inmates included Obersturmbannführer Paul Werner Hoppe, former commandant of Stutthof concentration camp, Obersturmbannführer Max Wünsche, Hitler's one-time orderly and officer in the 12th SS Panzer Division *Hitler Jugend*, Oberführer Otto Baum, last commander of the 2nd SS Panzer Division *Das Reich*, and Standartenführer Gunter d'Alquen, head of the Waffen-SS propaganda *Standarte* and editor of its magazine *Das Schwarze Korps*. The inmates of Compound O were subjected to 'de-Nazification programmes', which often involved repeated screenings of newsreel of the horrors perpetrated in the name of the Third Reich and highlighting Germany's total defeat by the Allies.

Months after transfer to Camp 165, Kretschmer was moved once again and ended up hospitalised with a stomach complaint in 252 Military PoW Hospital, Abergwili Road, Carmarthen, South Wales. Here he was informed that, once again, the Berndt affair was being pursued by British investigators apparently keen on Kretschmer's scalp. If he could be found guilty of being directly responsible for the death of the young officer, he could face court martial and a possible death penalty. Interrogations began at the hospital and continued after his recovery and subsequent transfer to PoW Camp 18, Featherstone Park, Haltwhistle, Northumberland. There he was held with twenty-four other U-boat captains still deemed unfit for repatriation.

However, Featherstone was operated in a completely different fashion to his previous incarceration, virtually an open installation with no visible wire and few, if any, guards. It was in effect a final step towards the rehabilitation of Germany's most stubborn warriors. Despite expecting a court martial for his illegal trial of Berndt, he was instead prepared for return to Germany. Taken by train to Harwich, Kretschmer and his fellow prisoners were shipped to the Hook of Holland and then onward first to Munsterlager, the former Wehrmacht training ground that had been transformed into the largest prisoner of war release camp in Germany. From there he was held for a brief time in the buildings of Neuengamme concentration camp before being moved to Hamburg's new Royal Navy headquarters building. There, the familiar routine of questioning about his past and present attitudes to German militarism, National Socialism and 'war guilt' continued, though evidently the British authorities had finally heard enough. On 31 December 1947, after six years, nine months and fourteen days of captivity, Otto Kretschmer was released.

The Germany to which he retuned was markedly different. His family home in Ober-Heidau now lay within the Soviet zone of occupation and had become Golanka Dolna, Poland. The country had been devastated by years of bombing and the subsequent ground war that finally officially ended on 8 May 1945. One year after his return, Kretschmer enrolled in a course in maritime law at Kiel University and graduated with ease. He married in 1948, wedding Doctor Luise-Charlotte (Lieselotte) Mohnsen-Hinrichs (née Bruns) who had previously been married to a doctor of the Afrika Korps who had been killed in action. During 1953 Kretschmer became President of the Deutscher Marinebund (DMB, German Navy League) and two years later was amongst those veterans who answered the call for volunteers when the Bundesmarine (Federal Navy) was established.

Largely formed for coastal defence, the Bundesmarine grew from the postwar German Minesweeping Administration and came to be mostly comprised of small surface craft along with a scattering of destroyers that had been loaned by the US Navy. Five small coastal U-boats were also brought on strength. Kretschmer, and many of his colleagues who had served in the Kriegsmarine, found some difficulty in accepting the nature of the new navy. In the early days of the Reichsmarine and Kriegsmarine, fully 80 per cent of officer candidates were rejected as unsuitable, whereas the Bundesmarine accepted 60 per cent in a Germany that had become pacifist and demilitarised by nature. The Bundesmarine was comprised largely of 'citizens in uniform' rather than the naval careerists who had preceded them.

Nevertheless, Kretschmer threw himself back into naval duties. In 1957 he became commander of the 1. Geleitgeschwader (1st Escort Squadron), in November 1958 commander of the Amphibische Streitkräfte (Amphibious Forces). He even took part in amphibious training alongside elements of the US Pacific Fleet. Beginning in 1962 he served in several staff positions, including Director of Fleet Training and Exercises in Bonn, before becoming Chief of Staff of the NATO COMNAVBALTAP Command (Naval Forces Baltic Approaches) in May 1965, a position he held for four years.

Amongst his duties was the difficult inquiry into the loss of the 232-ton submarine *Hai* and death of its nineteen crewmen in September 1966. *Hai*, a Type XXIII U-boat that had been scuttled in 1945 and subsequently repaired and returned to service, had been heading for Scotland on a goodwill mission. Kretschmer found considerable technical faults and deficiencies in the training and command of the crew, though his report did not gain him friends amongst the upper echelons of the Bundesmarine.

In 1970, West Germany had a new government and the Department of Defence was under the leadership of Social Democrat Helmut Schmidt, a former artillery officer from the Wehrmacht. Schmidt desired younger blood in the military's highest positions and so Kretschmer finally retired in September 1970 in the rank of *Flottillenadmiral*.

Kretschmer retained his interest in all things naval and was frequently available to meet historians, amateur and professional, and provide information for documentaries and periodicals detailing the events of the U-boat war. He and his former crewmates of *U99* held regular reunions, though the numbers shrank as the years passed. He also attended the numerous funerals of men whom he had served alongside, delivering a brief speech at the funeral of his friend Herbert 'Vati' Schultze in 1987 in which he delivered his highest compliment: 'Deeply respected by friend and foe, revered by his crew, Herbert Schultze was an exemplary naval officer in the best tradition.'

In 1955 he was the subject of Terence Robertson's biography *The Golden Horseshoe* (published as *Night Raider of the Atlantic* in the United States). On 24 October 1955, Kretschmer was a guest of the 'Wooden Horse Club' in Hertford Street, London. The club, formed of British officers who had been Prisoners of War, invited Kretschmer to be guest of honour at a reception dinner, following the publication of Robertson's book. There, he met once more with Donald Macintyre, who returned his binoculars, to which he had added a small inscribed silver plate that read: 'Returned to Otto Kretschmer, a gallant foe. Donald Macintyre, Captain RN, Oct 24th 1955.'

Kretschmer's reputation and apparent notoriety remained long after the end of the war. He became a loose inspiration for the 1970 British film *The McKenzie Break* written by the colourful American screenwriter William W. Norton and directed by Lamont Johnson. German actor Helmut Griem plays a captured U-boat commander, Kapitän zur See Willi Schlüter, who challenges British authorities at every turn, instigating a mass brawl and rebellion against the British guards, murdering an outcast German PoW suspected of betraying escape plans, and leading an attempted breakout of prisoners set to rendezvous with a U-boat. Clearly not factual, and clearly not biographical, it is nonetheless easy to see where the inspiration for the plot originated.

The Kretschmers settled in Hans-Bockler Alle, in the pleasant Lower Saxon village of Hinte only six kilometres north of Emden. Like many of his contemporaries, Kretschmer became an unwitting member of a pseudo-historical research organisation based outside mainland Europe that gradually grew more and more right-wing in its creed. Kretschmer's fame preceded him and his membership was used as an endorsement and in advertising for new members, becoming a centre point for 'war tourism' of Europe. However, on 5 July 1998 he resigned all association with the organisation's 'Advisory Board' with 'immediate effect' after faxes sent to correct what he called 'so many major and minor errors' regarding his service were ignored. The organisation had developed a political stance which included unsubstantiated stories regarding Adolf Hitler's escape to South America peddled as 'fact' and increasingly frequent meetings with neo-Nazi organisations in Austria that Kretschmer told of 'strong government pressure' that put at risk his pension by association with a 'political anti-German magazine'. Kretschmer's was not the only name so attached, but it was certainly one of the most famous. His cause was later taken up by Volkmar König, attempting to restore the reputation of the commander to whom he remained dedicated until his final days

Sadly, Kretschmer was never to see the end of this sordid postscript to his career. While holidaying with his wife on a Danube river cruise as part of their golden wedding celebration, during summer 1998, he tripped and fell down a staircase and was severely injured. Unconscious, he was taken to hospital in Straubing where Otto Kretschmer, the 'tonnage king' of the U-boat service, died on 5 August 1998 at the age of eighty-six. Cremated, his ashes were later scattered on the waters of the Baltic Sea.

Kretschmer's reputation remains one based on military prowess. He appeared not to possess the convivial presence attributed to many of the U-boat service's most renowned members, such as Reinhard Suhren and Claus Korth. Neither did he demonstrate the poetic and somewhat philosophical nature of a man like Erich Topp, nor the wry view of the world possessed by the hospitable yet world-weary Jürgen Oesten. Instead he is remembered for his implacable calm and studious approach to each and every aspect of his life. While in the military he was the consummate officer, correct in every way in his dealings with friend and foe. He appears to have been contemptuous of weakness and harsh on the smallest transgressions of what he believed to be appropriate behaviour both on and off the battlefield. His period in captivity was laced with apparently unrelenting adherence to the codified conduct expected of a member of the Wehrmacht and, as Oesten later discovered, Kretschmer never really surrendered, even once behind barbed wire. However, he was not the automaton that these personality traits would seem to indicate. He did indeed possess a sense of humour and willingness to be open and hospitable – particularly in his later years – to any who cared to interact with him.

Ultimately, Kretschmer was a private man who remains something of an enigma: not politically driven, and yet rated as a 'hard-core Nazi' by several Allied captivity reports; shy and reserved and yet possessing an iron-clad commanding presence within his U-boats. Indeed, Kretschmer was a unique multi-faceted individual who, while not remotely conceited, had a strong sense of identity, firm resolve and absolute confidence in his abilities, which is why, in less than two years of war, he became the most successful U-boat commander of the Second World War. In fact, if we remind ourselves of the confidential report written of him by his flotilla commander in 1939, there seems little that had changed within the man himself by the time of his death: 'unusually quiet, but has an extremely strong and defined character'.

> Kretschmer became an ace because he was successful. And he was successful because he was cold-blooded and very intelligent. He was my commanding officer and I never lost my respect for him.
>
> Volkmar König, Kiel, 2000

> After all, the Battle of the Atlantic was grim but chivalrous warfare. The politicians make the wars and the people have to fight them out.
>
> Otto Kretschmer, Hinte, 1989

Notes

Foreword

1. Letter from Otto Kretschmer to Mr Priddey, 18 June 1989. Held by the Royal Navy Submarine Museum. Cited hereafter as 'Letter from Otto Kretschmer, 18 June 1989.'

Chapter One: Between the Wars

1. The twenty were († denotes Killed in Action):

Max-Hermann Bauer†	*U18, U50*
Udo Behrens	*U16, U24, U17, U845*
Otto von Bülow	*U3, U404, U2545*
Theodor Fahr†	*U567*
Siegfried Freiherr von Forstner†	*U59, U402*
Fritz Frauenheim	*U21, U101*
Wolfgang Heller†	*U842*
Otto Kretschmer	*U35, U23, U99*
Dietrich Lohmann†	*U554, U579, U89*
Karl-Heinz Moehle	*U20, U123*
Heinz-Joachim Neumann	*U372, U371*
Adolf Cornelius Piening	*U155*
Hellmut Rathke	*U352*
Wolf-Axel Schaefer†	*U484*
Joachim Schepke†	*U3, U19, U100*
Herbert Schultze	*U2, U48*
Wolfgang Schultze†	*U17, U512*
Werner Winter	*U22, U103*
Ralf-Reimar Wolfram†	*U108, U864*
Wilhelm Zahn	*U56, U69*

2. Letter from Otto Kretschmer, 18 June 1989.
3. Günther Prien, *Mein Weg nach Scapa Flow*, p. 111.
4. *Emden* was subsequently returned to the fleet at the beginning of 1932, though later global cruises would still provide a training platform for naval cadets.
5. Melanie Wiggins, *U-boat Adventures*, p. 28.
6. The covert deployment of two combat U-boats (*U33* and *U34*) to assist the Spanish Nationalist Navy – Operation *Ursula* – was also approved, resulting in the sinking of Spanish submarine *C3* by *U34* on 12 December 1936.
7. Rösing interview, quoted in Lawrence Paterson, *Second U-boat Flotilla*.
8. Wiggins, *U-Boat Adventures*, pp. 28–30, for Kretschmer's near-drowning and the other incidents during this stage of his career.
9. Dietrich von der Ropp took command of *U12* of the *Lohs* Flotilla on 1 October 1937 and was later promoted to *Kapitänleutnant* on 1 August 1938. The boat made two brief war patrols and was sunk by a mine near Dover on or about 8 October 1939 with all twenty-seven hands lost. Von der Ropp's body later washed ashore on the French coast near Dunkirk.

Chapter Two: Command: War in the North Sea with U23.

1. He was awarded the Medaille zur Erinnerung an die Heimkehr des Memellandes, commemorating the return of the Memel territory, on 26 October 1939, and the Medaille zur Erinnerung an den 1. Oktober 1938 on 20 December, for having been at sea during the Sudetenland occupation.
2. Terence Robertson, *The Golden Horseshoe*, p. 21.
3. FdU KTB, 21 August 1939.
4. Emden and his entire crew – Sergeant S. G. McKotty, Sergeant R. C. Grossey and Aircraftman First Class R. Evans – were all killed.
5. Filed March 1940, 2 AstO, FdU Staff West and FdU/SKL Staff as well as FdU/BdU Ops.

Chapter Three: 1940

1. Ernst Wollweber was a German communist who had fled Germany in 1933. He formed a small group, officially called the 'Organisation Against Fascism and in Support of the USSR', that committed at least twenty-one acts of sabotage against ships sailing from Scandinavia and other northern European ports that they deemed to be supporting the fascist cause. He survived the war, returned to East Germany and subsequently became the head of the Stasi: Ministry for State Security.

2. *U23* KTB, 11 January 1940.
3. Nigel Cawthorne, *Reaping the Whirlwind: Personal Accounts of the German, Japanese and Italian Experiences of WW II*.
4. Interview with Otto Kretschmer; recorded by Sharkhunters organisation.
5. BdU KTB, 17 January 1940.
6. Oblt.z.S. Günther Lorentz's *U63* was subsequently sunk on 25 February while attempting to attack convoy HN14. Lorentz and all but one of his crew (Maschinenobergefreiter Ewald Kopietz) survived and were captured.
7. SKL KTB, 18 February 1940.
8. The *Daghestan* was sunk on 25 March by *U57*.
9. *Western Morning News*, 27 February 1940.
10. *U23* KTB, 22 February 1940.
11. Interview with Otto Kretschmer; Youtube: https://youtu.be/dhlSx7_L64s.
12. KTB, 1st U-boat Flotilla.

Chapter Four: Into the Atlantic with U99

1. Navy Department, Office of the Chief of Naval Operations, Washington. ONI 250 – G/Serial 14: Report on the Interrogation of the Sole Survivors from *U521*; sunk on 2 June 1943, by Lieutenant Kuhn.
2. Ibid.
3. *U99* KTB, 21 June 1940.
4. The ship was requisitioned by the Royal Navy in September 1940 and rearmed with two 6-inch guns, one 12-pounder gun and an anti-aircraft gun. Sailing as HMS *Manistee* (F104) it had become an 'Ocean Boarding Vessel', one of seventeen merchant ships taken into military service for enforcing wartime blockades by intercepting and boarding foreign vessels. On 23 February 1941, *Manistee* was hit by torpedoes from *U107* and Italian submarine *Bianchi* south of Iceland while escorting convoy OB288. A chase ensued in which *U107* fired three more torpedoes at the zig-zagging damaged ship before another salvo of two torpedoes hit it and sent it under with no survivors from the 141 crewmen.
5. Robertson, *Golden Horseshoe*, p. 50.
6. *U99* KTB.
7. Wrecksite: www.wrecksite.eu/wreck.aspx?115673.
8. Andrew Williams, *The Battle of the Atlantic*, p. 71.
9. Letter from Otto Kretschmer to Jordan Vause, 15 October 1986, quoted in *U-Boat Ace, The Story of Wolfgang Lüth*, p. 90.

Chapter Five: Lorient

1. See www.bluestarline.org/auckland1.html.
2. Captain MacFarlane was later given command of Blue Star Line ship MV *Melbourne Star* which took part in Operation *Pedestal*, reaching Malta heavily damaged as the second ship to arrive on 13 August 1942. Fourteen crew members had been killed and MacFarlane was awarded the Distinguished Service Order, the *London Gazette* announcing the award on 8 September 1942: 'For fortitude, seamanship and endurance in taking his ship through to Malta in the face of relentless attacks by day and night from enemy submarines, aircraft and surface forces.' MacFarlane survived the war and passed away in 1984 aged eighty-nine.
3. BdU KTB, 2 August 1940.
4. The *Sonderführer* rank denoted a civilian specialist temporarily attached to the military. This allowed the Wehrmacht and Waffen-SS to incorporate experts in any given field into their units, without the need for them to be permanently conscripted to military service.
5. Letter from Otto Kretschmer, 18 June 1989.
6. *Ran an den Feind! Kampfberichte von unserer Kriegsmarine. Aus der Reihe: Kleine Kriegshefte Nr. 7/1940*, Zentralverlag der NSDAP Fr. Eher Nachf. Deutscher Verlag / Berlin, 1940.
7. BdU KTB, 16 August 1940.
8. Williams, *The Battle of the Atlantic*, p. 70.
9. *London Gazette*, 14 December 1940.
10. BdU KTB, 21 September 1940.
11. *U99* KTB, 21 September 1940.
12. Robertson, p. 74.
13. *U99* KTB.
14. Interview with Otto Kretschmer; recorded by Sharkhunters organisation.
15. Report by Commander E. Ford, RNR, Londonderry, 1 October 1940.
16. Interview with Otto Kretschmer; prepared by Stephen Ames; https://www.uboat.net/men/interviews/kretschmer.htm.
17. Joseph Byrne, service number 1105908, survived the war despite being torpedoed once more. He died of a heart attack in 1969.
18. 'Adequacy of Protection of Merchant Ships in Convoy', Memorandum by the First Lord of the Admiralty, 3 October 1940.
19. SKL KTB, 23 January 1940.
20. Interview with Otto Kretschmer; Stephen Ames, www.uboat.net.
21. Letter from Otto Kretschmer, 18 June 1989.
22. Interview with Otto Kretschmer, *The World at War*, BBC TV, 1973.
23. BdU KTB, 17 October 1940.

24. *U99* KTB, 18 October 1940.
25. Interview with Otto Kretschmer, *The World at War*, BBC TV, 1973.
26. See www.warsailors.com/singleships/snefjeld.html.
27. Don Kirton, Leading Supply Assistant, HMS *Bluebell*, quoted in Williams, *The Battle of the Atlantic*, p. 98.
28. BdU KTB, 20 October 1940.
29. Interview with Otto Kretschmer; recorded by Sharkhunters organisation.
30. *U99* KTB, 3 November 1940. The reference to the scuttles *not* having been plated over is a typist's error as the scuttles were indeed plated after the ship's conversion to military use.
31. Christopher Paddock, *The Sinking of HMS Patroclus and HMS Laurentic*. Paddock is the grandson of Able Seaman James Paddock who was badly injured during the sinking of HMS *Patroclus* and spent several months in hospital. See www.rootsweb.ancestry.com/~cannf/mil_hmspatlau.htm.
32. 'WWII Royal Navy Career of Alfred Miles', www.barry-miles.tripod.com.
33. It is probable that the British mistook the muzzle flash of *U99*'s 88 mm cannon for a hit on the U-boat.
34. By coincidence, the previously built SS *Laurentic* had also been used as an armed merchant cruiser during the First World War and had been sunk on 25 January 1917 by mines left by *U80* off Lough Swilly.
35. Robertson, p. 105.
36. Wolfgang Frank, *Enemy Submarine*, p. 116.
37. Karl Dönitz, *Ten Years and Twenty Days*, p. 171.
38. Ibid., p. 173.

Chapter Six: Oak Leaves

1. Robertson, p. 112.
2. *U99* KTB, 2 December 1940.
3. Morgan and Taylor, *U-boat Attack Logs*, p. 76.
4. www.bbc.co.uk/history/ww2peopleswar/stories/01/a1954901.shtml.
5. Ibid.
6. BdU KTB, 4 December 1940.
7. *U99* KTB, 7 December 1940.
8. Admiralty Report C.B.4051 (40), '"U 93", Interrogation of Survivors'.
9. Letter from Otto Kretschmer to Jordan Vause, 15 October 1986, quoted in Vause, *U-boat Ace*, p. 63.
10. Letter from Otto Kretschmer, 12 July 1989.

Chapter Seven: The Final Patrol

1. Interview with Volkmar König.
2. Robertson, p. 131.
3. BdU KTB, 2 March 1941.
4. Letter from Otto Kretschmer, 18 June 1989.
5. Ibid.
6. Ibid.
7. HMS *Vanoc*, After Action Report, 19 March 1941.
8. Letter from Otto Kretschmer.
9. Walter P. Edney, WW2 People's War. (www.bbc.co.uk/history/ ww2peopleswar/stories/88/a2626788.shtml). The above is an extract from *Fortune without Fame* by Lt.-Cdr. Walter P. Edney, written in 1993 for his children and grandchildren.
10. HMS *Vanoc*, After Action Report.
11. Edney, People's War.
12. Letter from Otto Kretschmer, 18 June 1989.
13. Donald MacIntyre, *U-boat Killer*, pp. 37–8.
14. Letter from Otto Kretschmer, 18 June 1989.
15. Letter from Otto Kretschmer, 12 July 1989.
16. Ibid.
17. MacIntyre, p. 42.
18. Herbert Werner, *Iron Coffins*, pp. 20–1. Though this book is frequently criticised for its inaccuracies, it is an interesting point of view of service aboard the later generation of U-boats of the Second World War, written by a man who went on to command his own.

Chapter Eight: Captivity

1. *The People*, Sunday 13 July 1941.
2. *U99* Interrogation Report.
3. On 15 July 1942, the CSDIC was relocated to No. 1 Distribution Centre (DC), Latimer House, Buckinghamshire and another facility, No. 2 DC at Wilton House, Beaconsfield, Buckinghamshire, on 13 December. The latter was used primarily for Italian prisoners. When the CSDIC moved, Trent Park became a base camp reserved solely for senior German prisoners of war.
4. Sönke Neitzel, *Soldaten – On Fighting, Killing and Dying: The Secret Second World War Tapes of German POWs*.
5. Ibid.
6. Jochen Brennecke, *The Hunters and the Hunted*, p. 71.
7. Robertson, p. ix.

8. Ibid.

9. Sacha Carnegie, 'Otto the Silent', *SAGA Magazine*, March 1999. Carnegie later rose to the rank of major and served in Italy and Malaya, was wounded three times and mentioned in despatches. He died on 6 September 1999 at the age of seventy-nine.

10. Ibid.

11. In January 1941 Werra escaped from a train in Canada while being transported to a PoW camp in Ontario, getting home to Germany via the then neutral United States and South America before returning to action. He was killed on 25 October 1941 by engine failure in his Messerschmitt Bf 109. Werra's story is told in the book *The One That Got Away*, subsequently made into a film starring Hardy Krüger.

12. Macintyre, p. 43.

13. Admiralty Report C.B. 4051 (31), '"U 570" Interrogation of Crew'.

14. Weir subsequently enlisted in the Royal Air Force, trained as a flight engineer and was posted as a sergeant to 635 Squadron, part of the Pathfinder force, operating Lancaster bombers. On 31 March 1945, he took part in a raid on Hamburg's Blohm & Voss shipyards, in which *U570* had been built, and was shot down aboard Lancaster PB958 (the only British member of an otherwise all-Australian crew), which crashed into the garden of a house at Steinkamp 23, Hamburg-Billstedt. Weir was captured by Volkssturm members. On the orders of their *Kompanieführer*, Heinrich Specht, Weir and two of his fellow crew-members were summarily shot.

15. Admiralty Record: C.B. 4051 (30) '"U 501" Interrogation of Survivors'.

Chapter Nine: Canada

1. Interview with Otto Kretschmer; Stephen Ames, www.uboat.net.

2. Author interview with Volkmar König.

3. Ibid.

4. Ibid.

5. 'World Battlefronts', *Time*, 26 October 1942, p. 32.

6. Interview with Otto Kretschmer, quoted in Jean-Guy Dugas, *Operation Kiebitz*, p. 216. Bowmanville to Chaleur Bay is some 700 miles. Kretschmer and his companions planned to take trains most of the way but would have to walk in the final stages.

Appendix

Much of the information contained within this appendix appears in other books and websites with some variation, particularly the list of ships sunk and credited to Otto Kretschmer's U-boats.

Otto Kretschmer's Kriegsmarine Ranks

1 April 1930	Offiziersanwärter
9 October 1930	Seekadett
1 January 1932	Fähnrich zur See
1 April 1934	Oberfähnrich zur See
1 October 1934	Leutnant zur See
1 June 1936	Oberleutnant zur See
1 June 1939	Kapitänleutnant
1 March 1941	Korvettenkapitän
1 September 1944	Fregattenkapitän

Kretschmer's Decorations

2 October 1939	Wehrmacht Long Service Award 4th Class
26 October 1939	Return of Memel Commemorative Medal
17 October 1939	Iron Cross 2nd Class
9 November 1939	U-boat War Badge 1939
17 December 1939	Iron Cross 1st Class
20 December 1939	Sudetenland Medal (1 October 1938 Commemorative Medal)
4 August 1940	Knight's Cross
4 November 1940	Knight's Cross with Oak Leaves
26 December 1941	Knight's Cross with Oak Leaves and Swords

Other Distinctions

Kretschmer was mentioned five times in the *Wehrmachtberichte*:

3 August 1940
A U-boat under the command of Kapitänleutnant Kretschmer has during one patrol sunk seven armed enemy merchant ships totalling 56,118 grt, three of them tankers sailing in convoy. Thus, this U-boat has sunk 117,367 grt of enemy merchant shipping plus the British destroyer *Daring*.

19 October 1940
German U-boats have sunk in the last few days thirty-one enemy merchant ships totalling 173,650 grt. Of these, twenty-six steamers were sunk from strongly defended convoys. Among these successes are those by the U-boat under the command of Kapitänleutnant Frauenheim with ten steamers totalling 51,000 grt, the U-boat of Kapitänleutnant Kretschmer with seven steamers for 45,000 grt, and the U-boat of Kapitänleutnant Moehle with seven steamers for 44,050 grt total.

4 November 1940
The U-boat commanded by Kapitänleutnant Kretschmer has sunk two British auxiliary cruisers, *Laurentic* (18,724 grt) and *Patroclus* (11,314 grt), as well as the armed British merchant ship *Casanare* (5,376 grt). With these victories, Kapitänleutnant Kretschmer has sunk a total of 217,198 grt and so becomes the second U-boat commander to destroy more than 200,000 grt.

17 December 1940
Just returned with his U-boat, Kapitänleutnant Kretschmer has sunk on this mission 34,935 grt of enemy merchant shipping. This brings the total amount of shipping sunk by this officer to 252,100grt and makes him the first U-boat commander to pass the 250,000 grt mark. In this total sinking tonnage are three auxiliary cruisers and the British destroyer *Daring*.

25 April 1941

The U-boats under the command of Korvettenkapitän Kretschmer and Kapitänleutnant Schepke have not returned from patrol. Both boats were recently instrumental in destroying enemy convoys under the toughest conditions and have increased their overall successes considerably.

Korvettenkapitän Kretschmer now has in addition to the destruction of three enemy destroyers – including two on his last undertaking – sunk a total of 313,611 grt, including the auxiliary cruisers *Laurentic, Patroclus* and *Forfar*. Kapitänleutnant Schepke sank 233,971 grt of enemy shipping.

The two commanders, awarded with the Oak Leaves to the Knight's Cross of the Iron Cross in recognition of their outstanding services in the freedom struggle of the German people, have won imperishable laurels with their brave crews. Korvettenkapitän Kretschmer was taken prisoner along with part of his crew.

War Patrols Commanded by Otto Kretschmer: U23

Departure date	port	Return date	port	Duration
25 Aug. 1939	Wilhelmshaven	4 Sept. 1939	Wilhelmshaven	11 days
9 Sept. 1939	Wilhelmshaven	21 Sept. 1939	Kiel	13 days
1 Oct. 1939	Wilhelmshaven	16 Oct. 1939	Kiel	16 days
1 Nov. 1939	Kiel	9 Nov. 1939	Kiel	9 days
5 Dec. 1939	Kiel	15 Dec. 1939	Kiel	11 days
8 Jan. 1940	Kiel	15 Jan. 1940	Wilhelmshaven	8 days
18 Jan. 1940	Wilhelmshaven	29 Jan. 1940	Wilhelmshaven	12 days
9 Feb. 1940	Wilhelmshaven	25 Feb. 1940	Wilhelmshaven	17 days

War Patrols Commanded by Otto Kretschmer: U99

Departure date	port	Return date	port

18 June 1940   Kiel   25 June 1940   Wilhelmshaven
8 days, 750 nautical miles surfaced, 130 nautical miles submerged.

27 June 1940   Wilhelmshaven   21 July 1940   Lorient
25 days, 3,900 nautical miles surfaced, 159 nautical miles submerged.

25 July 1940   Lorient   5 Aug. 1940   Lorient
12 days, 2,000 nautical miles surfaced and 93 nautical miles submerged.

4 Sept. 1940   Lorient   25 Sept. 1940   Lorient
22 days, 3,600 nautical miles surfaced, 137 nautical miles submerged.

13 Oct. 1940   Lorient   22 Oct. 1940   Lorient
10 days, 2,100 nautical miles surfaced, 46 nautical miles submerged.

30 Oct. 1940   Lorient   8 Nov. 1940   Lorient
10 days, 1,900 nautical miles surfaced, 102 nautical miles submerged.

27 Nov. 1940   Lorient   12 Dec. 1940   Lorient
16 days, 2,700 nautical miles surfaced, 64 nautical miles submerged.

2 Feb. 1941   Lorient   17 March 1941 Sunk

Sixteen patrols, 224 days at sea.

Kretschmer's Successful Attacks

Date	Ship	Tonnage (claimed)	Nationality
		U23	
		1939	
4 Oct.	*Glen Farg*	876 (3,000)	British
8 Dec.	*Scotia*	2,400 (5,000)	Danish
		1940	
11 Jan.	*Fredville*	1,150 (3,000)	Norwegian
12 Jan.	*Danmark*	10,517 (10,000)	Danish
24 Jan.	*Varild*	1,085 (1,500)	Norwegian
18 Feb.	HMS *Daring*	1,375	British
19 Feb.	*Tiberton*	5,225 (5,000)	British
22 Feb.	*Loch Maddy*	4,996 (7,000)	British
		U99	
5 July	*Magog*	2,053	Canadian
7 July	*Sea Glory*	1,964 (3,577)	British
7 July	*Bissen*	1,514 (8,401)	Swedish
8 July	*Humber Arm*	5,758 (10,000)	British
12 July	*Ia*	4,860	Greek
12 July	*Merisaar* (Prize)	2,136	Estonian
18 July	*Woodbury*	4,434	British
28 July	*Auckland Star*	13,212 (11,400)	British
29 July	*Clan Menzies*	7,336	British
31 July	*Jamaica Progress*	5,475	British
31 July	*Jersey City*	6,322 (8,000)	British
2 Aug.	*Strinda* (dam.)	10,973 (9,385)	Norwegian
2 Aug.	*Lucerna* (dam.)	6,556	British
2 Aug.	*Alexia* (dam.)	8,016	British
11 Sept.	*Albionic*	2,468 (2,300)	British
15 Sept.	*Kenordoc*	1,780	Canadian
16 Sept.	*Lotos*	1,327	Norwegian
17 Sept.	*Crown Arun*	2,372	British
21 Sept.	*Invershannon*	9,154	British
21 Sept.	*Baron Blythswood*	3,668	British
21 Sept.	*Elmbank*	5,156	British

18 Oct.	*Empire Miniver*	6,055 (6,500)	British
18 Oct.	*Niritos*	3,854 (6,000)	Greek
18 Oct.	*Fiscus*	4,815 (9,500)	British
19 Oct.	*Empire Brigade*	5,154 (7,000)	British
19 Oct.	*Thalia*	5,875 (6,000)	Greek
19 Oct.	*Snefjeld*	1,643	Norwegian
19 Oct.	*Clintonia* (dam.)	3,106	British
3 Nov.	*Casanare*	5,376	British
3 Nov.	HMS *Laurentic*	18,724	British
4 Nov.	HMS *Patroclus*	11,314	British
5 Nov.	*Scottish Maiden*	6,993 (8–10,000)	British
2 Dec.	HMS *Forfar*	16,402 (16,418)	British
2 Dec.	*Samnanger*	4,276	Norwegian
3 Dec.	*Conch*	8,376	British
7 Dec.	*Farmsum*	5,237	Dutch

1941

7 March	*Terje Viken*	20,638	British
7 March	*Athelbeach*	6,568	British
16 March	*Beduin*	8,136	Norwegian
16 March	*Franche-Comté* (dam.)	9,314	British
16 March	*J. B. White*	7,375	Canadian
16 March	*Korshamn*	6,673	Swedish
16 March	*Venetia*	5,728	British
16 March	*Ferm*	6,593	Norwegian

Forty-seven ships sunk (274,418 tons) and five ships damaged (37,965 tons).

U99's Crew on the Final War Patrol

Name	Rank	Position	Age

Seaman Branch

Name	Rank	Position	Age
Otto Kretschmer	Kapitänleutnant	Captain	28
Horst Hesselbarth	Kapitänleutnant	Captain under instruction	30
Hans-Joachim von Knebel-Döberitz	Oberleutnant zur See	IWO	23
Günther Rubahn	Fähnrich zur See	Midshipman	20
Volkmar König,	Fähnrich zur See	Midshipman	20
Heinrich Petersen	Stabsobersteuermann	IIWO	38
Rudolf Ellrich,	Obersteuermann	IIIWO	29
Gerhard Thoenes	Stabsbootsmann	Coxswain	31
Heinrich Quellmalz	Bootsmannsmaat		25
Josef Kassel	Oberfunkmaat	Senior Radio Petty Officer	26
Stohrer, Otto	Funkmaat	Radio/Hydrophone	25
Werner Gottschalk	Funkobergefreiter	Radio/Hydrophone	20
Johan Waltl	Matrosenobergefreiter	Combat Helmsman	21
Wilhelm Helling	Mechanikersobergefreiter	Torpedo mechanic	21
Wilhelm Börner	Mechanikersgefreiter	Torpedo mechanic	20
Ernst Kohlruss	Matrosenobergefreiter		19
Paul Teske	Matrosenobergefreiter		21
Franz Binder	Matrosenobergefreiter		21
Andreas Häger	Matrosengefreiter		23
Herbert Löffler†	Matrosengefreiter		21
Hans Lapierre	Matrose		20
Heinrich Graf	Matrose		19

Technical Branch

Name	Rank	Position	Age
Gottfried Schröder†	Oberleutnant (Ing.)	Engineer Officer	24
Armin Weigelt	Obermaschinist	E-Motor Chief	27
Karl Bergmann	Obermaschinist	Diesel Chief	35
Artur Popp	Obermaschinenmaat	Control Room Mate	27
Gerhard Heinrich	Maschinenmaat		25
Richard Jakubovsky	Maschinenmaat		24
Wilhelm Strauss	Maschinenmaat		24
Johannes Clasen	Maschinenmaat		26

Franz Wendt	Mechanikersmaat	24
Erich Uberscheer	Maschinenhauptgefreiter	23
Hans Pils	Maschinenobergefreiter	21
Hans Schiemang	Maschinenobergefreiter	21
Peter Berg	Maschinenobergefreiter	20
Emil Fleisch	Maschinenobergefreiter	20
Valentin Mäling	Maschinengefreiter	23
Hans Zender	Maschinengefreiter	21
Heinz Mock	Maschinengefreiter	20
Ernst Stellmach	Maschinengefreiter	20
Martin Krausch	Maschinengefreiter	20
Emil Karding	Maschinengefreiter	20
Heinz Schneider†	Maschinengefreiter	20

† Killed in action.

Bibliography

Bernard, Yves and Bergeron, Caroline, *Trop Loin de Berlin: Des prisonniers Allemands au Canada (1939–1946)*, Septentrion, 1995

Blair, Clay, *Hitler's U-Boat War*, 2 vols, Weidenfeld & Nicolson, 1999

Brennecke, Jochen, *The Hunters and the Hunted*, Koehlers Verlagsgesellschaft, 1956

Cawthorne, Nigel, *Reaping the Whirlwind: Personal Accounts of the German, Japanese and Italian Experiences of WW II*, David & Charles, 2008

Clutton-Brock, Oliver, *Footprints on the Sands of Time: RAF Bomber Command Prisoners of War in Germany 1939–1945*, Grub Street, 2003

Dönitz, Karl, *Ten Years and Twenty Days*, Weidenfeld & Nicolson, 1959

Dugas, Jean-Guy, *Operation Kiebitz*, Caraquet Editions Franc-Jeu, 1992

Frank, Wolfgang, *Enemy Submarine*, William Kimber, 1954

Hague, Arnold, *The Allied Convoy System 1939–1945*, Vanwell Publishing, 2000

Harr, Geirr H., *The Gathering Storm: The Naval War in Northern Europe September 1939–April 1940*, Seaforth Publishing, 2012

Herzog, Bodo, *Otto Kretschmer: Der erfolgreichste U-Boot-Kommandant des Zweiten Weltkrieges 1939–1945*, Klaus D. Patzwell, 2001

Hessler, Günter, *The U-Boat War in the Atlantic, 1939–1945*, HMSO, 1989

Isby, David, *The Luftwaffe and the War at Sea 1939–1945*, Chatham Publishing, 2005

Lohmann W and Hildebrand H. H., *Die Deutsche Kriegsmarine 1939–1945*, 3 vols, Podzun Verlag, 1956

Macintyre, Donald, *U-Boat Killer*, Wiedenfeld & Nicolson, 1956

Morgan, Daniel and Taylor, Bruce, *U-Boat Attack Logs*, Seaforth Publishing, 2011

Neitzel, Sönke, *Soldaten – On Fighting, Killing and Dying: The Secret Second World War Tapes of German POWs*, Simon & Schuster, 2012

Paterson, Lawrence, *Second U-Boat Flotilla*, Pen & Sword, 2002

Prien, Günther, *Mein Weg nach Scapa Flow*, Deutscher Verlag, Berlin, 1940

Raeder, Erich, *Grand Admiral*, De Capo, 2001 (first published as *My Life*, NIP, 1960)

Robertson, Terence, *The Golden Horseshoe*, Evans Brothers, 1955

Rohwer, Jürgen, *Axis Submarine Successes of World War Two*, Greenhill Books, 1999

Rohwer, J., and Hümmelchen, G., *Chronik des Seekrieges 1939–1945*, Gerhard Stalling Verlag, 1968

Rössler, Eberhard, *Vom Original zum Modell: Uboottyp II; Die 'Einbaume'*, Bernard & Graefe, 1999

——, *The U-Boat: The Evolution and Technical History of German Submarines*, Cassell, 2002

Schepke, Joachim, *U-Boot Fahrer von heute*, Deutscher Verlag, 1940

Stern Robert C. *Type VII U-Boats*, Brockhampton Press, London 1998

Uziel, Daniel, *The Propaganda Warriors: The Wehrmacht and the Consolidation of the German Home Front*, Verlag Peter Lang, 1 October. 2008

Vause, Jordan, *U-Boat Ace; The Story of Wolfgang Lüth*, Naval Institute Press, 1990

——, *Wolf: U-boat Commanders In World War II*, Naval Institute Press 1997

Werner, Herbert, *Iron Coffins*, Cassell, 1985

Wiggins Melanie, *U-boat Adventures*, Naval Institute Press, 1999

Williams, Andrew, *The Battle of the Atlantic*, BBC Books, 2002

Wynn, Kenneth, *U-boat Operations of the Second World War*, 2 vols, Chatham Publishing, London, 1998

Index